# Canoeing Wild Rivers

# Canoeing Wild Rivers

## By

### Cliff Jacobson

*Illustrated by James Zotalis*

ICS Books Inc.
Merrillville, Indiana

# Canoeing Wild Rivers

797.1
J
c. 1

**Published by:**
ICS Books Inc.
1000 E. 80th Place
Merrillville, IN 46410


**Distributed by:**
Stackpole Books
Cameron and Kelker Streets
Harrisburg, PA 17105

**Library of Congress Cataloging in Publication Data**

Jacobson, Cliff.
    Canoeing wild rivers.

    Bibliography: p.
    Includes index.
    1. White-water canoeing.    2. Canoes and canoeing.
3. Canoes and canoeing--United States.    4. Canoes and
canoeing--Canada.    I. Title.
GV788.J33   1984        797.1'22        83-26479
ISBN 0-934802-17-3

*To my father, Henry Jacobson, who taught me to love and respect the wilderness.*

# CREDITS

The author expresses thanks to the following:

CANOE Magazine for permission to re-print portions of his articles which appeared in the following issues:

THE GREAT COVER-UP (July, 1981)
MENDING THE TEARS (Used in entirety) (November, 1979)
FOODS THAT WORK TO KEEP YOU WORKING (March, 1979)
ON COURSE TO MAKING ROUTE DECISIONS (July, 1978)
SOLO RIGGIN' (February, 1981)
RAINY DAYS MAKE ME SMILE (April/May, 1980)
TASTY ROUTES TO DINING OUT (July, 1980)

RIVER WORLD Magazine (no longer in print) for use of material from his articles which appeared in the following issues:

CANOE TENTS ARE DIFFERENT (July, 1978)
CAMPING COOKBOOK (July, 1978)
PROPER PACKING CAN GO A LONG WAY (June, 1978)

CAMPING JOURNAL Magazine (no longer in print) for portions of his "Campcraft" column which appeared in the following issues:

March/April, 1981, and June/July, 1981

AUDUBON Magazine, September, 1981, for allowing him to re-print a paragraph from Eric Sevareid's article, "Return to God's Country".

NATIONAL AND PROVINCIAL PARKS AND ASOCIATION OF CANADA, for use of portions of "Access Roads", written by Don Mitchell and Bill Simpson, which appeared in the Spring, 1982 issue of PARK NEWS.

Alfred A. Knopf, Inc., for their permission to use the quote from Sigurd Olson's book, "The Lonely Land", which appears in Chapter 14.

# ACKNOWLEDGMENTS

I wish to extend special thanks to the following people:

My publisher, Dr. Bill Forgey, for his enthusiastic support and his permission to re-print information from his book "Wilderness Medicine".

Allen Todnem, Bob Brown, and Kent Swanson for their advice and patient reading of the manuscript.

Bob Dannert, Bob O'Hara, and John Lentz, for their recommendations on barrenland canoe travel.

Christie Buetow, Jill Bubier, Fred Gaskin, Ted Goddard, David Harrison, Kay Henry, Verlen Kruger, Hamilton Kurtz, Steve Landick, Carl and Margie Shepardson, Keith Thompson, John Turner, and Clint Waddell, for their anecdotes, trip logs, personal stories, advice, and testimonials.

Don Mitchell and Bill Simpson for revealing the truth about "bush roads".

Brian Thompson and Cecille Ward of "Travel Arctic" for their help is securing essential information about canoeing in the Northwest Territories.

John Viehman, editor of CANOE Magazine, for his encouragement and enthusiastic support.

Bjorn Kjellstrom, author of "Be Expert With Map & Compass", for his recommendations on the use of the compass in the far north.

Walt Tomascak, Fire Management Officer, United States Forest Service, for his advice on avoiding the dangers of wild fires.

Mike Link, Director of Northwoods Audubon Center, Sandstone, Minnesota, for his excellent definition of "the trip leader".

Bruce Hubbard, Inquiries Specialist, U.S. Geological Survey, for technical information used in the preparation of Chapter 13 (Bearings Into The Unknown).

Mad River Canoe Company and Old Town Canoe Company, for product information and photographs.

Grumman Canoe Company, for detailed procedures for the repair of aluminum canoes.

Blue Hole Canoe Company, for specific procedures used in the repair of Royalex canoes.

Coleman Company, for the methods used in the repair of polyethylene canoes.

Hastings and Burnsville, Minnesota branches of the Dakota County Public Library system, for their persistent professional efforts in locating obscure journals and out-of-print books.

Glen Hogarth, Chief Pilot, Parsons Airways Northern LTD, Flin Flon, Manitoba, and Ron Gibson, Thousand Lakes Airways, Upsala, Ontario, for their detailed information on bush planes.

Paul Swanstrom, for his technical drawings and advice.

Eugene Jensen, canoe racer and master strip canoe builder, for information regarding the repair of wood-strip canoes.

Dick Steinke, Senior Chemist for H.B. Fuller Company of St. Paul, Minnesota, for information regarding adhesives used to repair polyethylene and Royalex canoes.

Farid Saed, for custom photographic work.

VIA Rial Canada and the Algoma Central and Ontario Northland railroads for information on railway routes and procedures.

Dick Roberts of "White Water West" for his unique method of repairing Royalex canoes.

Minnesota Canoe Association, P.O. Box 14207, University Station, Minneapolis, MN 55414, and especially HUT magazine editor Mike Gilman, for encouragement and help in obtaining essential information.

Tom Todd who did the lay-out in this book; his attention to detail and artistry is evident everywhere.

# TABLE OF CONTENTS

## APPENDIX

# CANOEING WILD RIVERS

## by

Cliff Jacobson
Ilustrations by James Zotalis

## WHY THIS BOOK?

This book began as a dream over a dozen years ago after I completed my first substantial canoe trip into the Canadian wilderness. To my chagrin, I discovered that a decade of predictable paddling on local streams and mid-sized lakes was only marginal preparation for the harsh realities of northern rivers. And the canoeing literature wasn't much help either: Even the best books parroted the obvious and avoided the things I really wanted to know.

Sure, they all contained the expected chapters on paddling, lake travel, reading white water, using a compass, etc., but there were no specifics on how to research a dangerous river; where to get large scale monochrome maps and white prints; procedures for keeping warm and dry in the teeth of week long rains and snow! How to cope with persistent bears (I learned that hanging food from a tree *was not* the answer!) and bugs; methods for packing equipment that are *really* waterproof; ways to prepare freeze-dried foods so they always taste good; techniques for baking on a trail stove without a commercial oven; the mechanics for shipping your outfit by plane, train, and barge...and much more!

As you can see, this book is not just for those who would tackle the wild rivers of the far north. It is for paddlers everywhere who love wilderness waterways and want to learn some fresh new ideas as well as the nuts and bolts of canoeing remote waters.

A major failing of most canoe books is that they're the work of a single author. Input is limited to the ideas, methods, and biases of one person. There's no room for debate, for philosophy, for individual differences. In writing this book I sought to overcome this shortcoming by enlisting the help of many of the best wilderness canoeists in the United States and Canada (see the Ackowledgments section).

To make room for the obscure but important things you really need to know, I've necessarily cut some basics--namely, "the art of paddling and reading white water". This information is readily available in every elementary canoeing text and would require far too much space to do justice here.

I've begun the subject of canoeing wilderness rivers at the far edge of "square one"--assuming you have some familiarity with the most elementary canoe procedures.

For an ultra-basic approach to wilderness canoeing, see my book "Wilderness Canoeing & Camping", published by the E.P. Dutton Company.

# 1

# A Time for Reflection

I discovered the canoe at the age of twelve at a rustic Scout camp nestled deep in the cedar swamps of northern Michigan. It was 1951—too early to mourn the passing of wood/canvas canoes and solid ash paddles. I'd heard of aluminum canoes, of course, but I'd never seen one. Pack frames, lugged hiking boots, and lightweight down sleeping bags, were a novelty.

The outdoor life was simpler then. We had no tubes of "fire ribbon" or hurricane resistant nylon tents. No bullet-proof canoes, unbreakable paddles, or freeze-dried filet mignon. Canoe camping was a rough and ready endeavor, though not nearly so demanding as some modern writers suggest.

In those days my outfit consisted of a surplus military wool sleeping bag and poncho, canvas pup tent, aluminum cook-kit, Scout hand axe, and a rag tag assortment of second hand woolens. Even if sophisticated equipment had been readily available, my friends and I had no money for it. So instead of buying gear, we practiced camping skills. Skills for rigging a snug camp in the teeth of icy April rains; skills for making fire with a *single* match! We had to cope with what we had. So we read every wood-craft book in print, listened intensely to the advice of those more experienced than ourselves. Ultimately, we learned "woodsmanship".

Things are different today. Now the emphasis is on "equipment" not know-how. (I recently checked the contents of a popular backpacking book. Over 90 percent of its pages were devoted to camping gear and its use.) Polyester sleeping bags and garments become a substitute for ones inability to keep down gear dry in a rain or canoe upset. Fire-starting chemicals are the alternative to correct fire making. And sledge tough canoes take the place of proper paddling technique. Somehow I think we've lost something of value in our search for "better ways".

Three decades ago places like the "Quetico-Superior" and "Alagash Waterway" were still very wild--their waters unpolluted by acid rain, their campsites untarnished by litter and free of Forest Service conveniences like fire grates and wooden box latrines. Only

James Zotalis

canoeists well experienced in the ways of the wilderness dared
venture far from popular routes without guides. How I yearned to go
there--to canoe those haunting lakes, camp amidst the fragrant
balsam and pine, hear the lonely yodel of the loon.

But Maine and Minnesota were a long way from my boyhood
home in Chicago, Illinois. Besides, I was too young to make the trip,
too poor and inexperienced.

The years passed- college, a job with the Bureau of Land
Management, the army, and marriage. But my desire to see America's
finest canoe country did not wane. So in 1967, a friend and I loaded my
then new Sawyer Cruiser atop his station wagon and headed north to
Grand Marais, Minnesota--gateway to the famed Boundary Waters
Canoe Area.

Our trip lasted ten days and traversed 100 miles--fairly
substantial for first-timers. We began at Seagull Lake, swung west
almost to Ely, then dashed back to the border, occasionally dropping
down into lakes that looked interesting on the map. I was naturally
overwhelmed by everything--the sheer grandeur of it all; the endless
procession of dazzling beauty; the proud, unafraid attitude of the
wildlife; the awesome quiet.

But even before the trip's end a measure of disappointment set in.
There were simply too many people around to suit me (not a day went
by when we didn't see at least one passing canoeist). There were other
annoyances too: navigating the big lakes was too easy--if we misread
the map there was always a sign at every portage to guide the way.

Finding campsites was no challenge either: their locations were all neatly marked with little red dots on the Fisher Company maps we carried.

Fishing was only mediocre. Not at all like the vivid description given by the old Quetico-Superior guide who entertained us one evening when we were boys at that camp in Michigan. He told us that fish were so easy to catch here that commercial lures weren't necessary. Laughing, he told how he'd bet his clients five bucks he could catch a fish *without* a hook. His method was to tear a strip of cloth from his bright colored bandana and tie it directly to the fishing line. Then he'd cast out his "lure", jiggling it as he slowly reeled it in. "A northern's (northern pike) teeth slant inwards," he explained. "They catch in the cloth and I get 'em every time."

Then he warned us not to wear any shiny rings on our fingers when we were up in "that country". "You jiggle your ring finger in the water and a northern'll hit it for sure!" he said. It all seemed too incredible to believe.

Perhaps we just weren't fisherman; our catch for that ten day trip consisted of two small mouth bass, three northern pike, and one walleye. And the biggest of the lot couldn't have weighed more than three pounds. (Many years later I would discover that "fishing that good" does indeed exist in the waterways of the far north. The oldtimer hadn't lied.)

I returned home from my first Boundary Waters trip with mixed emotions. Certainly the area was beautiful beyond words, its waters still unspoiled. But there was no challenge to it, what with portage signs, marked campsites, fire grates, box latrines, cleaned portage trails, canoe rests, picnic tables, and lots of other people to depend on if our own resourcefulness failed. It just wasn't wild enough, isolated enough, for my tastes.

My thoughts turned to the waterways of the far north. Rivers like the Albany and Hays, Missinaibi, Moose, and Fond du Lac. Places like James and Hudson's Bay, Athabasca, Fort Chippewan, Yellowknife. Were they real or just a figment of passing fancy?

I read all the wonderful old canoeing books I could find. Sevareid's "Canoeing With The Cree", all the works of Calvin Rutstrum, John Malo, Sigurd Olson. The journals of Thompson. Simpson, Tyrrell, and Alexander.

But I knew I was not yet ready to tackle the unforgiving waters of the far north. I needed much more knowledge, more experience. So I joined a canoe club (The Minnesota Canoe Association) and took lessons on "how to paddle". For awhile I became interested in covered slalom canoes (C-1's and C-2's), but found these craft too specialized for the type of touring I had in mind. But the skittish slalom boats taught me valuable lessons about paddling white water--lessons that helped me to better negotiate turbulent wilderness waters in years to come.

I attended seminars by the outstanding wilderness canoeists of the day: Bob O'Hara, Dr. Robert Dannert. Christy Buetow and Katie Knopke, Verlen Kruger and Clint Waddell. Each contact was another notch on my pistol. My thirst for canoeing knowledge was boundless.

I soon discovered that every "super canoeist" had his or her own definite ideas about how things should be done, though there was general agreement on the basics that affected one's comfort and livelihood. For example, canoes should be much bigger and stronger than those used for recreational paddling. Clothing should be wool, boots of rubber. I listened and questioned, and kept an open mind. Ultimately, I developed my own tripping style.

I made seven more trips into the BWCA before I felt ready to tackle a remote Canadian river. Then I proceeded cautiously, armed to the teeth with research. I had little money to spend so I selected a route with a road at the start and a railroad at the end. A combination of rivers--the trip began on the Groundhog River near Foleyet, Ontario. It traversed the Mattagami and Moose, finishing at Moosonee on arctic tide water some 300 miles away.

The weather was bad, the black flies were worse. And the river was in flood, which made the run extremely dangerous. Only two other parties attempted the river that year and neither completed it. One group "totaled out" in the quarter mile wide Grand Rapids of the Mattagami and walked forty miles through black-fly infested spruce bogs to reach the safety of the rail head. The other team experienced a drowning when they upset while attempting to run a falls that we portaged.

But we had no "adventures" or serious difficulties. Even our close calls were predictable. We had done our homework well. We were prepared--in equipment, skills and positive mental attitude. Our detailed research, training, and respect for the river brought us home safely with hundreds of memories and pictures to share.

Canadian rivers are addictive. Once you've done one you'll be back for more. Each year I try a new river--some distant and challenging (the two don't necessarily go together), others close to home and less intimidating. In either case, I choose my routes carefully and so experience all the wonderful qualities for which Canadian rivers are best known: Isolation, freedom to camp and build fires when and where I please, excellent fishing, and the relative absence of "Improvements"--signs, picnic tables, fire grates, and the like.

I still make an annual pilgrimage to the Boundary Waters Canoe Area to guide teenagers as part of the junior high school summer program where I teach. And sometimes I return again with my solo canoe in late autumn when the air is crisp and the people and bugs are gone. But my first love is the rivers of the far north, and that's what this book is all about.

**2**

# Researching
# A River

English River. Motel, gas station, small cafe. That's about it. Nothing spectacular, just a jumping off place for a delightful canoe trip down a picturesque river that bears its name.

Some pretty lakes with creative names and varying personalities; a few interesting rapids, an awesome falls, generally good fishing, and lots of wildlife. Campsites? Great! Not at all what you'd expect from northern Ontario. Plenty of space--level space!--for the biggest tent you'd want to carry. In all, a nice predictable run, just right for sharpening your backcountry skills or introducing your family to the wonders of those magnificant Canadian waterways.

That, in essence, is what I told the man who called to ask about canoeing the English River with his wife and two teenage boys.

I laid out the details as best I could recall (it had been four years since I'd done the river) and suggested he write the MNR (Ministry of Natural Resources) for a trip guide. I also added that the shuttle was *expensive!*

"How expensive?" he asked.

"Eighty bucks for 60 miles. Plus two bucks a day to store your car. Town's got the business down to an art: One guy does all the driving... and he won't negotiate."

"I s'pose a lot of people do the river, huh?"

"I don't know. We didn't see a single canoe. Two fishing boats, that's all."

"Any other way in?"

"Just the train out of Thunder Bay--crosses the river about 20 miles down--but you'd still need a shuttle."

"Mmmm. What about further north, up around Dryden and Grassy Narrows?"

"Don't know," I replied. "There's lots of routes up there . . . and Dryden's a "real" town, so you might find a cheaper shuttle. You'll just have to check it out."

"Thanks, Cliff. I'll get on it."

Several months later the fellow called again, bubbling with the usual enthusiasm that always accompanies a good canoe trip. "Great weather, didn't rain once. . . good campsites. . . no bugs!"

"How was the fishing?" I asked.

A long silence. Then . . . "Pretty good but we couldn't eat'em. Mercury poisoning from some paper mill in Dryden!"

Further conversation revealed that the man had done a reasonably good job of "doing his homework". He had good maps, an MNR trip guide, and a contact person in the Dryden area who would shuttle his car for a whole lot less than 80 dollars, but he had omitted one small detail--*he hadn't asked anyone about the water quality!*

Moral? Get *all* the facts before you wet the paddle. All parts of the same river may not be equally appetizing. Failure to check out everything ahead of time is a sure recipe for running into a hydro dam, logging operation, pulp-choked stream, recent burn, high water, low water, no water, or polluted water. Research should begin six months or more before you make the trip!

First, pick your province. Then get out the typewriter and compose a letter to the appropriate government agency (addresses in Appendix "B"). Request a provincial road map, a list of canoeable rivers in the area of your interest, and whatever tourist information is available.

If you can narrow your choice to two or three rivers, your letter may bring exactly what you want—monchrome (black and white) printed route maps (not suitable for navigation) and specific trip guides. At the very least, you'll get the addresses of MNR offices or other government agencies who have knowledge of canoeable routes.

MNR district managers are especially accomodating. When they can't provide a ready answer to a question, they'll often tell you where to write to secure the information; sometimes they'll even forward your letter to the appropriate individual.

Besides canoeing specifics, your "tourist packet" will contain a wealth of details about local fishing, road conditions, hiking trails, service stations, availability of lead-free gasoline, etc. So don't discard anything until you've read it all.

While you're waiting for materials to arrive, write the *Canada Map Office,* Depatment of Energy, Mines, and Resources, Ottawa, Ontario K1A OE9.* Request an index to topographic maps for "your province"*and the free brochure "Maps and Wilderness Canoeing"--a marvelously informative publication that's invaluable for anyone planning a canoe trip in the far north.

---

*For Alaska maps, write: U.S. Geological Survey, Federal Center, Denver, Colorado 80225. Or order directly from the Alaska Distribution Branch, U.S.G.S., 310 First Ave., Fairbanks, Alaska 99701.

*Three indexes cover all of Canada. Might as well get them all. They're free!

When indexes arrive, you're ready to order maps. At this point, I like to simultaneously research two or three nearby rivers that look promising--helps dispel disappointment if my first choice turns out to be unacceptable for one reason or another.

So I order a small scale (1.1,000,000) map of the general locale first. This is really too small for serious navigation but it is good enough to help me discover a wealth of nearby routes not covered in the governmental publications or too distant for inclusion on a large scale map of limited area.

The Canadian government is working feverishly to expand its offerings of river guides, but frankly, it's an overwhelming job, one which may never be completed--much to the joy of those of us who still like to explore!

Some of the best rivers have no guides--but they do exist on maps, and you'll find them if you look hard enough.

The absence of a river guide does not indicate a route is unacceptable: it only means that government voyageurs haven't yet mapped it for canoe travel.

Similarily, if like me, you're the solitary wilderness type--one who reacts negatively when you see another canoe on "your" water--don't give up just because your prospective route is detailed in a fancy brochure. Some of the most remote, spectacular rivers I've paddled are described in well written trip guides.

A good example is the "Fond du Lac" in northwest Saskatchewan. In his wonderful book "Canoe Canada", Nick Nickels describes the Fond du Lac as a "remote challenging river for expert white water canoeists". The river is all of that and more, but the provincial guide which describes it is so fancy (printed on rag paper, complete with photos), that you'd expect to find the area over-run with canoeists. It isn't. We spent nearly two weeks on the Fond du Lac in 1979 and saw only one other canoe party. There was little evidence the route was paddled much at all.

A good guide *may* indicate heavy use. On the other hand, it may be little more than a governmental effort to stimulate the economy of a remote impoverished community.

When you've decided on a specific river section or sections, consult your index and order the appropriate 1:250,000 scale (about one inch equals four miles) maps. This scale has sufficient detail to permit a reasonably accurate analysis of a river's characteristics.

When maps arrive go over the route carefully with a large magnifying glass. Mark with pencil all potential dangers--rapids, falls, and dams. Next comes the river "profile"--essential to determine "drop per mile".

Begin by drawing a broad line along each side of the river, parallel to your route. The lines should be about an inch apart so they won't

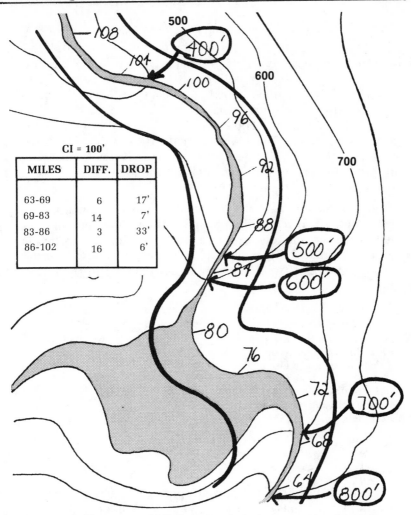

CI = 100'

| MILES | DIFF. | DROP |
|--------|-------|------|
| 63-69 | 6 | 17' |
| 69-83 | 14 | 7' |
| 83-86 | 3 | 33' |
| 86-102 | 16 | 6' |

**Figure 2-1** "The Map Profile" illustrates the technique used to determine the drop of a typical river. Handwritten circled numbers indicate contours. Distances (miles) are not circled.

obscure important topographical features. I use a felt tip "hi-liter" pen--the kind college kids prefer for marking important passages in text books. Hi-liter ink is translucent so you can read through it.

Next, consult the map scale and mark the miles along your route. The common procedure is to "tick off" every ten miles, but this is awkward and may lead to navigational errors later. Instead, I mark each four miles, which, on a 1:250,000 map, works out to a mark every inch. Scale relationships are easy to maintain this way since average cruising speed for a loaded wilderness canoe is about four miles an hour, or "one inch to the hour".

Four mile units are also easier to split mentally than ten mile ones. And as you'll discover, a watch is an essential tool for navigating northern rivers. If you keep track of precise time you'll always know your exact position (well . . . almost always).

When you've finished marking mileage, stand back and take a hard look. Are you too ambitious? Do you have enough vacation days to cover "all those miles"? Have you alloted extra time in the event you become windbound (the standard rule is one day in five)? The answers to these and other questions will become clearer as the planning stage proceeds. Nevertheless, you should be able to make some preliminary decisions now.

Next procedure is to draw a small arrow everywhere a contour line crosses the river. Write in the elevation of each contour near the penciled arrow and circle it. Be sure you indicate whether the elevation is in feet (') or meters (M). The "Contour Interval"--or vertical distance between contour lines--is given in the lower map margin.

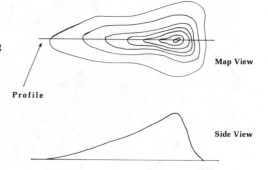

**Figure 2-2**
Basic contour of a long sloping hill that gives a rough idea of interval spacing. Note the significant drop on the right side of the hill and the gentle slope at left.

Map View

Profile

Side View

You don't need to be a cartographer to interpret contours. An understanding of these basics will get you through:

1. Contour lines connect points of *equal* elevation. Thus, closely spaced lines indicate lots of elevation change (drop), whereas wide-spaced lines show the opposite (figures 2-2, 2-3, 2-4).

2. The closed or "vee" end of a contour line always points *upstream* (figures 2-3, 2-4).

3. Where the contour lines cross or run very close together, you'll find an abrupt drop--a falls or canyon (figures 2-3, 2-5).

4. The Contour Interval ("CI") *is not* the same for all maps, so look closely! Convert meters (all the new Canadian maps are metric) to feet (10 meters equals 33 feet) if you're confused by the metric system.

5. The larger the contour interval, the less clear are the river's characteristics. In short, a map whose "CI" is 10 feet, gives a clearer picture of the topography than one whose "CI" is 100 feet.

RIVER—⁀ Direction of flow ➤   CONTOUR LINES

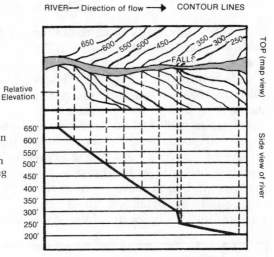

**Figure 2-3**
Falls are easy to spot on the contour map. Closely spaced "vee" points indicate a sudden drop. Notice the difference between the extreme elevation change at 300'- 250' and the long decline between 250'- 200'.

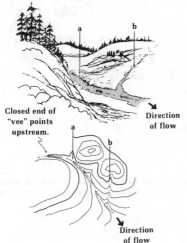

Closed end of "vee" points upstream.

**Figure 2-4**
Stream (b) flows into river (a).

**Figure 2-5**
"Beware the Canyon!" Contour lines that run very close together and parallel to river banks indicate canyons. Be sure to identify the canyon! Once inside, you are committed!

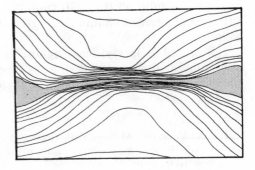

# The Drop

You're now ready to compute "drop". Do the computations in a table similar to that in figure 2-1. For example: the 800 foot contour crosses the river at mile 63, while the 700 foot line interacts at mile 69. This is recorded in the table as "63-69". The mileage difference is six (69 minus 63). Dividing six into 100 (the value of the contour interval)· yields a drop of 17 feet per mile.

From mile 69 to 83 the river drops less--seven feet per mile, etc.

To the experienced canoeist "drop figures" conjure up a vivid picture of a river's personality. Three to five feet per mile is nice cruising; better than 10, things get hairy. Fifteen means a probable portage. And 20 or more is about the limit for a loaded open canoe.

Equally important as "drop per mile" is how the drops occur--whether uniformly, or at a falls, dam, or major rapid.

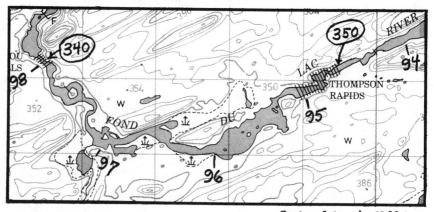

**Figure 2-6**                                    **Contour Interval = 10 Meters**

This map and the map in Figure 2-7 are of sections of the Fond du Lac River, N.W. Saskatchewan. Handwritten circled numbers indicate contours. Distances (miles) are not circled.

Consider the section shown in figure 2-6. The river drops 10 meters (about 33 feet) from mile 94.5 (junction of the 350 meter contour) to mile 98 (the 340 contour). Dividing 33 feet by 3.5 (the difference between 98 and 94.5) gives you 9.4 feet per mile--not too significant.

Runnable? Barely! Look again. Virtually all the drop occurs in two places--the rapid at the 340 contour (a set of formidable sandstone ledges that will swamp you for sure)* and Thompson

---

*Maps aren't perfect. Manitou Falls (legend above incomplete) shown at the 98 mile marker, which will grind you up and spit you out, is actually located three-quarters of a mile downriver at the falls marked "F".

rapids (runnable with high risk if the water level is right). The midsection, however is quite placid--easily paddled by inexperienced Boy Scouts.

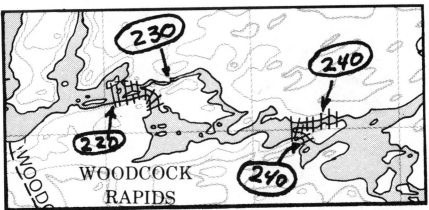

Scale: 2½" = 1 mile                              Contour Interval = 10 Meters

**Figure 2-7**
River drops 33ft/mile between 230-240 contour, and 120ft/mile at Woodcock Rapids section.

A more spectacular example is shown in figure 2-7. Here the river drops 33 feet per mile between the 230 and 240 contour, while further west (Woodcock rapids section), it spills violently at about 120 feet per mile and creates one of the most awesome pitches of white water imaginable. But again, the quiet water between the two drops is easily canoeable.

Okay, now that you've got the basics, it's test time! Study the river map (Figure 2-8) and determine which (if any) sections are runnable.

**Answers are at the end of this chapter.**

# RIVER MAP

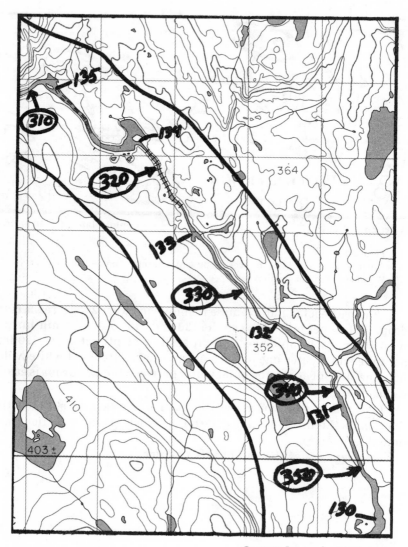

Contour Interval = 10 Meters

**Figure 2-8**
**IS IT RUNNABLE?** Figure the average drop in *feet per mile* (Don't forget to change meters to feet!). Mile marks indicated in dark black as 130, 131, etc. Values of contours (in meters) are circled.

Canyons (figure 2-5)--places where the contour lines run close together--are another hazard you must check out thoroughly before you commit yourself to a river. Maps aren't perfect, so don't depend on drop figures or topographic hash marks (the symbol for rapids) to influence your decision of whether to run or portage. Once you enter a canyon you're committed, so it's imperative that you know what's there *before* you proceed! See Chapter 17 for a discussion of canyons and their dangers.

Expect also to encounter difficulties (rapids!) at every place the river narrows. Maps occasionally overlook some dandy drops here. Conversely, expect to portage most marked rapids. I've never seen a rapid indicated on a Canadian topo that rated less than a high Class II on the International scale which, if you've forgotton, includes rapids with waves up to three feet high!* And most of what's marked is much more formiddable than that.

Granted, you can *always* portage the obstacles, but it may not be easy. Contrary to popular belief and the misguided statements of some writers, there's no such thing as a falls or rapid that *can't* be portaged. The rivers of the far north are littered with the bones of unfortunate canoeists who disagreed. Portage trails along the northern rivers are less used than those further south and so tend to be overgrown with vegetation. Rule of thumb for negotiating cleared trails like those in the BWCA, is 20 minutes per mile. But these figures are meaningless where the path is uncertain. It's not uncommon for an anticipated mile long portage to become a day long endurance contest!

Some years ago I portaged 16 hours to get into a remote section of Ontario's Steel River. Thank goodness I was carrying my 40 pound solo canoe and not my 80 pound Old Town Ranger. Whether that kind of exercise is worth it depends, of course, entirely on your physical conditon, mental make-up, and desire for punishment.

You should also realize that maps don't tell the whole story. Imagine how you'd feel if, after just completing a five mile carry into an isolated lake, you discovered dozens of people who had effortlessly got there by driving a logging road that wasn't indicated on your map. Or perhaps after months of planning you arrive at the headwaters of your river only to discover that the ice hasn't gone out yet-and perhaps won't for another two weeks!** This is why you need to contact a local person who has first-hand knowledge of the river.

So back to the typewriter. If there's a Chamber of Commerce in the town, a letter will bring fast results, but for many small villages, the best procedure is to simply address the mayor.

*See Appendix "E" for a description of this rating scale..

**Most Canadian rivers within the timberline are ice-free by mid-June, but those above the 65th parallel (tundra rivers) frequently remain frozen well into July.

Be sure to ask specific questions and let correspondents know you're an experienced canoeist not a beginner. You can do this by making a casual statement to the effect or by naming a river you've canoed. Acknowledging your experience is not bragging; it is a subtle way of letting your contact know that you have the skills to make a successful trip. Community and government officials receive dozens of canoe trip inquiries each year, mostly from novice canoeists. They don't want to steer a beginner into a route that's too difficult. So your admission of competence will allay concerns and eliminate some of the usual tourist responses.

Many years ago I requested general information about Ontario's Gull River from the Ministry of Natural Resources office in Nipigon. I said nothing about my canoeing background. What I received was a generally useless strip map of the route and a discouraging letter which read:

Dear Sir:

In answer to your request we have forwarded copies of the Gull River Route and in addition a copy of the Master Map for the District which is self explanatory.

If we might suggest, an alternative route to the Gull River should be cosidered as it is a fairly difficult trip.

We hope we have been of some service.

Very truly yours,

G.O. Koistinen, District Manager
Nipigon District

Sometime later I wrote another letter which was much more specific. Needless to say, I was well pleased with the response. It was detailed and directly answered routing and access questions.

If you have a lot of people to contact, you may prefer to send a formal questionnaire instead of a personal letter. But keep the questions short and to a single page. People don't like to answer long forms

Canadians should enclose a self-addressed stamped envelope when writing private individuals, but Americans had best stick with a simple "thank you".

I once requested information about a certain river from Eric Morse--famed Canadian canoe man. I included a stamped return envelope with my request. Eric was anxious to help and supplied what he could. But he also enclosed a note which read: "Thanks for your thoughtfulness in providing the stamp, Cliff, but it's time you realized that Canada is a separate country with its own postal service and its own stamps!"

A foolproof way to get replies is to address the local Catholic church. Even the smallest village usually has a Catholic church with a priest who is willing to help. Equally important, the local clergyman usually knows who has intimate knowledge of "your river" and for that reason, may be your best contact.

In all likelihood, the Catholic diocese which services your own community can supply names and addresses. Or you can direct your request to the appropriate Canadian archdiocese. You'll find these addresses in the "Official Catholic Directory"--a voluminous publication that's in the library of every American Catholic church.

You'll also discover that a professional looking letterhead or rubber stamp will speed up all your correspondence. Personalized stationery suggests you're serious and competent, so it is more likely to get a prompt reply.

As the information rolls in, the picture of your river will begin to enlarge. Barring unforseen obstacles like a drought, flood, or a crew that backs out at the last minute, you're nearly ready to commit yourself to a specific route.

But first you must iron out the solutions to the physical difficulties (those canyons, falls, and rapids, mentioned earlier) you may encounter. Time to shift gears--or rather map scales, to 1:50,000 (one and one-fourth inches to the mile). These large scale maps provide exacting detail--just what you want for locating an obscure portage or a route through the maze of islands on a complex lake.

However, 1:50,000 maps have one serious drawback; they cover so little area that you may need many of them to cover a lengthy route. And at several dollars a sheet, costs mount up quickly. One answer is to order these maps for specific areas of concern and to stick with the larger 1:250,000 maps for less intricate navigation.

Colored maps in 1:50,000 scale are available for almost all the populated parts of Canada, while remote areas are commonly mapped only in monochrome. The monchrome maps are less expensive and their high contrast makes them easier to read under typical field conditions. Additionally, monochrome maps reproduce beautifully, so inexpensive copies can be made for everyone in the party.

I usually purchase a complete set of monochromes and then cut and paste the sections together to form a long strip map that covers the entire route. Then I make copies of this strip map for each member of the crew. This method is much less expensive and bulky than buying additional maps.

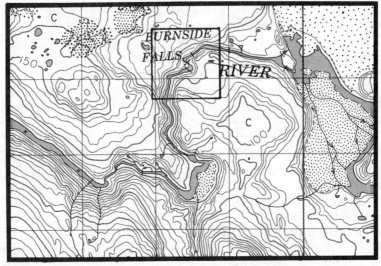

**Figure 2-9**
1:50,000 monochrome map showing Burnside Falls, NWT. Compare this map with the aerial photo (Fig. 2-10) of the same aera.

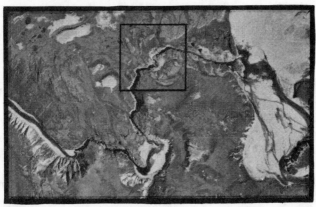

**Figure 2-10**
Shown here is Burnside Falls (Burnside River, NWT). This is a small portion of an aerial photograph that can supplement the use of a monochrome map by providing a better idea of the river's terrain.

Still concerned about a particular obstacle? Then order the aerial photographs from which the map was made, from the National Air Photo Library, 615 Booth Str., Ottawa, Ontario K1A OE9.*

*Alaskan photos may be obtained from: Rocky Mountain Region Engineer, U.S. Geological Survey, Bldg. 25, Federal Center, Denver, Colorado 80225.

Photos are extremely large scale--somewhere between 1:24,000 (one inch equals two-fifths of a mile) and 1:60,000 (one inch to the mile). And since there are more than four million of them on file in the Air Photo Library, getting exactly what you want requires precise identification of the specific area.

The most satisfactory way of getting the right photo is to outline the area on a topo map and send it along with your check to the Air Photo Library. They'll return the map with your order.

Or you can also state the *exact* latitude and longitude, to the nearest five minutes of arc, of the specific feature--falls, rapids, dam, etc.--about which you're concerned.

Incidently, it's a good idea to order your photos as stereo pairs. This enables you to see the topography of the river in three dimension with the aid of an inexpensive stereoscope, available at forestry and surveying supply houses. 3-D makes it real!

You don't actually need a stereoscope to see in three dimension. As a forester with the Bureau of Land Management many years ago, I learned to adjust my eyes to get a 3-D picture. It takes practice but the procedure is simple: Set the two photos on a flat surface side by side with the object you want to study about three inches apart. Then stare boldly "into" the photos--as if you're looking through them. Each eye should be focused straight ahead, independent of the other eye. Slowly move the two photos around--a few centimeters each way-- until the object comes into 3-D focus. The procedure will sting your eyes a bit while you're looking but the pain will cease instantly when you quit. Foresters commonly leave their stereoscopes at home and use this method in the field.

It would be unfair to leave the subject of maps without mentioning "base maps" and "land use" maps.

Base maps, sometimes called "white prints" or "logging" or "mining" maps, are simply paper prints of forest resources inventory maps. They're drawn from the latest aerial photos, usually on a scale of 20 or 40 chains to the inch. A chain is an old surveying measurement: There are 66 feet or four rods to a chain, 80 chains to the mile. Each map sheet commonly covers about 10 to 20 miles.

Many of the Canadian provinces are scarred with a network of logging and mining roads, most of which are not shown on topographic maps, but which are sometimes visible on the latest base maps. If there are recent base maps available, the Canada Map Office will know where to find them. And where land adjacent to a river is owned by a paper or mining company, some sort of provisional map

*The most complete source of forestry/surveying/mapping supplies I know of is "Forestry Suppliers, Inc." 205 West Rankin St., Jackson, Miss. 39204. Write for their gigantic catalog.

which shows road access is bound to exist. Occasionally, large scale paper prints which indicate roads and trails are available directly from the company which owns the area.

Land use maps, which are not available for all parts of Canada, do what their name implies--they tell you how the land is used. Basically, they're standard 1:250,000 topo maps that are overprinted with information about wildlife, vegetation, hunting and fishing, climate, and places of interest. They tend to be pretty cluttered with data and so are only marginally useful for navigation. But they do provide a wealth of interesting data--reason enough to carry one.

Order these maps from the Canada Map Office (same place you get all the others) and be sure to specify "Land Use Information Series".

Finally, don't overlook "tourist maps" when planning your trip. These maps--commonly available from local Chambers of Commerce and area businesses, may be extremely useful. One of the best tourist maps I ever had cost one dollar at a gas station in Kakabeka Falls, Ontario. The map showed the location of every logging road and horse path, and there were lots of'em. It even indicated by lake, the species of fish you might expect to catch. Wish we'd known about that map *before* we canoed the English River. It might have saved us a seven mile portage!

At this point your research is pretty complete. What you've learned should keep you from running into too much of the unexpected. However, if you want to be really thorough, you'll attempt to locate the journals of early explorers--Tyrrell, Raddison, Thompson, Mackenzie, and others--who paddled your route. Here's an example:

"Immediately above the portage the channel is very crooked, and there is a stiff rapid with a fall of about twelve feet, which we ascended with a line, above which is a stretch of moderately easy water, up which we paddled with the assistance of a stiff breeze, to the foot of Thompson Rapid, one of the heaviest rapids on the river. The lower part, in which the banks are low, was readily ascended with a line to a short portage thirty-five yards long, across a point on the north side, where we camped for the night of August 12th. Above this short portage, almost to the top of the rapid, the banks are from ten to fifteen feet high and consist of flat-lying sandstone, generally undercut by the water. Past part of this cascade we portaged all our stuff for 300 yards on the north bank,

merely tracking up our empty canoes. The total fall in the
rapids is about thirty feet."*

Though these trip logs are frequently more than 100 years old,
they're still valuable, for most major rapids, falls, and portages, have
changed little over the course of time.

Certainly it's not necessary to do an exhaustive journal search to
insure a successful canoe trip. On the other hand, the writings of a
perceptive explorer might give you just the edge you need to quickly
locate a hard-to-find portage or a route through a tricky rapid. If
nothing else, the old diaries lend historical perspective to what might
otherwise be "just another canoe trip".

Unfortunately, there's little demand for the old   journals so don't
expect to find them sitting boldly on the shelves of your county
library. Moreover, many of the old journals are bound in books which
are frequently hundreds of pages long and span many years. Seldom
do you need all that. Fortunately, librarians are wonderful people--
they'll go the extra mile to help you find exactly what you want. In
research as with other things, patience has its own rewards.

Another place to look for accounts of early explorers is the local
historical society which serves the area of exploration. Again,
historical librarians are more than willing to help.

Whew! That about does it--river researched, planning complete.
Right! Not hardly. You've got the river nailed down all right but
there's much more to do. Like a crew to pick--one that likes your route
and your tripping style; food to buy and pack; equipment to round up;
a time and distance schedule to calculate; and transportation to
consider. And don't forget money--the stuff that makes it all happen.
How will you carry enough for a four week trip? Travelers checks?
Cash? Money orders? Credit cards? Can everyone in your party
"afford" your trip? What about fishing licenses, CB permits, wildlife
refuge travel permits?

Just the thought of all that's left to do makes you want to abandon
the operation and opt for a friendly float down a local stream, doesn't
it? No way! Planning is outright fun, almost as much as the trip itself.
Besides, planning makes you an active participant in the trip rather
than just a tag-along who was picked up at the last moment to fill out
the crew. Making a successful expedition is meaningless if you don't
take an active part in putting it together. After all anyone can follow
"their guide" through the wilderness!

*From the Journal of J.B. Tyrrell. Report on the country between Athabasca Lake and
Churchill River with notes on two routes travelled between the Churchill and
Saskatchewan Rivers. Canada. Geological Survey, Annual Report, Volume 8, 1895,
pages 82D - 83D.

Granted, you can be pretty haphazard about planning if your route is well traveled and not dangerous. So what if you get confused for a few hours or run a Class II rapid without first scouting it? Penalties are not severe: a bit of extra paddling, perhaps a dunking. Nothing serious.

But if your dreams take you to the distant north, where rivers run cold and wild, and help is many miles away, then you better put your efforts into rigorous planning!

# Answers to "EXERCISE" Fig. 2-8
## ("Is it runnable?")

**Contour Interval Equals 10 Meters**

| MILES | DISTANCE (miles) | DROP/MILE (feet)* |
|-------|------------------|-------------------|
| 130.5-131.3 | 0.8 | 41 |
| 131.3-132.5 | 1.2 | 27.5 |
| 132.5-133.7 | 1.2 | 27.5 |
| 133.7-135.4 | 1.7 | 19.4 |
| **Total miles = 4.9** | | **115.4 feet (total drop)** |

Total drop/mile = 115.4 feet
Average drop/mile = 115.4/4.9 = 23.6 feet

Is it runnable? **No way!** A few isolated sections might be canoeable for short stretches. But this river is *really* moving!

*Don't forget to change meters to feet. Remember, there are 3.3 feet in one meter, or 33 feet in 10 meters.

# 3

# Picking A Crew

Picking a crew is like buying a used car: What you see outside only suggests what you get inside. Only miles of driving under a variety of conditions will tell you the true nature of the beast. "You pays your money and you takes your chances", as the saying goes. So it is with canoe teams. A good friend at the office may be incompatible in the wilds, and vice versa, Responsible performance under city stress is not a measure of level-headedness afield. The two variables are quite unrelated.

A canoe crew has an investment in the safety, joy, and well-being of all its members. There's no room for loners or ego-maniacs. It takes lots of time, on the river and off, to find enough skilled, responsible, and caring people to fill out a crew-- the reason why experienced groups are so possessive about keeping their members together on subsequent trips. When a proven individual drops out of a successful team for one reason or another, a semi-panic often ensues. After all, filling the void with someone new is like buying boots by mail: Even when you know your size there's no guarantee of a perfect fit!

Foremost in selecting a crew is "compatibility". All other factors--paddling skill, age, physical abilities, woodsmanship, etc.--take a back seat to this requirement. The literature is filled with tales about trips which nearly ended in disaster because canoe partners simply couldn't get along. Intolerance of the views of others spells danger, or at best an unwholesome acidic experience.

## BASIC SKILLS

There are two kinds of skills--those you have and those you think you have! An honest appraisal of your own abilities is essential to insure a successful canoe trip, so begin by taking a long hard look into the mirror. Twenty years of canoeing experience in the Allagash or Minnesota Boundary Waters doesn't qualify you for an arctic adventure. Neither does equal time spent paddling slalom gates on the national white water course. Certainly these experiences are

**Figure 3-1**
A canoe crew has an investment in the safety, joy, and well being of all its
members. Taking a break is (left to right) Kent Swanson, Marc Hebert,
Reb Bowman, Bob Dannert, David Dannert, and Cliff Jacobson near a
small nameless falls on the Hood River (NWT).

valuable, but what you really need is "variety", not years of rote
practice in the same environment.

Canoeists new to the wilderness game don't realize that learning
"when to portage" is more important than developing talents for
paddling the near impossible. A back country canoeist's greatest skill
is "good judgement"--a quality which takes many years to develop.

High tech canoeing skills are useful of course, and the tougher the
river, the more essential they become. But more important are the
answers to these fundamental questions: Can you thread your way
through the maze of islands on a 40 mile long fog-shrouded lake? Or
rig a snug camp in the teeth of an icy rain? Are you able to sniff out a
coming storm and locate an unmarked portage in a mess of tangled
alders? Have you the mental discipline to keep going in the face of all
obstructions--foul weather, grueling portages, persistent insects?

These skills plus your own mature judgement are what will keep
you safe and comfortable on a wild and distant river.

Still looking into the mirror? Perhaps you're getting somewhat
frightened at your own inadequacy. Good! It's normal. And healthy.
Shows that beneath that staunch outward appearance there's a
warmly beating heart. *You're not alone!* Virtually every backcountry
canoeist I know secretly admits some inner fear (call it profound
anticipation, if you will) that his  or her own skills are inadequate to
meet the challenge.

Mild controllable fear is nature's way of telling you to slow down and think before you act. At the other extreme is foolhardiness, and every white water club has some of these people, many of which are excellent technical paddlers. Follow them down a local river clad in wetsuit and helmet if you like. But keep'em out of the wilds. They'll kill you for sure!

Dr. Bill Forgey, veteran north country canoeist and author, sums it up:

"Somehow on long trips, the uncertainty of the next days travels, the food supply, the amount of time, all seem to gnaw at me--perhaps in many ways spoiling the trip... Why do I take these things so seriously? Perhaps I'm not cut out for wilderness travel. I asked Sigurd Olson one day about this. He laughed and said that he'd put the same question past Camsell* at the Explorer's Club one day. Camsell replied that he'd spent most of his adult life exploring the bush and had been scared during nine-tenths of it."

The point of foregoing discussion is elementary: Select your crew members for their maturity and level-headedness. Avoid technically competent hotdogs who don't have all their mental faculties. And if the skills of your party suggest you're not ready for a certain river, don't be disappointed. There's a world of lesser routes out there waiting for you to learn on. And these waterways are often just as beautiful and remote as the awesome bone-chillers of the far north.

It takes years to develop the "proper" wilderness canoeing sense. Don't rush it!

It's interesting to note that the best wilderness canoe experts usually don't consider themselves as such. Despite their proven abilities they know there's still much to learn. Now compare this attitude with that of equipment shop arm-chair experts who know it all. Humbling, isn't it?

## PADDLING SKILLS

The tougher the river, the better you and your crew had better be! Most of the time you can get by okay if one person per canoe is a skilled paddler. This individual usually takes the stern and trains his

---

*Charles Camsell, noted Canadian explorer, former commissioner of the Northwest Territories, died in 1958.

bow partner during the course of the trip. If the river's not too violent the procedure works well enough--a few scrapes and dings on the hull during the learning process, but that's all. Most novice bow paddlers become acceptably proficient after the first week of white water travel.

Only when the river becomes dangerously demanding does the "train as you go" philosophy fail. It's then that your bow person becomes invaluable--he or she must "understand" the why's and how's of moving water and react instantly, precisely, without error. Failing this, you'd better portage, and there's no dishonor in that. So again, the bottom line is compatibility.

Another characteristic of a matched crew is "similiar sociological backgrounds." Mix five deep thinkers with one non-intellectual and you've got a recipe for problems--not due to snobbery or insensitivity of the majority, but because the person who is "different" may magnify unimportant subtleties. For example, a series of lofty discussions carried on for days can make a person who "doesn't understand" feel genuinely inferior--an outcast. Sensitivity towards each others feelings can over-ride the difficulties, but it takes conscious and continuous practice.

Ideally, each crew member should contribute some special skill-- cooking, white water technique, map reading, first-aid, biology/geology/meterology/photography, etc. When the days turn to weeks you'll discover that there's simply no substitute for good stimulating conversation. And the more interesting, unique, and diversified are your friends, the more memorable your canoe trip will be.

Other considerations which affect your choice of crew are time, money, and purpose. The more time you have, the less costly your trip can be. For example, if you have five weeks to do a river, you may have enough time to start and/or end your run at a town that has road, rail, or commercial air  transportation back to your starting point. Obviously this is much less expensive than a shorter route which requires a flight in or out on a charter float plane.

Charter flights are incredibly expensive. It's not uncommon for a one way air shuttle to consume more than half of your tripping dollar! Cars, boats, and trains, are a much cheaper way to travel. But they're also more time consuming.

The cost versus time relationship should be fully explored by all prospective crew members. In general, younger folks--especially college kids--have more time than money. As age, with its accompanying responsibilities overwhelm, the situation reverses, for few jobs allow long periods of time off. Here again, the importance of similar backgrounds comes into play.

Equally important, is "purpose". Will this be a fishing trip, a canoe adventure, or something inbetween? You've just got to get this one nailed down tight at the start. A lot of canoe trips have been ruined because some people wanted to paddle while others wanted to fish or photograph.

Personally, I don't like to fish. And on the rare occasions I do, I never catch anything. Once on a small tributary of the Moose river, five friends caught over 100 Northern Pike in just 90 minutes (of course we didn't keep them all). I caught three. . . and lost two. One friend felt so sorry for me that he played a tired yard long fish to shore, handed me the pole and said, "Here Cliff, have some fun. . . catch a fish!" Nice buddy, huh?

Nevertheless, I do relish fresh batter-fried fish. So I always like to have someone in my crew who understands the ways of the rod and reel. But I make it perfectly clear *before* the trip that *we canoe until we stop for the day!* Then the fishing begins!

More than once I've paddled out after sunset in search of a friend who lagged behind to fish. For safety sake it's important that a canoe group stay close together at all times. And you can't do that if  one pair is miles behind casting hopefully into a quiet pool.

Agree on a purpose--a traveling philosophy. Then stick to it. And write the rules in technicolor so everyone understands!

## WHAT SIZE CREW?

The safest and least expensive way to go is with a crew of six. This gives you two rescue boats in the event of an upset, but more important, there's ample room to get everyone out if you lose a canoe in a rapid.

Six is also the cheapest way   to fly. A Twin Otter will carry six passengers, three canoes, and all your packs for little more than flying four plus gear on two smaller Cessna's. And carrying canoes inboard is obviously a safer way to fly than tying them alongside pontoons.

On the negative side, it's not easy to find enough level open sites to erect three six by eight foot tents. Certainly you can sleep everyone in two tents this size, but what happens if you lose a tent in a rough water upset? Is your remaining tent large enough to accomodate the overload?  It happens!

It's also more of a hassle to feed six than four--mainly because freeze-dried foods come pre-packed in units   of four servings.

But the greatest detriment to six person crews is getting to and from the river. It's almost impossible to stuff six adults, three canoes, and nine or more bursting Duluth packs into today's small cars. A station wagon isn't much help either. Three canoes can be carried atop a full size wagon but it's a messy operation. What you really need is a van and canoe trailer.

What about crews larger than six? Frankly, the farther you get from the standard four person group, the more difficult things become. I've traveled with many parties of nine over the years and I've had compatibility problems with at least half of them. If you've led many Scout or church groups you know exactly what I mean. Adults are no easier to manage than teenagers--believe me, you'll still experience your share of problems. Simple mathematics suggest that the larger the crew, the more and varied the difficulties.

In summary, safety and low cost favor large groups; logistics favor small ones. Except for trips into the remote arctic, my preference is four.

All this philosophy looks good on paper until you realize that even small crews invariably emerge solely from the ranks of those "who are free to go". Besides, there's always someone who backs out at the last minute and leaves you scrambling for a warm replacement—one who "might like to go on a canoe trip". As I think back over the imperfect crews I've had over the years, I wonder why I find it so difficult to follow my own advice. But I'll keep trying!

## WHAT ABOUT TAKING CHILDREN ALONG?

Not everyone enjoys having children along on a canoe trip. The factor here seems to be whether everyone's child is involved or just a select few. Thus it's "okay" if each canoe is manned by a father/son or mother/daughter team. The problem arises when there's just one boy or girl in the company of a crew of adults. Telling a parent his or her child "isn't wanted" may be the most difficult of all crew problems to solve. But the situation can be worked out to satisfaction if everyone is open and honest with their feelings. Remember, you're "family" on a canoe trip. And no fighting please!

You should also realize that even the most mature, level-headed youngster has far poorer judgement than the average rational adult. So pick your river with this thought in mind if you're taking children along. Make sure the experience is *well within* their capabilities.

# DUTIES

Okay, you've got yourself a crew! Time to celebrate with a good dinner and fine wine. And afterwards you can hit the maps again, assign specific work duties, and get down to the serious business of solving the 101 problems which still remain.

### THE TRIP LEADER

"The group leader is the intermediary between the participants and their surroundings. The leader is the facilitator, the dependable decision maker, the first-aid administrator, the group phycologist, and naturalist. The leader is a little bit mother, a little more example, a source of knowledge, and the great anticipator.

The object of any trip is to meld people with the land and to develop a satisfaction from an experience. The leader is usually more capable than the group, and more concerned with the experience of the whole group, rather than his or her own personal satisfaction.

The skill level of participants must be built with mild nudges and steady progress so that the individuals find satisfaction. The mix of emotions and personalities must be blended with concern for the whole. Ethics must come naturally and each part of the experience must be an unspoken lesson.

There is no room for the leader to have a bad day, to become disgusted with the weather, or to succumb to a general bitchiness. The leader must call on extra adrenalin and find an emotional release after the trip.

What is done on the trip must allow the participant to develop a feeling for the land, a recreation to the flow of the river, and a comraderie for the life that surrounds the trip. The leader allows the experience to transcend the physical realm into the realm of recognition, knowledge, emotion and commitment. The leader is the spokesperson for the environment."

MIKE LINK
Director, Northwoods Audubon Center
Sandstone, Minnesota

By and large, canoe trips proceed along democratic lines. What to fix for supper, when to stop for the day, whether to traverse a windy bay or wait it out, is all the result of mutual discussion and consent. But often there's disagreement. And the majority is not always right. That's why every group needs an experienced leader who is not afraid to make decisions.

In 1979, I led a CANOE magazine sponsored trip down Saskatchewan's Fond du Lac river. When we arrived at Black lake near the end of our journey the wind was howling murder and the lake was kicking up four foot white caps. We fixed a hasty supper and retired to the shelter of our tents intent on making the necessary 20 mile crossing later in sub-arctic twilight when the wind died down.

When we arose at midnight the waves were much smaller than before but were still running steadily from the west (our direction of travel). Minutes passed. Finally, my friend Darrell Foss had had enough. "You're the trip leader, Cliff,"he said, "Make a decision!"

"Okay...we go!" I replied. And without another word we dropped camp and in 30 minutes we were waterborne.

It was a rough wet ride but we made it to a protected narrows just minutes before the wind vented its full fury. A delay of even a quarter hour would have seen us caught on open water in a dangerously running sea. Probably we should have stayed the day and waited it out. But the fact that the decision was made quickly, saved the day.

Generally I go with the majority on matters not directly concerned with safety and opt for the cautious course, reagardless of vote, when the occasion demands. For example, if three of four want to run a questionable rapid, I'll side with the minority and portage even if I think the drop is safe. I don't like to cajole someone into doing something they feel is dangerous.

Other crews approach the matter on a partnership rather than crew basis. Thus, one team runs the rapid if they choose, another portages or lines.

## TREASURER

The treasurer handles all money and keeps track of expenses. He or she should convert the necessary amount of the expedition's dollars to Canadian currency in advance of the trip. Conversion should be made at an American bank to insure the highest rate of exchange.

It's essential that the expedition have some working capitol on hand early in the planning stage. This lets you take advantage of special pre-season dried food and equipment sales and a fluctuating foreign exchange rate. Besides, "money down" means *committment*-- it keeps people from backing out at the last minute.

The crew should agree on some sort of graduated payment schedule like the one shown below:

Total cost of trip (hypothetical)_____ $500

### Payment Schedule

February 1 .............. $100 (non-refundable deposit)
March 15 ........................................... $200
May 1 .............................................. $200
Trip dates: July 2-26
Note that all money has been collected *two months in advance* of trip!

## RESEARCH TECHNICIAN

Someone must take responsibility for writing all those letters mentioned in Chapter two. Invariably this duty falls on the trip leader, who out of necessity, must leave no stone unturned.

## TRANSPORTATION CHAIRPERSON

This person secures the appropriate road maps and plans the route to and from the river. If special tires or vehicle modifications are required, the cost should be borne in part by the crew. The transportation chairperson is usually the one who owns the vehicle. Owner of the vehicle *does not* pay for gas or oil en route.

## WEATHER FORCASTER

You can make this job as easy or complex as you like. Either way, weather forcasting is fun and practical. Instruments range from low cost thermometers and cloud comparison charts to the sophisticated Sager Weathercaster which requires an expensive barometer. Every expedition should have a weather man or woman. Gives you someone to blame for a week long rain.

## MENU MAN/WOMAN

Best handled by two people with dissimiliar tastes. The idea is to work up a low cost efficient menu for the trip (ideas in chapter 11).

## SUPPLY OFFICER

Someone must develop a thorough equipment list of personal and group essentials. Absolutely nothing must be left to chance. Invariably, this is another responsibility for the group leader.*

## PUBLICATIONS OFFICER

Essential only if you want to advertise your trip. Local newspapers are always searching for interesting items. Possibly you can get some sponsorship in return for a short story or trip log and photos.

---

*Perhaps you're beginning to discover that most of the burden of organizing a canoe trip ultimately falls on the leader. Effective delegation of responsibility can help lighten the load, but only if those who undertake the duties are sufficiently knowledgeable to rise to the challenge. All too often the leader finds himself in the unfortunate position of "doing it all"!

Now that you have an anxious working crew, the solutions to problems will come much easier. After all, many heads are better than one. But don't let things stagnate until trip time. Keep the pot boiling with a meeting each month.

No one can tell you how much time you need to plan a successful canoe trip. That depends on a long list of variables--the general difficulty of the route, remoteness of the area, distance from home, length of stay on the river, etc. Nine months is probably the *minimum* you should allot for planning a major trip; a year or more is not uncommon.

It's *never* too early to plan a canoe trip!

# 4

# Loose Threads

"A compendium of unrelated things you need to do before the wheels role north."

It was September 14, 1955 on the Dubawnt River in the Northwest Territories, and already there was a crispness in the air. Each day, frost grew heavier on the morning ground. Arctic summer, so intense in early August was gone now and autumn with its sub-freezing temperatures and fierce polar gales had begun. Arthur Moffat, experienced trip leader, was worried; he knew the snows of winter were not far away.

Moffat unfolded his map and stared unbelievingly at the thin ribbon of blue that was the Dubawnt river. Two hundred fifty miles lay between his campsite and destination--the isolated settlement of Baker Lake. After some discussion there came a monumentous decision. To save time the party would run any rapid which "looked safe from the top".

Later that day they came upon a substantial rapid. Moffat stood up in the canoe to check it out. "Looks okay",he said. "Let's run it!"

Almost immediately it happened. Capsize! Another canoe followed suit close behind. Four men now struggled for survival in the icy waters of the Dubawnt.

Everyone was rescued quickly so there should have been no problems. But there was not enough wood to build a warming fire and the crew knew little about hypothermia. We can only speculate why Moffat died on that September day and his friends did not. Perhaps he was concerned for the safety of the others and so neglected his own treatment until it was too late. Or maybe he was in poorer health than his friends.

Arthur Moffat was buried at Baker Lake in the land he loved best. A simple wooden cross in a lonely cemetary marks his grave.

Canoeists were stupified by the untimely death of this competent outdoorsman. Surely barren land rivers were unsafe places, fit only for supermen of incomparable stamina and skill. The myth persisted for a decade after Moffat's death. Even today, few canoeists dare venture north of sixty (the sixtieth parallel).

Nonetheless, Moffat's crew made many serious errors, all of which are easily avoidable by perceptive men and women with cautionary sense. Most unforgiveable was recklessness--failure to carefully check a rapid before running it. Arctic rivers are no place for impulsive decisions. There was also an inability to maintain a travel schedule. Indeed, Moffat's diary, later published in "Sports Illustrated" magazine, gave no indication that he had a trip plan at all. Freeze-up comes early in the barrens. September is no time to be in the middle of a tundra river!

Good maps and common sense are not enough to insure your safety on a difficult river. You need a realistic travel plan that takes into account the physical characteristics of the route--stoppers like rapids, falls, low water, ice, and the experience and goal of your crew. In every case, the bottom line is the same--be conservative, don't break off more than you can swallow!

How many miles can you expect to average in a ten hour day on a typical northern river?

--Average fast river with few portages .....30 to 50 miles.
--Average fast river with frequent portages 15 to 20 miles.
--Lakes, no wind ........................30 to 40 miles.
Upstream with occasional rapids ......less than 10 miles.

Of course these are averages and they're affected by so many variables that they're probably meaningless.

For example, you'll make much better time if you paddle a fast cruising canoe than a slow white water boat, even if you have to carry around most rapids. It usually takes more time to check a rapid than to portage it so you're almost always ahead in the faster canoe.

A good plan is to cover 15 miles a day. This gives you a day off now and then, an opportunity to explore all that beautiful backcountry you've come to see, and a chance to fish and photograph. And it allows for the unexpected--storms, high winds, navigational blunders, difficult portages, injuries. These are the realities of wilderness tripping--realities which should be taken seriously and planned for.

Figure 4-1                              SCHEDULE

| Day (on water) | Day's run -miles | Distance to Date -miles | Time- % of Total | Distance- % of Total | Comments |
|---|---|---|---|---|---|
| 1 (July 19) | 4.4 | 4.4 | 5.3 | 1.4 | 3 hours on water only |
| 2 | 8.8 | 13.2 | 10.5 | 4.3 | |
| 3 | 4.8 | 18.0 | 15.8 | 5.9 | |
| 4 | 18.0 | 36.0 | 21.1 | 11.8 | |
| 5 | 12.8 | 48.8 | 26.3 | 16.0 | behind |
| 6 | 19.6 | 68.4 | 31.6 | 22.3 | schedule |
| 7 | 13.2 | 81.6 | 36.9 | 26.7 | |
| 8 | 25.6 | 107.2 | 42.1 | 35.1 | |
| 9 | 16.4 | 123.6 | 47.3 | 40.4 | |
| 10 | 35.6 | 159.2 | 52.6 | 52.1 | on schedule |
| 11 | 22.4 | 181.6 | 57.9 | 59.3 | |
| 12 | 20.4 | 202.0 | 63.2 | 66.0 | |
| 13 | 26.4 | 228.4 | 68.4 | 74.6 | |
| 14 | 19.6 | 248.0 | 73.7 | 81.1 | |
| 15 | 19.6 | 267.6 | 79.0 | 87.5 | ahead of schedule |
| 16 | 11.6 | 279.2 | 84.3 | 91.2 | |
| 17 | 8.8 | 288.0 | 89.4 | 94.2 | |
| 18 | 8.8 | 296.8 | 94.8 | 97.0 | |
| 19 (Aug. 6) | 8.8 | 305.6 | 100.0 | 100.0 | |
| **TOTALS** | **305.6** | **305.6** | **100.0** | **100.0** | **Mean 16.1** |

Figure 4-1 indicates the daily mileage of the Keith Thompson* party on their 1971 canoe trip from Rawalpindi Lake via the Coppermine River to the Arctic Ocean.

Figure 4-2
**CROSS CONTINENT CANOE SAFARI——TIME AND DISTANCE SCHEDULE**

| Place | Projected Date 1971 | Miles Between Points | Total | Travel Time | Actual Dates |
|---|---|---|---|---|---|
| Montreal | 4 April | 0 | 0 | — | 17 April |
| Ottawa | | 110 | 110 | 4 days | 23 April |
| Mattawa | | 210 | 320 | 8 days | |
| North Bay | | 45 | 365 | 1 day | 1 May |
| Georgian Bay, Lake Huron | | 110 | 475 | 2 days | |
| Sault Ste. Marie | 8 May | 195 | 670 | 5 days | 11 May |
| Fort William | | 420 | 1090 | 15 days | 27 May |
| Atikokan (route changed) | 3 June | 180 | 1270 | 6 days | |
| International Falls | | 100 | 1370 | 2 days | 4 June |
| Lake of the Woods | | 90 | 1460 | 2 days | |

*Keith Thompson is an experienced arctic canoeist who lives in Yellowknife, NWT. Copies of his complete trip log may be obtained by writing "Travel Arctic", Yellowknife, NWT X1A 2L9.

| | | | | | |
|---|---|---|---|---|---|
| Kenora | | 80 | 1540 | 2 days | |
| Lake Winipeg | 12 June | 160 | 1700 | 5 days | 14 June |
| Saskatchewan River, Grand Rapids | | 315 | 2015 | 10 days | |
| The Pas | | 140 | 2155 | 5 days | |
| Cumberland House | | 80 | 2235 | 3 days | |
| Amisk Lake, Flin Flon | 1-5 July | 60 | 2295 | 2 days | 30 June |
| Churchill River, Frog Portage | | 116 | 2411 | 4 days | |
| Buffalo Narrows, Peter Pond Lake | | 369 | 2780 | 11 days | |
| Clearwater River, Methye Portage | | 125 | 2905 | 3 days | 27 July |
| Athabasca River, Fort McMurray | | 80 | 2985 | 1 day | |
| Lake Athabasca, Fort Chipewan | | 200 | 3185 | 4 days | 2 Aug |
| Fort Smith | | 125 | 3310 | 3 days | 5 Aug. |
| Great Slave Lake, Fort Resolution | | 195 | 3505 | 3 days | 11 Aug. |
| Mackenzie River, Fort Providence | | 165 | 3670 | 3 days | |
| Fort Simpson, at Liard River | | 140 | 3810 | 3 days | |
| Fort Norman at Great Bear River | | 305 | 4115 | 6 days | |
| Fort Good Hope, 25 mi. S. Artic Circle | | 175 | 4290 | 3 days | |
| Arctic Red River | | 215 | 4505 | 4 days | 29 Aug. |
| Peel River, Ft. McPherson | | 60 | 4565 | 2 days | |
| McDougal Pass (over the Rockies) | 5 Sept. | 130 | 4695 | 10 days | 8 Sept. |
| Porcupine River by Bell River | | 115 | 4810 | 2 days | |
| Old Crow | | 100 | | 1 day | |
| Alaska Border, Ramparts House | | 55 | | 1 day | |
| Fort Yukon, jct. Yukon River | | 225 | 5190 | 4 days | 18 Sept. |
| Tanana, jct. Tanana River | | 320 | 5510 | 5 days | |
| Galena | | 165 | 5675 | 3 days | |
| Koyukuk River | | 30 | 5705 | 1 day | |
| Kaltag | | 52 | | 1 day | |
| Anvik | | 140 | | 2 days | |
| Russian Mission | | 110 | 6007 | 2 days | |
| Mountain Villate | | 130 | 6137 | 2 days | |
| Bering Sea, Norton Sound | 10 Oct. | 85 | 6222 | 2 days | 10 Oct. |
| Akumsuk | | 23 | | | |

This TD schedule, **put together nearly one year before the trip**, may seem a bit ambitious. But it was right for Verlen Kruger and Clint Waddell-seasoned racers who made the voyage from Montreal to Alaska in a 21 foot epoxy/fiberglass wood strip canoe of Verlen's design. On some days the pair covered more than 60 miles, as you can see for yourself.

Note that they arrived at the Bering Sea on the precise date they predicted. Exceptional planning!

*Projected date included lay-over for filming (a full length movie was made) and recreation. The original starting date was moved back to April 17 because of the late winter and persistent ice. Clint and Verlen also made two side trips--a 250 mile race at Flin Flon (six days) and a diversion from Peel River to the Arctic Ocean and back (300 miles, 8 days).

A time and distance schedule need not be as fancy as the one used by Verlen Kruger and Clint Waddell on their epic 7000 mile voyage to the Bering Sea (figure 4-2), but it should provide the basic information:

1. Miles between check points. I like to indicate the exact distance I expect to make each day.

2. Date you plan to arrive at each check point or mile marker. The schedule should reflect planned lay-over days and provide at least one day in five for wind and the unexpected.

Computing a realistic time and distance schedule is just one of the many loose threads you'll need to tie before the wheels roll north. Here are some others which are less obvious:

# WHO FURNISHES THE GEAR?

It would be nice if every crew member would contribute an equal share of equipment. You know, John furnishes the tent, rain tarp, and cook-set; Tom and Al supply canoes, Jim contributes the packsacks and stove, etc. But it never works out that way. There's always one or two people who provide everything. And that's both unfair and expensive. There's a lot of wear and tear on canoes and gear on a major trip and the farther you get from the beaten path, the greater the abuse.  It's all part of the game, of course, but it's one everyone should play!

Some expeditions solve the problem by renting items to group members for a few dollars each day. The fee "insures" the user against all damage and loss, even if he or she is directly at fault.

Other crews assign damages to those who are directly responsible. Thus, tent partners split the cost of repairing a wind-torn tent; canoe teams pay an equal share towards replacement of a demolished canoe, etc. But everyone chips in for a lost stove, cook-set, camp saw, etc.

The rental plan has the advantage of paying full compensation for normal wear but it doesn't account for the unexpected, like loss of a canoe while lining.* On the other hand, the "fair share" method provides for major damage but has no provision for expected wear. As you can see, there's no just solution; the   owner of the gear almost always comes out the financial loser.

---

*Lining is the art of working a canoe downstream with the aid of a rope attached to the bow and stern. Hauling it upstream is "tracking". Both procedures require perfect coordination between those who are controlling the lines. If the stern of the canoe is allowed to get out too far in the current while lining, the canoe may broach and upset and suffer serious damage.

Whichever plan you choose, make it clear at the start that everyone *must* supply at least these personal items:

--All clothing, rain gear, and bedding.
--A comfortable foam-filled life jacket.
--Two paddles.
--Proper foot gear.
--Maps and compass.

And *demand* that everything be durable enough to last the trip! You may laugh when your friend shows up with a cheap rain suit and hardware store canoe paddle. But the humor will fade when these things destruct along the route and you have to repair them. A canoe party can travel only as fast as its slowest member. One person's problem--equipment or otherwise--is everyones!

I can't stress enough the importance of selecting good rugged equipment. It's easy to let your sentiments fog your better judgement when you hear "I can't afford it!" But stand firm. The price for equipment failure along a remote river is high .

## SHOULD WE RENT CANOES OR BRING OUR OWN?

It may actually be less expensive to rent canoes on the spot than to haul your own hundreds or thousands of miles on a car or airplane. The Hudson Bay Company offers the most complete canoe rental service in Canada. You can pick up canoes at one store and leave them at another, hundreds of miles away. At this writing, seventeen foot standard weight Grummans are all you can get and cost 95 Canadian dollars per week. Minimal rental time is two weeks and a 50 percent non-refundable deposit is required. You are responsible for all damages to canoes other than that which results from normal use.

Despite the high prices, HBC "U—PADDLE SERVICE" canoes are in great demand. Place your reservation early if you want one. For further information, write or telephone:

The Bay
National Stores Department
77 Main Street
Winnipeg, Manitoba R3C 2R1
Phone: 204: 943-0881

There are dozens of routes that have HBC stores scattered along the way. Here are a few for the *experienced* canoeist:

| ROUTE | TOTAL MILES | TIME/ WEEKS |
|---|---|---|
| Yellowknife-Thelon River-Baker Lake | 800 | 6 |
| Yellowknife-Lac de Gras-Coppermine | 600 | 4 |
| Ile a la Crosse to Pelican Narrows | 340 | 2 |
| New Osnaburgh to Albany | 500 | 3-4 |
| Fort Providence to Inuvik or intermediate points... | 700 | 4-6 |

# MONEY MATTERS

I've always been very apprehensive about carrying large sums of money on canoe trips. What frightens me most is the thought of watching a pack filled with cash disappear down a foamy rapid.

The money belt is much safer than packing money away. In the old days, money belts were cumbersome and easy to detect. But now, only the invisible zippered compartment in back suggest they're anything but ordinary wide dress belts. You can carry hundreds of dollars in a money belt without fear of losing it on a river or in town.

Travelers checks are another alternative. But they're only safer than cash if you don't lose the serial numbers. An obsure place in your car is more secure than the bottom of a wilderness packsack or your own back pocket.

Nearly everyone from French Canada to the north slope of Alaska, recognizes VISA and American Express credit cards. But again, a credit card is no good if you lose it. One friend punched a hole in a corner of his VISA card and attached a small metal key chain. He wears the card around his neck on a loop of parachute cord!

A real advantage of using a credit card in Canada is that you're billed at the current rate of foreign exchange. There are no "special fees" for converting American dollars to Canadian.

Another solution, more commonly suited to the long trip than the short one, is to establish credit with the Hudson Bay Company. The procedure is simple: You write a check to HBC for whatever amount you choose. They in turn send you a letter of credit (Figure 4-3). Expenditures incurred at company stores along your route are noted on the letter and a running total is kept.

Write HBC in Winnipeg for details.

**Figure 4-3**
The Hudson Bay Company can supply your expedition with equipment and
a convenient source of credit for the expedition. This particular credit
voucher is from Verlen Kruger and Clint Waddell's 7000 mile Cross
Continent Canoe Saffari.

# HOW MANY CAR KEYS DO YOU NEED?

Many years ago when I was a boy, my family spent three weeks touring northern Canada by automobile. One night while we were asleep in an Ontario campground, we were robbed. The thief came right into the tent and stole my father's trousers and my mother's purse. Both sets of car keys were gone. The next day provincial police gathered keys from dozens of similar make cars in an effort to find a mate. Ultimately, they found a key that fit and had a duplicate made. But it would have been much easier if Dad had kept an extra set of keys in a magnet box under the hood!

# HOW DO YOU FIND A RELIABLE PERSON TO SHUTTLE YOUR CAR?

A lot of nice rivers don't get paddled simply because canoeists can't find someone to shuttle their car. Actually, getting a shuttle is easy. It just takes persistence.

First, exhaust the standard resources--Chamber of Commerce, local fishing lodges, Ministry of Natural Resources, community churches, etc. Failing this, write the Superintendent of schools in the area. The Chamber of Commerce or mayor can supply the name. A note in the monthly school bulletin will reach almost everyone in the community--you're sure to get a reply from an interested parent.

Your letter should include all essential details--date of shuttle, time, and exactly where you want to go. Be sure to tell what type of vehicle you're driving and whether it has an automatic or stick shift. If you're pulling a trailer say so. A lot of drivers don't want the responsibility for a trailer. And don't forget to mention that you're willing to pay a reasonable fee for this service.

# WATERPROOF YOUR MAPS

Everyone should have a complete set of waterproof maps onto which they've copied all pertinent data--drop figures, portage locations, dangers, etc. You can waterproof maps with contact paper or chemicals. Contact paper, available at most dime stores, resists abraision best and is absolutely waterproof. But it is expensive and bulky and you can't write on it.

Chemicals are cheaper and easier to apply. They make maps *water-resistant* rather than waterproof. But you can write over them- -a real plus if you plan to make notes on your map later.

I've had good results with "Stormproof"--a chemical that's specially formulated for use on maps and charts (available by mail from the Martensen Co., P.O. Box 261, Williamsburg, VA 23185), and

"Thompson's Water Seal"--an industrial strength compound that's used for sealing concrete block. You'll find Thompson's Water Seal on the shelves of most hardware stores in aerosol cans and tins. I buy it by the quart and apply it to maps and journals with a polyurethane foam paint brush. The product also does a fine job of waterproofing hats and clothing. Just attach a plastic pump spray head to the metal can and you're in business. Thompson's Water Seal is inexpensive and highly effective.

Water resistant maps should be further protected by sealing them inside a plastic map case.

## SALT WATER CHARTS AND TIDE TABLES

If your route terminates at salt water, such as James or Hudson Bay, Chantrey Inlet, etc., you should obtain a local tide table and possibly a navagational chart of the estuary.

For example, the mouth of the Albany River is affected every six hours, twelve and one-half minutes by tides which range from two to eight feet. Naturally, islands, bays, and channels in that area will look much different as the water level changes, and of course, camping along tidal flats requires special techniques (See chapter 17).

Conversely, tides along the Arctic Sea coast at the mouth of the Back, Coppermine, and Hood River, are much smaller--a foot or two. An up-to-date tide table will give you the specifics.

The Department of Fisheries and Oceans, in Ottawa, is the place to write for tide and current tables and nautical charts of Canada. The National Ocean Survey office in Anchorage, Alaska, is the source for information about Alaskan waters.*

## NATIONAL ATLAS OF CANADA

This is the place to look for hard-to-find specifics about everything from climate and exploration to posts of the Canadian fur trade. You can buy the entire Canada atlas or select the individual sheets you need. Write the Canada Map Office in Ottawa for a free table of contents.

## ALASKA CATALOG

If you're going to Alaska you'll want to read the Alaska Catalog-- a giant 140 page publication that contains road maps, camping

*Get Canadian charts and tide tables from the Hydrographic Chart Distribution Office, Dept. Of Fisheries and Oceans, 1675 Russell Rd., P.O. Box 8080, Ottawa, Ontario K1G 3H6. For Alaskan charts, write: Chart Sales and Control Data Ofice, National Ocean Survey, 632 6th Ave., Anchorage, Alaska 99501.

information, tips for preparing your vehicle for driving the Alaska highway, procedures for traveling to remote villages, addresses of charter air services, what to do in case of attack by a grizzly bear, and much more. Makes enjoyable reading even if you never visit the 49th state.

The Alaska catalog is available by mail from "The Alaska Catalog", Box 4-907, Anchorage, Alaska 99509.

## REGISTER YOUR ROUTE

Canoeing in a remote part of Canada? Then file a trip plan with the Royal Canadian Mounted Police (RCMP). Registration is a form of life insurance; it guarantees that someone will come looking for you if you're "not out" within a reasonable time after your predicted date. The more isolated your route, the more seriously you should take registration, and the specific date you set as a deadline.

There is no official procedure for registering Alaskan canoe trips. However, you won't get far into Alaska's backcountry without a float plane so your pilot will invariably know where you are.

If you're meeting a charter float plane at trip's end, you'd better be at the appointed place on time. If you're not, your pilot will contact the RCMP or Alaskan authorities and file a "missing persons" report which may initiate an air search.

On the other hand, you can be more liberal with your arrival date if your trip terminates at a town or rail line. Being a *few* days off schedule is only serious if you're meeting an airplane.

In the heat of excitement of a new trip, it's easy to drive past the last town, and RCMP office, and thereby neglect to register you route. So plan accordingly! And if you forget, use the telephone, or relay your plans through the provincial police.

## YOU CAN'T FISH WITHOUT A LICENSE!

Some friends and I once drove 500 miles to canoe a certain Ontario river near Lake Nipigon. We left after work on a Friday evening and drove all night Several times we stopped and tried to buy fishing licenses, but it was too late--all the stores were closed.

At about three a.m., we arrived at our launch site--a shallow creek by a dirt logging road, 60 miles from the nearest town and source of fishing licenses!

If you want to fish, you'll need a license, and you can't get one in the wee hours of the morning. So schedule a daylight stop at a town or tourist lodge on the drive up. Or if that's impossible  purchase your license by mail (where permissible). The Provincial Bureau of Tourism can supply details. Alaska fishermen should write to the Alaska Department of Fish and Game at the address below:

Alaska Department of Fish and Game
230 South Franklin Street
Juneau, Alaska 99801

## FIREARMS--A PERMIT TO CARRY?

There's really no reason to carry a firearm on any canoe trip, even those in Alaska and the Northwest Territories. The only exception might be in certain parts of the arctic where grizzly and polar bear encounters are common. Even here, it's unlikely you'll ever be attacked. Most bears will take off at a fast run at the first smell of you!

Nevertheless, some canoeists feel more secure in bear country if they are armed. According to Alaskan guides, the best bear gun is a twelve guage shotgun loaded with 00 buck. Most non-hunters just aren't accurate or fast enough to kill a charging bruin with a single shot from a high powered rifle.

Another solution is the over/under rifle-shotgun made by Savage Arms Company. One version, called the "Camper's Companion" breaks apart for easy packing and gives you an instant choice between .22 rimfire (top barrel) and 20 guage below. There's even room in the stock for extra shells. The Camper's Companion would make a much better survival weapon than a standard shotgun, if the need arose.

Firearms regulations vary from province to province, so write for specifics before you pack your gun. Ontario, for example flatly prohibits guns during summer when no hunting is allowed. The Northwest Territories, on the other hand, has no restrictions. However, pistols of any kind are strictly forbidden to Americans everywhere in Canada.*

Just about any gun that's legal, including pistols, can be carried in Alaska. Indeed, possession of firearms is encouraged in certain parts of the 49th state.

Be sure to check with the Canadian Wildlife Service** (or Alaska Department of Fish and Game, as the case may be) if you're going armed down a river that passes through a wildlife sanctuary. It's

*You must pre-register rifles and shotguns with U.S. Customs before you enter Canada. If you don't pre-register your guns they'll be confiscated before reentry into the United States!

**Environment Canada, Canadian Wildlife Service, Room 1000, 9942-108 St., Edmonton, Alberta T5K 2J5.

flatly illegal to hunt or bring any unsealed rifle or shotgun into a wildlife preserve. Law breakers may receive stiff fines and jail terms.

# MIGRATORY BIRD SANCTUARIES

You should contact the Canadian Wildlife Service or Alaska Department of Fish and Game if you intend to canoe through a migratory bird sanctuary. Migratory birds are very fickle during the nesting season and may abandon their nests if disturbed. The danger period runs roughly from mid-May to early July--heart of the canoeing season. Wildlife authorities can provide particulars on what areas, if any, are closed to canoe traffic if you advise them of your route and travel dates.

# CANOEING IN NATIONAL AND PROVINCIAL PARKS

You must have a permit  to camp and canoe in Alaskan and Canadian parks. Some parks require a substantial fee, others insist only on formal registration. If you plan to fish in a Canadian National Park, you'll need a special fishing license in addition to your non-resident angling license. Contact the Bureau of Tourism or specific national park for details.

# CITIZEN'S BAND RADIO PERMITS

Listen to your "CB" radio all you like in Canada, but don't transmit without a permit! Thanks to a recent change in Canadian regulations, you can now obtain a permit to transmit without filling out a special form. Here are the details:

Write to COMMUNICATIONS CANADA, 200-386 Broadway Ave., Winnipeg, Manitoba R3C 3Y9, and request a permit to operate your radio. Include the following information in your letter:

--Class of FCC lincense.

--Call sign of FCC license.

--Date current license expires.

--The specific areas of operation in Canada and the approximate date or dates you'll be in Canada.

Canadian authorities will stamp your letter and return it. The letter will then act as your official permit while you're in Canada.

It takes three to four weeks during the spring/summer season for CB requests to pass through official channels. So apply early!

# GET YOUR OWN ACT TOGETHER!

It's only common sense to be in good physical condition before you embark on a canoe trip. This means regular work-outs during the winter months--jogging, swimming, cross-country skiing, jumping rope, etc. Portaging your outfit over rugged trails--or no trails--is part of the game, and all too often the worst carries come early in the trip.

You should also get a good physical exam before you set out on a major trip. A doctor's okay won't guarantee there'll be no problems later, but it is some assurance.

Equally important is a thorough dental exam. Nothing will spoil your fun faster than a gnawing toothache.

Some years ago a friend developed a terrible toothache midway down the Kanaaupscow River in Quebec. For days he pleaded with the crew to pull it out. Finally, one man agreed. He doped my friend with a cup of "Yukon Jack" then yanked the tooth with a small parallel jaw fishing pliers.

The operation was a success; my friend felt much better *afterwards!* Needless to say, a dentist could have done the job *before* the trip.

# DAILY JOURNAL

It's almost impossible to keep the facts and sequences of events correct on a long canoe trip if you don't write things down when they occur. A rapid to one person is a major falls to another; a grueling portage early in the trip becomes a cake walk later. And of course the fish you catch increase in size logarithmically with each mile north you travel.

This is why you should keep a daily diary. It won't make or break your trip if you don't, but it will keep you honest when the weeks merge into years.

At this point you may be overwhelmed by all the many things you need to do before the wheels roll north. There seems to be an unending array of problems to solve and skills to accumulate. Details, skills, dangers. Is it really worth the effort?

The first time you startle a moose that's feeding quietly among the lily pads, silhouette emblazoned against a backdrop of new born sun and morning mist, or watch a thousand caribou do a thunder dance across the endless tundra, you'll "know".

A wild river is not all dangerous rapids and creature discomforts. It is often quiet and beckoning. There is time to swim and fish and photograph; long stretches where you can lay your paddle down, lean against a pack, and for a time let the world and its important thoughts float idly by.

**Figure 4-4**
A wild river is not all dangerous rapids and creature discomforts. Often, there are long stretches where you can lean against a pack and let the world float idly by. ( L: Kent Swanson, R: Reb Bowman.  Along the Hood River, NWT. )

Canoeing the wild rivers of the far north makes you understand why primitive man felt so close to God.

# 5

# The Wild River Canoe

"In the canoes of the savage one can go without restraint, and quickly, everywhere, in the small as well as large rivers. So that by using canoes as the savages do, it would be possible to see all there is, good and bad, in a year or two"

Samuel Champlain (1603)

My first canoe was a disaster. It measured 15 feet long, weighed an honest 90 pounds, and was slopped together from chopper gun* fiberglass. As an added insult it was trimmed in plastic and painted to resemble the honorable birchbark craft of a bygone era. In all it was a cheap ugly canoe that excelled at nothing.

I thought it was beautiful--"a canoeists canoe".

I paddled that canoe in blissful ignorance for two years. Then I joined a canoe club and rubbed shoulders with experts. Suddenly my beautiful, wonderful, do everything canoe, was a "dishpan", a "meatplatter"...an ugly boring pig. It was apparent I'd been had!

I put the tub up for sale. It went within a week to an unsuspecting canoeist.

A hundred bucks plus what I got for the old scow bought me a sleek new Sawyer Crusier--a 17 foot, 9 inch U.S. Canoe Association competition canoe that tipped the scales at barely 65 pounds. The Sawyer was a "real" canoe. There was absolutely nothing ugly or boring about it. But my dream boat had a single fault: it was so fine at the ends that it cut cleanly through waves rather than climb confidently over them. Paddling bow on a wind-tossed lake was invigorating; water leaped into my lap by the bucket full with each oncoming wave. It was even worse in big white water. Nevertheless,

---

*Chopped fiberglass and resin is sprayed into a mold and the whole allowed to harden. The canoe that results is heavy, inexpensive, and not very strong.

the Sawyer was fun to paddle--reason enough to keep any canoe. And to buy another.

The new addition was a 17 foot shoe-keeled Grumman--state of the art for white water boats in the mid-sixties. At last I had all the canoes I'd ever need. Or did I?

Deep within me was the yearning desire to paddle the wild rivers of the far north. I wondered which of my canoes was best suited to the challenge. The Sawyer was unalloyed joy to paddle flat out along the non-intimidating rivers near my southern Indiana home, but it wouldn't handle big water or carry much of a load. And the tank tough Grumman though admittedly doggy on the flats, was king in white water even with two weeks supply of camping gear aboard. Once I sunk the Sawyer in a rough water crossing on Ontario's Northern Lights Lake; I had no desire to repeat that experience. And the Grumman? Well it would get me there and back, but without precision, grace, or flair. Or even speed.

It began to appear that the north country was a highly diversified place. There was everything I could imagine--lakes of ocean size, tiny beaver streams and ponds, salt water seas, shallow rocky creeks, deep lazy rivers, mile after mile of heart-pounding rapids, deep mucky portages, and mean rocky ones. And the list went on. Each trip north brought into play new dimensions, new ideas, and a growing dissatisfaction with the canoe I paddled. Slowly a picture of the perfect wild river canoe began to emerge.

It should be long enough to track well but short enough to fit between the waves; broad and deep enough to carry a good load but with low ends so it wouldn't catch the wind. There should be no keel to catch on rocks and the bottom would be slightly rounded or with a subtle vee to enhance stability in rough water. The ends would be fine enough for good speed below the waterline and deeply flared above to climb the waves. The canoe would be fast on the flats yet turn instantly on command. It would run dry in the wildest white water with the heaviest load of camping gear aboard, weigh less than 70 pounds, and be impossible to puncture.

I've been searching for my ideal canoe for 20 years now and still haven't found it. That's because no single canoe can do everything well. Often what's right for one tripping condition is wrong for another--a reason why experienced canoeists often own several canoes. (I have five which isn't nearly enough!) Those who regularly trip the wild waters of the far north are very opinionated as to "what is best". And these opinions vary widely as you'll discover later. For this reason I'm reluctant to recommend specific canoe dimensions or even materials. What works perfectly for one person is all too frequently unacceptable to another.

Everyone has a notion of the kind of wild rivers they want to paddle. Some envision vast open waters with few rapids and portages--rivers like the Mackenzie, Yukon, and Abitibi. Others conjure up dynamic white water runs--the South Nahanni, Burnside, and Hood. And of course there's the more common middle ground-- Missinaibi, Thelon, and Fond du Lac. Each river is different, and so too is the best canoe for paddling it. If you can identify your own tripping style and the specific kind of waters you plan to paddle you'll have no trouble finding the right canoe to meet the challenge. But if you want to canoe "all of the above", you'll need to be more liberal in your thinking and select a more generalized craft--one which you can trust in all types of water.

Amidst your confusion you'll ultimately discover that the bottom line is your own safety. The rivers of the far north run very cold, even in early August. A capsize may be fatal. Suddenly the reality of it all appears. A wild river canoe must be trustworthy and forgiving; strong enough to stay intact after you've hung it up on a mid-stream ledge with a month's load of gear aboard; big enough to ride the waves of a giant lake or formiddable rapid, yet light enough to portage without breaking your back. And it must be bolted together to stay that way after a thousand miles of river and a hundred over land.

A wild river canoe is a pick-up truck, not a sports car. Sports cars are fine for the easy rivers down home, but they're too flighty for use in the rugged and changeable environment of the far north.

Enough. Let's get down to the basics of wilderness canoe design:

## HOW LONG IS LONG ENOUGH?

Canoes are basically displacement hulls so their maximum speed is a function of their length. Thus, the longer the canoe the faster it will run.*

You can compute the relationship mathematically by applying the over-simplified formula:

$$S = 1.55 \text{ X } \sqrt{WL}$$

(Speed in miles per hour equals 1.55 times the square root of the waterline length, measured in feet.)

Thus, an 18 1/2 footer will peak out at around 6.7 miles per hour while a 16 footer will run about 6.2 miles per hour. The difference is seven and one-half percent--significant only at the end of a ten hour day or when you're pushing hard into a wind.

*Lightweight canoes can be planned for short distances and exceed their displacement speed.

Speed and ease of paddling *are not* the same. The formula tells you only the *maximum* hull speed, not the amount of effort required to get it there. It's quite possible for a sophisticated 16 footer to paddle more easily than a workhorse 18 footer. But the longer canoe will always have a higher top speed.

A long canoe will also ride the waves of a wind-tossed lake more smoothly than a short one. A 15 footer is an abomination in a quartering sea--it "torques out" with each oncoming wave and leaves you fighting to keep on course. Add a foot more length and you gain stability and a better ride. Now you're beginning to feel like you're paddling a canoe rather than a washtub. But increase the length to 18 or 18 1/2 feet and as if by magic the craft becomes completely manageable. It rises and falls gently with the waves like a monster battleship on a rolling ocean.

Okay, long canoes are more manageable than short canoes in a running sea, but they don't always run drier. If the wave phase (distance between waves) is shorter than the canoe's own length, the canoe may plow and take on water. Under these conditions, a shorter canoe--one that fits between the waves--would be more seaworthy even though it might make for a rougher ride. Seaworthiness and manageability are not the same. In boats of equal volume, seaworthiness is in fact the *reciprocal* of length*. Merely a matter of math: A 15 foot canoe will more easily fit between two waves or clear a low ledge than will an 18 1/2 footer. And it'll be more maneuverable too--simply because there's less boat to turn. All of which explains why whitewater slalom canoes are always less than 16 feet long.

It would seem that you really need two canoes--a 16 footer for running technical white water and closely spaced waves, and an 18 1/2 footer for everything else. And a magic genie to switch them on command!

The "appropriate" length is also programmed by how you'll get the canoe to and from the river. If you plan to tie it to the outside struts of a Cessna float plane, you'd better limit your length to 17 feet. (Some Cessna pilots won't carry canoes that are longer than 16 feet!) Of course you can always fly your big 18 footer on the floats of a "Beaver" or in the belly of a ten passenger "Otter". But these planes aren't always available and they're much more expensive than the tiny Cessna's.

Another variable which will affect your choice of canoe length is the amount of gear you'll carry. Sit down now and figure best you can, exactly how many number three Duluth packs you'll need *per canoe* to outfit a four week trip. You might get by with four packs, but I'll bet you'll need one more. Really now, just where will you put five packs in

---

*Obviously, there's a point of diminishing returns.

a 16 foot canoe? If you remove the forward and aft thwarts you might be able to stack two packs north of the yoke and three behind it. But it will be tight. Very tight! And what about the camera packs and extra paddles?

Loading a 16 foot canoe for a four week trip is akin to traveling across America in a Volkswagon Rabbit with a family of four. It can be done, but not comfortably. On the other hand, there's *plenty* of room in a good sized 18 footer!

Ultimately, you'll come to realize that for all around use in the north country, a high volume 17 to 18 foot canoe is best. Certainly shorter and longer boats offer advantages, but what you'd "like to paddle" and what you may have to paddle, are too frequently dictated by conditions beyond your control.

## SHIP SHAPE

A canoe's personality is shaped by its ends. A craft with narrow ends will run fast but plunge deep and get you wet when the waves begin to roll. Conversely, a stout-ended boat will do the opposite: It'll be a pig to paddle on the flats but will run dry in the rough. At the far extreme are canoes with ends too wide--most 15' and 17' aluminum models--which pitch badly and slap violently into waves.

What you need is a pleasant compromise--plenty of buoyancy above the waterline, substantial fineness below. Such "flare" permits the craft to fall gently to its deepest most buoyant point before it rises predictably skyward. Untamed buoyancy has no place in a wild river--or any other canoe. Flared ends are much better and safer.

**Figure 5-1a**
Nearly all the carrying capacity of a canoe is borne in the middle two thirds of the hull. Here, canoe **A** will handle a load much better than canoe **B** because its buoyant ends will ride up over waves rather than cut through them. But canoe **B** is definitely the faster of the two canoes.

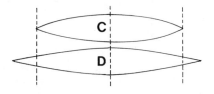

**Figure 5-1b**
Canoes **C** and **D** have the same carrying capacity. Canoe **D** is faster than **C**, but **C** will ride the waves and rapids better (run drier).

It's interesting to note that nearly all the carrying capacity of a canoe is borne in the middle two thirds of the hull. Thus, end shape has little real effect   on the actual freeboard with a maximum load. Figure 5-1 shows the relationship. Nevertheless, the rough water characteristics of the two canoes are much different. Load both canoes to capacity and "B" may sink with the first oncoming wave while "A" rises confidently above it.

The differences become even more exaggerated when you change the length. For example hulls "C" and "D" in figure 5-1 have the same carrying capacity even though they're not the same length. With an identical load aboard, the longer canoe will be faster, of course, but the shorter one with its more buoyant ends will ride the waves and rapids better. Manufacturers "capacity ratings" are only meaningful if you understand these relationships.

## WIDE OR NARROW

**Figure 5-2**
Width is measured at four places on a canoe--at the gunnels or rails; at the widest point (called maximum beam), and at the three and four inch working waterline.

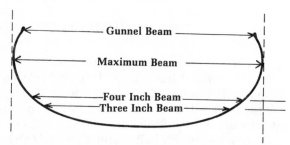

Width is commonly measured at four places on a canoe. (figure 5-2). At the gunnels or rails; at the widest point (called maximum beam) and at the three inch and four inch working waterline. It's pointless to talk about width until you understand how these variables are related. A canoe can be wide at the working waterline and narrow at the gunnels or vice versa. Or it can be narrow down low, wider midway up, and narrow again at the rails. Each configuration affects performance differently, and every design is dependent on the shape of the bottom.

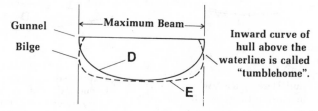

**Figure 5-3**
The typical "sportsman's" canoe usually follows the outline of canoe **E** which feels rock stable but becomes unpredictable when the waves begin to roll. Canoe **D** is much safer.

Note that both **D** and **E** have the same maximum beam. This maximum occurs at the gunnels on canoe **D** and at the bilge in canoe **E**.

Manufacturer's specifications are meaningless unless you understand the difference.

For example, the typical "sportsman's canoe" usually follows the outline of canoe "E" in figure 5-3: It's flat and broad down low and has extreme tumblehome or inward curve higher up. Such a craft feels rock stable initially but it becomes unpredictable when the waves begin to roll. Lean a highly tumblehomed canoe even slightly in rough water and it'll unhorse you instantly.

Canoe "D" is a much better design. The bottom is slightly rounded and the sides flare outward. The flare is there for a reason--it directs oncoming waves away from the hull rather than into it. And the more you lean the craft, the more stable it becomes. In canoeing terms, it "firms up"--exactly the opposite of what happens in a canoe with lots of tumblehome.

Okay, flared hulls with gently rounded or vee bottoms have better sea manners than those with lots of tumblehome and flat bottoms, right? Well, yes...other things being equal. Surprisingly, some of the best wild river canoes flatly defy design logic, or at least so it seems. The 17'2" Old Town Tripper, 18 and 20 foot Grummans, and 18 1/2 foot Alumacraft, are a few. That these canoes do so well with heavy loads in big water is due partly to their large size, and for the Old Town and Alumacraft at least, relatively fine, vee--shaped ends *below* the waterline.

Canoe design is much too complicated to "tell it all" in a single chapter. So keep an open mind and be aware that there *are* exceptions.*

# KEELS--A DANGEROUS AFFECTATION

A keel will make any canoe track (hold its course) better. But it will also catch on rocks and upset you. Most of the canoe accidents in the far north have been attributed to keeled canoes which hung up on a ledge or rock and dumped its occupants.

Good tracking is achieved by proper canoe design, not by an afterthought tacked lengthwise along the bottom. If keels had value the Indians and voyageurs would have used them on their canoes. The "real" reason manufacturers use keels is to stiffen a badly designed, flat, floppy canoe bottom. More than anything else, a keel is one feature you should avoid in a serious river canoe. Put your faith in good canoe design and your own paddling skills. Your *keeless* canoe will do the rest!

Perhaps the one exception to "no keels" is the optional shoe keel offered by the makers of some aluminum canoes. Shoe keels are shallow rounded affairs and so are less likely to catch on underwater

---

*Experienced canoeists are fond of judging the performance of a canoe by the shape of its hull. But canoeing is full of surprises. The only way you can be sure of a canoe's real performance is to paddle it!

obstacles. Nonetheless, they're still more dangerous than "no keel at all"!

# TURN ABOUT IS ESSENTIAL PLAY

The upward curve at each end of a canoe is called *rocker*. The greater the rocker, the more maneuverable the hull, the easier it will rise with waves, and the poorer it will track. A wild river canoe is usually very heavily loaded--the weight of all your camping gear presses the hull deep into the water (acts like a keel) and makes it difficult to turn. Consequently you need a fair amount of rocker--1 1/2 inches at each end is not unreasonable. A canoe that tracks like a mountain cat when empty will turn with impudence when heavily loaded--which is exactly what you don't want for all around wilderness use. Don't let some flat water racing enthusiast talk you into buying a canoe with near zero rocker. A wild river canoe and a racing canoe are not the same. Adequate rocker is essential for good performance in white water and running seas.

# ADEQUATE DEPTH

Shallow depth is a real mistake in a wild river canoe. You need at least thirteen and one-half inches of sidewall at the center to keep out big waves. And often this isn't enough. Most of the best tripping boats are built to a maximum depth of around fourteen and one-half inches--essential if you want a margin of safety in the rough stuff. Some canoe "experts" recommend a minimum safe freeboard of six inches, which is ridiculous: A boat that heavily loaded will drown you in the first big rapid if you don't have a fabric splash cover. Open canoes should maintain *at least* nine inches of freeboard for safety in turbulent waters.

# STRONG OR LIGHT--TAKE YOUR PICK

A wild river canoe must be light enough to carry long distances but built strong enough to stay intact when you slide it down a ravine, drop it on a boulder, or smash headlong into a rock with a full outfit aboard.

Unfortunately, weight and strength are closely related. You can have a strong heavy canoe or a light fragile one, but you can't have it both ways. Certainly there's a middle ground, but it's much narrower than you think. A canoe that's *big enough* and *strong enough* for running difficult rivers will   probably weigh around 65 to 75 pounds in Kevlar, 75 to 85 pounds in aluminum or Royalex, and 85 or more in hand laid reinforced fiberglass. And some of the best big water canoes weigh more than this.

There are some really nice lightweight high performance, high volume tripping canoes on the market which weigh under 60 pounds. These are fine for canoeing the Boundary Waters of Minnesota, the out-back of the Allagash, and the like. Use'em in the gentle north of Ontario and Manitoba if you like, but watch out if you head into remote country with them. They may not hold up!

I'd flatly reject any deep hulled 17 - 18 1/2 foot canoe that weighed much less than 70 *honest* pounds, regardless of claims made for it by the manufacturer. Either the maker is stretching the truth about the weight (a most common practice) or the boat is just too fragile for serious wild river use.

Remember, northern rivers are not local streams. If your canoe destructs along the route you may have a long difficult walk out. And no matter how skilled you are, you'll make mistakes, which is precisely why you need strength and dependability.

Still confused about what to buy? Stay tuned; things will become clearer after we've reviewed the basic canoe building materials.

## ALUMINUM

Still the most abrasion resistant and weather-proof material available. You can leave an aluminum canoe in a snow bank all winter and it'll come out looking like new in the spring. Aluminum is easy to repair too. Most every bush pilot carries a rivet kit to fix his plane, and what works for him will mend your canoe. Aluminum doesn't lend itself to the most sophisticated hull shapes (though one manufacturer--Beaver Canoes--has shown it can be done). Aluminum also dents, sticks to rocks, and is noisy and cold to the touch. But it's the longest lived of all the canoe building materials.

Aluminum canoes remain the workhorse of the far north; you'll see them at every fishing lodge and Indian village from Ontario to the Yukon. Look for heat treated aluminum and flush rivets. And check out the hull shape. Invariably, 18-18 1/2 footers are much better wild river canoes than the more popular 17 footers. Avoid lightweight construction and standard deep keels.

## FIBERGLASS

Some of the best and worst canoes are constructed of fiberglass. There's no such thing as a "good, cheap" fiberglass canoe. Avoid chopper gun specials which are heavy and break easily. Instead, look for all hand lay-up construction--the tell tale is the crisp outline of the fabric weave inside the hull.

Sight along the hull for signs of "cheek" (indents) and examine the inside of the canoe for bubbles, resin-starved (chalky) areas and resin-flooded areas. Any of these defects indicates careless workmanship.*

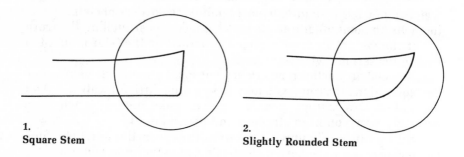

1.
**Square Stem**

2.
**Slightly Rounded Stem**

**Figure 5-4**
Canoe **1** has square stems; canoe **2** has rounded ones. Square stems are fine for racing but they're fragile and they catch seaweed.

Check out the stems (ends) of the canoe. They should be slightly rounded and not too square (figure 5-4). Square stems are fine for racing as they allow the canoe to reach its longest legal length at the waterline. But they catch every thread of seaweed and are prone to break when you hit rocks.

Fiberglass lends itself to the manufacture of the most highly refined hull shapes, so it's natural that enthusiastic manufacturers will try to produce the most efficient paddling canoes possible. However, as I've pointed out repeatedly, the best paddling canoes don't necessarily make the best wild river canoes. High performance features have no place on a canoe if they detract from its versatility or ruggedness.

A fiberglass canoe must be carefully constructed to be strong enough for wild river use. Stick to the most respected manufacturers in the industry and you can't go wrong.. And remember that a good tough fiberglass canoe will be neither ultra-light nor inexpensive!

---

*Some of the very best canoes exhibit one or more of these defects. An occasional "cheek" or small resin flood, etc., is permissible as these defects are cosmetic and don't affect hull strength or perfomance.

# KEVLAR 49

Contrary to popular belief, canoes built of Kevlar 49* are not bulletproof. The lay-up used on a canoe is much less substantial than that of a policeman's flak vest. You *can* put a hole in a Kevlar canoe. All it takes is a real sharp object and a good head of steam!

Kevlar isn't magic. Unit for unit it's about 40 percent stronger and half the weight of fiberglass but the real strength to weight difference of a finished canoe is not as great as you think. That's because much of a canoe's weight is in the resin and trim--seats, decks, and rails. There's also a considerable difference in the way Kevlar and fiberglass is used.

For example, consider an impeccably built 85 pound all fiberglass canoe. Now build that same canoe to an *equal weight* with Kevlar. The Kevlar version will be *considerably* tougher than its glass brother. But most manufacturers don't build them this way. Instead you get a 50 pound canoe that is easy to carry but possibly no stronger than the 85 pound glass model. "Kevlar is not Kevlar." There are all sorts of different lay-ups--some strong, others barely adequate.    The more Kevlar you use in construction, the higher the price, and you get just what you pay for. It's unrealistc to compare the strength of a 1000 dollar Kevlar canoe to a similar one which costs twice as much.

Kevlar has an unusual property--it can't be sanded like fiberglass. The stuff just frizzes up like cotton candy when it's abraided, which is why Kevlar canoes are always patched with fiberglass. Examine the bottom of a well worn all Kevlar canoe sometime--it will look like it needs a haircut! A layer of S-glass (a very abrasion-resistant form of fiberglass) on the outside hull would solve the "hair" problem and make cosmetic repairs easier. But only a very few canoe makers build boats this way. Why? Possibly because North American canoeists are on an "all Kevlar kick". So long as sales

**Figure 5-5**
No canoe is indestructable. These remains of what appears to be a 17 foot Grumman canoe, were found by Bob Dannert and party along the remote Back River in the Northwest Territories. Photo: Bob Dannert

*Kevlar is an incredibly strong and very expensive gold-colored fabric that's manufactured by the Dupont Co. It's commonly used in the construction of tires and bullet-proof vests. The product has wide industrial applications.

of pure Kevlar canoes continue to sky-rocket, manufacturers will keep building them, even if a far less expensive and only slightly heavier modified lay-up will work as well.*

Some manufacturers will build you a modified Kevlar/glass canoe if you specify it. Expect to pay a special order fee and to save a substantial amount of money over the cost of all Kevlar construction.

Colors: Color is a matter of preference, though green is most popular and outsells every other color by a wide margin--a consideration if you buy and sell canoes as often as I do. But red and yellow are best from a safety standpoint. Try locating an overturned blue or green canoe in a river sometime and you'll understand why.

Once I "lost" my green Old Town Ranger along an undefined--and unrefined--portage in  Saskatchewan when I set it down to scout the way. When I returned, it took me nearly thirty minutes to locate the canoe--its green color blended perfectly with the scrub-green vegetation. Now I always snap on my sunshine yellow cover whenever I leave the canoe in the bush.

My own color preference is white because it doesn't show scratches and generally makes for a lighter boat. Colored  Kevlar and fiberglass canoes all scratch white, so it doesn't take long for the bottom of a shiny red canoe to become a mass of white claw marks. White canoes "scratch white" so at least the damage doesn't show. It's also easier to get a good color match on a white boat than a colored one when the time comes to refinish small areas.

The weight difference, which is seldom more than a couple pounds, is due to the fact that fewer pounds of color pigment are needed to get a white color than a solid red, blue, or green one, etc.


## ROYALEX

*Royalex* is an ABS thermolastic from Uniroyal Co. The number of thicknesses and laminations used are specified by the canoe maker. Some Royalex lay-ups are quite substantial, others are merely adequate. Again, you get just what you pay for. One popular lay-up consists of seven layers of material--an expanded ABS foam core, two thicknesses of ABS plastic sandwiched to each side of the core, and an outer sheath of colored cross-linked vinyl to protect the ABS from decomposing in the sun. Royalex is extremely tough and very

---

* Charlie Walbridge, the guhru of American white water boat building, flatly states in his *Boatbuilders Manual*, ". . . that Kevlar has excellent flexural strength but poor compressive strength. (When you break a stick over your knee, you are elongating it on the top and compressing it on the bottom.) This means that the outer layer of Kevlar frequently breaks, creating soft "hinge points" in the hull. An all-Kevlar lay-up is not very durable for the money spent."

slippery. It will slide over ledges that stop aluminum canoes in their tracks and break or damage glass or Kevlar craft. A swamped Royalex canoe will often come through the toughest rapid unscathed and pop back into near perfect shape even after being folded completely around a mid-stream boulder.

Royalex can withstand severe impact but only limited abrasion. Continued dragging through shallows reduces the smooth vinyl skin to a mass of deep cuts. Nonetheless, the product is incredibly durable, and for this reason is the favorite of many white water daredevils and arctic canoe trippers.

## POLYETHYLENE

Basically the same stuff they make poly bottles out of, only thicker and with added color. Polyethylene (Ram-x, Xylar, etc.) is very strong stuff and it's easily molded into the most complex of shapes--though manufacturers of open canoes have been less than daring in this respect.

Polyethylene is very floppy so it must have lots of curves and/or ribs, keels, struts, etc., to keep it in shape which defeats the advantages of the material. A flexible material will give when it strikes a rock but not if it's held in place with a rib or strut.

Polyethylene, like Kevlar, fiberglass, and Royalex, is very slippery; it slides over rocks with scarcely a murmur.

## FIBERGLASS COVERED WOOD-STRIP CANOES

Nearly every new canoe began life as a cedar or redwood strip prototype. To date, modern technology has not produced a material that is as lightweight, rigid, and beautiful as fiberglass covered wood strips. If properly built, wood strip canoes are much stronger than most people think. My two redwood strip solo canoes are used regularly in white water. They require frequent patching but they hang together. I've used "strippers" on tough northern rivers, but I've been extremely careful with them. They're not really strong enough for a major trip down a rocky river.

## WOOD-CANVAS

Wood-canvas canoes are a dying breed. They're beautiful, very expensive, and considerably tougher than the canoeing literature suggests. Even experts who prefer ultra-light Kevlar or wood-strip boats will admit that there's a joy in paddling a canvas covered wood canoe that is experienced in no other watercraft. Now that the

Chestnut Canoe Company of Canada is no longer in business, there is no real source of wood-canvas canoes in North America. Even Old Town—grand daddy of them all--is now covering their impeccably crafted wood-ribbed canoes with fiberglass instead of canvas. The Thompson's, Shell Lakes, Whites, and others, ring nostalgically from the past. There are a few scattered custom builders of wood-canvas canoes but basically these crafts are relics, though ones which are emminently suitable for use on any river if manned by competent paddlers. I mourn their passing.

Except for some exotic custom shop products, that's about it for canoe building materials. Read the preferences of the experts that follow. Then sit down and put your thoughts in order.

# BOB O'HARA

Bob O-Hara has been paddling the remote rivers of the high arctic since the 1960's. His accomplishments include the Back, Coppermine, Dubawnt, Thelon, Kanaaupscow, and others too numerous to mention. Bob's trips generally last for five weeks or more, and because of their remoteness, he often has to leave canoes at a remote village or in the bush. Bob O'Hara is a most competent arctic traveler. Neither he nor his crew have ever suffered a serious injury and he has never lost a man to drowning. He works as a biology teacher and outdoor education instructor for a Minnesota school district.

"Each of us has a "special canoe" that we've come to favor. It may not be the ultimate or best, but one we're comfortable with and trust. My favorite is the 18 foot standard weight Grumman with shoe keel. I've also used 17 and 20 foot Grummans in the Arctic, but the 18 footer is the most versatile. It will fit nicely inside a Twin Otter or outside a smaller float plane*, or I can load a half ton of gear for a five week trip and still maintain adequate freeboard. The 18 foot Grumman with shoe keel weighs about 90 pounds--not too heavy for the occasional one to three mile hike around a canyon. But it's very strong and can be repaired by any bush pilot with a rivet gun in an hour or so.

*Few bush pilots will carry canoes over 17 feet long on a Cessna or 18½ feet long on a Beaver.

Major repair of fiberglass and Kevlar canoes is often difficult in the Arctic as liquid polyester and epoxy resins don't always cure properly at the cold arctic temperatures.

Frequently, I need to leave my canoes at a remote village over the winter, and neither snow, wind, nor sub zero temperatures affect them. I suspect a plastic canoe would destruct under the same conditions. The Grumman isn't fast, but it is reliable. It will safely handle all the large waters of the central Arctic, and with a partial or full fabric cover, it keeps me out of trouble in the roughest rapid. The 18 foot Grumman is also less expensive than a glass, Royalex, or Kevlar canoe of similar capacity. I've never had my 18 foot Grumman fail me; which, I guess is why I continue to use it."

# FRED GASKIN

Fred Gaskin is  one of the most experienced Barren Lands canoeists in the world. He has paddled all the classic canoe routes and most of the major rivers in the Canadian Arctic, in addition to scores of challenging routes within the timberline. Articles about his experiences have appeared in "Backpacker" magazine, "Hand In Hand" (Great Britain), "Royal Canadian Geographical Society", "Arctic in Colour", "Canadian Boating", and many more. Fred lives in Ontario and is a fellow of the Insurance Institute of Canada, and a partner in the firm of Bradley Gaskin Marshall Insurance Brokers Limited, in Cambridge, Ontario.

"Eighteen foot canoes are the best by far in rough water. Our "fraternity" has used four types. In the early years we used cedar plank covered with fiberglass, and also fiberglass canoes, and until 1974 we used aluminum canoes. Now we use only Old Town ABS Royalex canoes. No other canoe provides the safety, efficiency, utility and maneuverability of the Royalex canoe. Our canoes absorbed tremendous punishment on our ascent of the Yellowknife River on our way to the Coppermine River in the Northwest Territories. We dragged them loaded up ledges and rock-filled rapids mile after mile, yet they seemed to shrug off every scrape and impact given them. On one occasion a canoe was dropped several feet onto projecting rocks--it merely bounced and showed no scar. We have used both the 17'2" Old Town Tripper and the 18 foot Voyageur and they are both marvelous canoes, ideally suited to the harsh requirements of the north. The 18 ft. Voyageur provides a smoother run through rough water and its lower 13 1/2 inch depth gets you more distance against those inevitable headwinds."

# DAVID HARRISON

David Harrison is well known in canoeing circles as a writer and serious north country canoeist. His articles have appeared frequently in outdoor magazines, especially CANOE. He and his wife Judy, have recently published two new books-*Canoe Tripping With Kids* (The Stephen Greene Press), and *Sports Illustrated Canoeing* (Harper and Row).

"Minimum length is 17 feet; beam 35 to 37 inches, depth 14 to 16 inches, weight 60 to 85 pounds. Kevlar, fiberglass-- custom lay-up" or ABS Royalex is fine. Wood and canvas will work. But I will not use any aluminum canoe that has a standard deep keel. In 1975 we lost a 17 foot Grumman on the Back River when it's deep keel hung up on a ledge. We finished the trip--all six of us--in the remaining two canoes--an Easy Rider TSL-1 and a Mad River Kevlar Explorer. Aluminum canoes with shoe keels are acceptable, though I'm not much of an aluminum fan.

For the past few years we ve used an all Kevlar Mad River Explorer on our major trips. It performs superbly on rivers and lakes of all sizes and difficulty even though it's only 16 and one-half feet long. It's a very well designed canoe and is quite strong. It paddles easier than the 17 foot Grumman and carries a heavy load more gracefully. And it's light enough (65 pounds) to carry long distances without breaking your back."

# Dr. BILL FORGEY

Dr. Bill Forgey is known all over North America as the author of "Wilderness Medicine"--the definitive work on back country first-aid. He is also founder and president of Indiana Camp Supply, a unique mail order shop that specializes in freeze-dried foods and hard-to-find items for the medical emergency.

Bill has paddled thousands of miles on the bush rivers of northern Canada. His trips generally last at least a month. Canoeing and camping is more than just a "summer vacation" to Bill Forgey; it is a life style which he pursues with gusto at every opportunity.

"My 20 foot Grumman* can't be beat for a two month trip in the big lake country and wide open rivers of northern Canada. The big Grumman has tremendous buoyancy and will ride over the biggest waves with less chance of swamping than any canoe I've ever used. I have a cabin along the Churchill River in Manitoba and I can haul in enough gear in my 20 footer to keep me provisioned for a complete summer if need be. And I frequently travel with three in my canoe, which would be impossible in a smaller craft. So the 20 footer is right for me, though admittedly it may be too much boat for others who make less substantial trips."

# BOB DANNERT

Each year, Bob Dannert canoes somewhere in the far north. He's done the Back, Coppermine, and Hood Rivers in the Northwest Territories, the Fond du Lac and Clearwater in Saskatchewan, the Missinaibi and English in Ontario, and scores of lesser routes. Bob is a research foods scientist for General Mills in Minneapolis. His on-the-job thoroughness is evident in the way he plans his trips. Bob leaves nothing to chance. Ever! He researches his trips like he's writing a

---

*Rumors that Grumman has discontinued the 20 foot canoe are false. Demand for these big boats has decreased so that they are being built only twice a year or so, when dealers have accumulated enough orders to warrant shipment. If you want a 20 footer, be patient!

Ph.D. thesis. Many of the suggestions for canoeing tundra rivers that appear in this book are taken directly from Bob's first-hand experience. Bob and I have canoed many miles together--most recently on the Hood River. Bob is competent, jovial, and always concerned about the welfare of his crew. Safety is his number one concern.

"I've used standard weight 18 foot Grummans and 17½ foot Old Town Trippers. They're both good boats but I prefer the Old Town by a wide margin. The slick ABS skin slides over rocks with scarcely a murmur which really speeds up travel in rocky areas--and also when lining. And there's no keel to catch on rocks. Equally important, the Old Town is really tough. The bottom of old "Akaitcho"* is pretty beat up but I've never put a hole in it. The Old Town is very forgiving and predictable too--important in the Arctic where a capsize in cold water can be fatal.

I also like the Royalex hull because it's a good insulator. My feet used to get awfully cold when I paddled an aluminum canoe. Royalex is always warm.

I think you need at least a 17 footer so you've got enough room to fit in all the gear for a long trip. And the canoe should have enough volume for the big waters of the tundra rivers. Actually, most any canoe will get you through if you're very careful with it and understand it's limitations. I trust the Old Town. I haven't found a better boat for what I do."

---

*Akaitcho was chief of the Copper Indians about 1820. A band of his Indians rescued Sir John Franklin and party from starvation along the Hood River. Akaitcho means "big foot".

# VERLEN KRUGER

Verlen Kruger, perhaps more than anyone else, knows and understands wilderness canoes. His canoeing accomplishments are so gigantic they defy the imagination. Verlen's first really significant trip was in 1971 when he and Clint Waddell paddled from Montreal to the Bering Sea in just five months! Then in 1980, he and Steve Landick--his son-in-law--began a 28,000 mile cross continent voyage in solo canoes that would ultimately take them nearly three years to complete.

Verlen cut his teeth flying P51 Mustangs during the Second World War and later began a plumbing and heating business in Michigan. To keep fit he took up canoeing--and canoe racing--at the tender age of 40. Verlen is one of North America's most colorful canoeists. He is not a macho type even though the nature of his trips suggests otherwise. Rather, he is a quiet unassuming man who has a profound appreciation for nature and respect for God.

"I've got a shedful of canoes at home and I like'em all. Jenny (my wife) and I have paddled all over the Canadian bush in an old Sawyer Cruiser. And I still have my old 17 foot Grumman, though I seldom use it. I like fast canoes and my favorite is an unusual looking 18 1/2 footer I designed myself. It's a big volume wilderness cruiser; it's got low ends for wind resistance and a partial deck to keep out the waves. There's enough rocker so it'll turn with a month's load. I believe a wilderness canoe should be built strong, so I make my canoes pretty substantial. I build them from Kevlar and vinylester resin and use a layer of S-glass on the outside for abrasion. I think that's the way a Kevlar canoe should be built. I'm thinking of manufacturing canoes when I return from the big trip and I'd like to make this boat available. I think it's the fastest, most seaworthy big tripping canoe around.

If I had to buy a big canoe for northern waters, I don't know what I'd get. It's been a long time since I've bought any canoe. But I'd probably go with a Sawyer Charger (18 1/2 foot) constructed according to my specifications. There are a lot of good big canoes on the market. We used a 21 footer of mine on the 7000 mile trip, and with the splash cover in place, it worked great, even on Lake Superior."

# STEVEN LANDICK

At 28, Steven Landick has already logged more canoe miles than most of us will experience in a life time. Since 1980, he and Verlen Kruger have been realizing their impossible dream--to criss-cross the continent by solo canoe.

Preparations for the "big trip" included six trips to the BWCA of Minnesota, a solo kayak trip from Maine to Michigan (1,400 miles), and 900 miles by kayak up the Columbia River. Like Verlen, Steve is a seasoned and very competitive canoe racer.

I had the privilege of meeting Steve in 1981 when he paddled his solo "Loon" up the Mississippi River through my home town of Hastings, Minnesota. Steve is a quiet, confident, warm-hearted young man--one who captures the good will of all who meet him.

It's hard for me to say what the best canoe is for use in the far North. I guess it depends on your philosophy--how fast you want to go, how comfortable you want to be, the amount of gear you'll carry, the time and distance, whether the route is mostly white water or flat water. etc.

Basically, I like fast canoes. The best tripping canoe I've found is a partially decked 18 1/2 footer that Verlen designed. It carries a big load gracefully and runs dry in the heaviest stuff. And because it has low ends it doesn't blow around in the wind. Verlen is thinking of manufacturing it. I hope he does. It's a *very good* boat!

Right now I don't own a tandem canoe. If I were pressed to buy one, I'd look hard at the We-no-nah Jensen "X" Boat.* I haven't paddled one, but it looks plenty big enough. And I like Jensen's designs. There are a lot of good canoes around. I just like long boats."

Okay, now that you've read the preferences of the experts, you're no longer confused about what canoe is best, right? Hardly! It's obvious that there's complete disagreement among everyone. Or is there? Let's take a closer look:

---

*A sophisticated 18½ foot high volume white water racing canoe designed by Eugene Jensen and manufactured by We-no-nah Canoes in Winonah, Minnesota.

# POINTS EVERYONE GENERALLY AGREES ON

1.Length: Except for the 16½ foot Mad River Explorer, 17 feet is considered the absolute minimum. Most like 18 or 18 1/2 foot canoes even though they can't be carried on the pontoons of small float planes.

2. The canoe should have substantial depth and high volume. Big canoes provide a margin of safety on rough water. Canoes that are too small are dangerous.

3. Keels are dangerous, avoid them! If you paddle an aluminum canoe it should be equipped with a shoe-keel not a standard fin keel.

4. Favored materials are ABS Royalex, Kevlar, and standard weight aluminum.

5. The overall weight of the canoe is second to strength. You need a good strong boat...period!

6. Slipperiness is an important factor: Everyone likes canoes which slide easily over rocks.

7. If you plan to over-winter your canoe in a snowbank, get an aluminum canoe. Canoes built of other materials may not withstand the intense (minus 50 degrees Farenheit or better) cold of northern winters.

8. The canoe must be trustworthy and forgiving on all types of water. If it has unusual quirks (acts spooky in certain types of water) you and your partner must be sufficiently skilled to overcome them.

9. Almost any canoe of adequate size and strength will get you through if you're careful and understand its limitations.

In summary, the major concern is safety. The rivers of the far north are no place to experiment with specialized canoes that offer a slight technical performance edge at the expense of strength or predictability.

# SOLO CANOES ARE DIFFERENT

Recently, there's been a revival of interest in canoeing alone: Most paddlers simply solo their big "wild river canoe", but that's not very efficient. Tandem canoes are for tandem crews: They're too big, too heavy, too wind-susceptible, and too awkward for one person to handle. If you're serious about going alone, you'll want a craft that's designed for it--a true solo canoe!

Compared to the big canoes we've been talking about, a craft that measures only about 15 feet long, 11 inches deep, and 27 to 31 inches wide, appears grossly inadequate, even for one person. You'd think a

canoe that small would sink in the first big wave. It won't. Hardly
ever! That's because you paddle a solo canoe from the center or
fulcrum which leaves its near weightless ends free to rise and fall
with the rhythm of the waves. Solo canoes are *immensely*
seaworthy—they'll go anywhere bigger canoes will go but with more
precision and flair. . . and fun!

Solo canoes are different, so the   traditional rules of tandem
canoe design don't apply. For example, most variables--speed,
tracking, turning, portability, seaworthiness, and general handiness-
-will be maximized in a canoe of 15 to 16 feet, a width at the gunnel of
28 to 30 inches, and a center depth of 11 inches. Except in the biggest
white water--stuff you should be carrying around anyway--
additional depth is unnecessary and unwise. High sides spell
crankiness when the wind comes up--remember, you're your own
partner in a solo canoe!

Frankly, there's a limited market for solo canoes, so the majority
of what you'll find in the stores parrots inefficient utility designs
which paddle poorly but sell well. At the other extreme are ultra-light
high performance racing canoes which are ideally suited to carrying
light loads rapidly across calm water but not heavy ones through
turbulent rapids and churning seas.

As interest develops, more and better solo designs are bound to
appear. At this writing, I am aware of less than a half dozen solo
designs from a handful of manufacturers that I'd trust to use on a
lengthy trek across dangerous waters.

Other solo canoes I've seen are either too big, too small, too heavy,
too flimsy, too slow, or too tempermental for serious wilderness use.
And the list goes on. But perhaps I'm simply as opinionated as those
whose testimonials you just read.

# 6

# Tandem Rigging

Some people are turned on by beautiful cars. With me it's canoes. So it was natural that I pour on the coal when just down river I saw what appeared to be a gleaming new wood/canvas canoe. I hailed the paddlers--a middle-aged couple from Nebraska--and slipped quietly along side. Sure enough, it was wood and canvas--and a 1928 Old Town to boot. She was an 18 foot guide, and every inch, from ribs and planking to the polished brass bands on her stems was like new.

"Restored her myself", said the man proudly. "Took me three years." I glanced along the oiled ash rails of my sophisticated Mad River TW Special, then focused on the ventilated hand-rubbed mahogany gunnels of the Old Town. The TW was pretty to be sure, but the old timer was *beautiful*. It was no contest.

"Sure would like to try your boat," I said wishfully to the man. "Yeah, and I'd like to paddle that racy boat of yours," he responded. Turned out we were going the same way, so we struck a bargain; we'd trade canoes until the next portage.

We talked enthusiastically about each other's canoes for maybe 20 minutes. All too soon the portage came into view. "Hey, how's about trading boats on the portage," I asked, "I've never carried a canvas canoe."

The man smiled knowingly and almost instantly said . . . sure!

We unloaded our canoes and the man took off down the trail, securely imprisoned beneath the contour padded yoke of my TW. His wife hung behind still struggling with a pack. I looked down into the Old Town--there was no yoke, only a straight ash thwart. "Where's the yoke", I called casually to the woman. "Oh that", she responded, "Jim just uses two paddles and that foam pad over there," she said pointing to a rolled trail mattress near her pack. I got the message! That "knowing smile" told everything. Well, too late now, the guy was long gone, probably humming happily beneath my yoke.

It was not a long portage--maybe half a mile, but it was a tough one. And the old canoe must've weighed at least 90 pounds. Half way through I developed shortness of breath, felt a severe tightening in my chest. My legs began to wobble and the pain at the base of my neck became unbearable. I had neither the strength to put down the canoe nor to continue on. But somehow I managed to struggle forth. Sweating, panting, bleary-eyed, I finally reached the next lake. Ahead was the faint outline of a human at the water's edge. I attempted composure, but it was impossible. "God this thing is heavy!" I blurted. "Can you. . .please. . .help me?" Instantly the man jumped into action. Together we struggled to unhorse what had now become a loathsome green canvas dinosaur. Finally I was free. Oh glory! I collapsed on a damp cedar log with incredible joy!

It seemed like an eternity before I was able to speak again, and then the words came slowly: "How can you stand to carry that thing?" I asked. "Ain't easy. . .you get used to it," replied the man. "Say, where can I get a neat yoke like yours?"

Now it was my turn to smile. "You can't" I replied, a bit sarcastically. "There's no such thing as a good store-bought yoke. You'll have to make your own."

The point is, even the best canoe--factory fresh or faithfully restored--is unsuitable for serious use in the backcountry until it's properly rigged. And the first step in proper rigging is to fit a well designed yoke.

## MAKING THE YOKE

If you've never used a wood yoke you're in for a pleasant surprise. There's a warmth and springiness to wood that's equalled by no other material. Aluminum yokes are unyielding affairs--much like jogging on cement while wearing ski boots. Wood yokes, on the other hand, are resiliant--they take "some" of the sting out of a nasty portage.

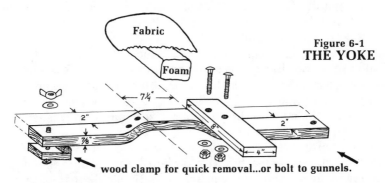

Figure 6-1
**THE YOKE**

wood clamp for quick removal...or bolt to gunnels.

You can make an acceptable yoke out of almost any straight-grained, clear hardwood, but white ash is by far the best. Ash has just the right amount of strength and flexibility. I prefer to use seven-eights inch thick wood when I can get it--cut to the dimensions shown in figure 6-1. If I can't obtain a seven-eights inch board, I'll use three-quarter inch stock and make the yoke a bit wider--about 2 1/2 inches to insure adequate strength.

It's doubtful you'll ever break a 2 1/2 inch by 3/4 inch solid ash yoke along its length, but it might split out where it bolts to the gunnels. So to eliminate any chance of breakage here, laminate a quarter-inch thick slab of one-inch by 2 1/2 ash to the underside of the yoke at each end. Run the lamination cross grain to the yoke bar and secure it with a good grade of waterproof glue. This will give you a full inch of wood to bolt through.

Don't make your yoke wider or thicker than I've suggested. The idea of going to wood in the first place was to gain flexibility-- something you'll lose if you increase dimensions substantially.

Your yoke must also have a curved neck piece to enable you to carry the mass of the canoe directly over your shoulders. I've found that a two-inch inset (see figure 6-1) is ideal. More than this is awkward while less isn't much better than a straight bar.

Follow this procedure to complete the yoke:

1. Cut two 4-inch by 8-inch by 3/4 inch yoke pad blocks from clear pine or Douglas fir (stronger). Don't use plywood; it delaminates with age.

2. Decide on the spacing of the blocks. Seven and one-fourth inches--inside to inside--is about right for most adults. Drill quarter-inch bolt holes through the yoke blocks and bar.

3. Drill a few 3/8 inch diameter drain holes through the face of each yoke block. Commercial yoke blocks don't have drain holes so water which accumulates in the foam pads stays there, and the wood blocks eventually rot.

4. Varnish the blocks, especially the insides of the bolt holes.

5. Install large carriage washers on quarter-inch bolts and run them through the holes in the yoke blocks.

6. For each yoke pad: Cut a 12 inch by 14 inch piece of naugehyde and set it face down on the floor. Pile about 8 inches of polyurethane foam pillow padding on the naugehyde and set the yoke block bolts up on the foam. Compress the foam to a 3 inch thickness and staple the naugehyde in place. Varnish the staples so they won't rust.

7. Bolt the pads to the yoke bar. Use a standard washer and lock washer under each nut.

8. Secure the finished yoke to the gunnels with quarter-inch diameter stainless steel bolts (brass bolts aren't strong enough). Use a carriage washer and lock washer beneath each nut.

The yoke I've described is strong, resiliant, and very comfortable. I've used it without incident on canoes of every size and description from the timid waters of the Mississippi to the toughest rivers of the north. Anyone who tells you a solid ash yoke isn't strong enough for a wild river canoe has a lot to learn about the capabilities of wood.

## TIE POINTS FOR YOUR GEAR

Opinions vary: Some say tie in your gear so tightly that the pounding of a rapid on the contents of a swamped canoe can't possibly tear anything loose. Others claim the opposite: "If you capsize and your canoe dives for a deep current or wraps around a rock, you may lose everthing--canoe, packs, the works. Better to waterproof your gear so it floats and can be picked up later in the quiet water downstream. Besides. . . 'your friends will salvage your gear!' "

Don't you believe it!

Really now, just what do you suppose are the chances you'll ever find packs which float free in a rough water upset? Maybe they will wind up in a quiet eddy not far from your mishap, but more than likely they'll continue down river for miles, ultimately to be lost in the gathering flow. And that hokum about "your friend salvaging your gear". Perhaps true enough on a local stream but not on a wild river where their *first responsibility is to rescue you* . . . then your canoe, and last, your packs!

Then there's the matter of "flotation". Every white water canoeist knows that the difference between a swamped canoe that survives a rapid unscathed and one that doesn't, is flotation. The principle is simple: The higher a swamped canoe floats, the less likely it will be damaged on rocks. So white water paddlers respond heart and soul by filling every nook and cranny in their boats with anything that floats--closed cell foam, air bags, innertubes, and the like.

Obviously, float bags and foam blocks are out of place in the wilds, but packs aren't. Waterproof your packs, lock'em tight in the canoe, and they'll perform the same miracle as an air bag when you swamp or capsize. But they won't work if they dangle out of the canoe in an upset or bob ominously when you swamp. That's why you need an effective tie-in system--one that's absolutely foolproof yet fast to rig.

Over the years I've come to favor a unique combination of rubber ropes and parachute cords. I can rig my outfit rock-solid in less than 30 seconds and unstring it to portage in half that time. We'll look into the specifics in chapter 9. Right now we're concerned only with the basics of rigging the canoe to accept the system, which is easy enough--all you need are attachment points along the gunnels.

If you have an aluminum canoe with broad flat inwales (inside gunnels), drill quarter-inch diameter holes four to six inches apart along the length of each gunnel. If your gunnels are tubular aluminum, plastic, or wood, drill smaller one-eighth inch diameter holes through the inwale or just below it, and thread short loops of parachute cord through the holes.

Now you've got lots of places to attach your security system and tie in small items.

**Figure 6-2**
After a month on the trail your canoe might look like this! Note shock-corded thwarts and rubber ropes hooked at gunnels. Parachute cords run fore and aft as an added safety precaution. Canoe is an 18' Grumman.

## SHOCK-CORD YOUR THWARTS AND DECKS

The best way to store maps, wet socks, and oddities in your canoe is to stuff them under loops of shock cord strung through thwarts (Photo 6-2). Shock-corded items will stay put in a wind and on portages. And they'll usually remain with the canoe in an upset.

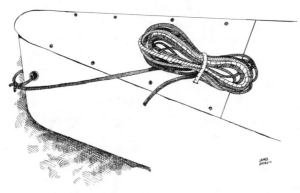

**Figure 6-3**
Coil your lines and stuff them under a loop of shock cord strung through holes in the deck.

Shock-cord your decks too. Bow and stern lines should be coiled and stuffed under the deck cords when they're not in use (Illus. 6-3). Never leave lines loose in any boat--they could wind around your arms or legs if you overturn in a lively current.

# LINING RINGS

Shorelines along rivers within the timberline are usually too brushy to permit much lining, but in the tundra where there are no trees, lining is a way of life. Deck mounted rings or eyes are generally worthless for lining as they place the pulling force of the lines too high above the mass of the canoe. If you pull hard on a deck secured rope while working a canoe through a tricky current, you'll upset it for sure. But get the force closer to the waterline (lower on the mass) and you've got no problem at all.

For this reason, some canoe books insist that you abandon deck mounted rings when lining and instead rig a towing harness around the hull. But a better procedure is to simply install the lining rings where they belong--mid-way down the stem of the canoe. Aluminum canoe makers have been doing it properly for years, but manufacturers of other canoes somehow haven't caught on.

You can buy fancy brass lining rings or plated steel ones, or simply bore a hole through the stem of the canoe a few inches above cut water. The latter method is least expensive and most reliable. Drill the hole large enough to accept a length of half-inch diameter plastic water pipe. Glue the pipe in place with quick-setting epoxy. The pipe will prevent water from leaking into the canoe when the ends plunge deep in rough water.

Granted, it takes some courage to bore a hole through the stems of an expensive canoe, but it only hurts for a second and in the end looks fine.

# LINES

To sea-faring folk, any rope used aboard ship is a "line". But to canoeists, lines are specialized ropes used for hauling a canoe around obstacles (such as rocks, logs, and water falls) in the water. In canoe parlance, "lining" implies downstream work, whereas "tracking" indicates the opposite. In either case, the ropes used must be strong, non-slippery, snag-resistant, and relatively inelastic. And for ease of handling they should measure at least 1/4 inches in diameter. Favored materials are bright colored polypropylene--because it floats, and "Gold-line"--a hefty stiff braided climbing rope. The woven nylon utility rope sold in hardware stores is bad news; it snags in its own coils when you throw it and has too much stretch--makes your canoe feel like it's dangling on the end of a rubber band. The "braid on braid" dacron sheet-line used on sailboats may be the best lining rope of all.

A good lining rope should have a "stiff hand". The stiffer the rope the better it will fly when you toss it to a friend on a distant boulder.

My own preference is 3/8 inch bright yellow, three-strand braided polypropylene. This is the same stuff they use in some of the best life-saving throw ropes.

Twenty-five feet of line for each end of the canoe is enough. The longer the line the less control you'll have of the canoe. Things get pretty hairy when you've got more than 25 feet of rope out. I know some very experienced "liners" who regularly handle 50 foot lines with only occasional difficulties. But not me--I'll portage before I trust my outfit to that kind of uncertainty.

At any rate, if you need more length, just extend what you have by tying on some of the extra rope you should always bring along on a wilderness trip.


## KNEELING PADS

If you're an avid reader of the canoeing literature you know that the modern way to run rapids in an open canoe is to sit--not kneel--in the canoe. White water racing teams never kneel in an open canoe, even in the toughest drops. So why should you?

You *shouldn't* if you paddle a skinny high performance cruiser whose seats are strung six or eight inches off the floor.

You *should* if you paddle a more forgiving boat with typical high mounted seats.

It's purely a matter of "CG" (center of gravity). The lower the CG the greater your stability on all types of water. And it matters little whether you get that stability by kneeling low or sitting.

Since it's more comfortable to sit in a canoe than kneel, it makes sense to simply lower your seats and always paddle on your duff. Right? Not entirely. Whether you sit or kneel or alternate between the two depends mostly on the type of canoe you have and how it's rigged.

For example, a typical 18½ foot high performance tripping canoe like the Mad River TW Special, Sawyer Charger, We-no-nah Jensen "X", etc., with its narrow bows and eight inch high seats feels tippy until you get used to it. And it would be even more tippy if you raised the seats to a comfortable kneeling height of 11 to 13 inches. So best leave the seats where the manufacturer put them and not mess with what works best. Besides, even if you do jack up the seats high enough to fit a pair of size twelve's beneath, the bows of these and other fine-lined canoes are too narrow to give your knees good purchase for kneeling. If there's insufficient space in a narrow bow to let you spread your knees wide for a good grip on the hull, then you might as well sit.

On the other hand you won't gain by lowering the seats on a high volume Grumman or Old Town Tripper. There's nothing worse than sitting low in a high-sided canoe and paddling with a gunnel in your arm-pit. And there's no contesting that the higher you sit the better you feel.

As you can see, whether you sit or kneel is less a matter of philosophy than canoe design. If you paddle the typical high seated wild river canoe, you'll have to kneel!

And that means you must have knee pads of some sort. Many white water paddlers prefer strap-on pads like those used by gardeners. But loose items which can get lost are unwelcome on any wilderness trip. Better to glue your pads in. Any type of waterproof foam will work, except Ensolite which crushes badly and crumbles in the sun*.

Contact cement your knee pads firmly to the canoe hull and glue rough canvas (old blue jean material works well) to the top surface so they'll take the beating of being stepped on.

Knee pads are essential even in aluminum canoes with non-slip floors. Try kneeling for very long in the bottom of a metal boat in the bone chilling waters of the far north and you'll see why.

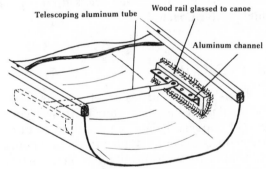

Telescoping aluminum tube    Wood rail glassed to canoe

Aluminum channel

**Figure 6-4**
There are dozens of ways to construct a suitable foot brace. This method provides a wide latitude of forward and aft adjustment and does not weaken the hull. The footbrace is easily remove-able.

## FOOT BRACES

Foot braces are useful in any canoe but they're downright essential in a high performance wilderness cruiser that you can't kneel in. The only way to lock yourself firmly into a low slung seat is to jam your feet against an immoveable object.

A foot brace need not be exotic. For the stern, a heavy pack placed strategically will work fine. But a more permanent solution is a telescoping aluminum tube, crushed at the ends and bolted to a pair of aluminum shod wood rails that are glassed into the canoe (figure 6-4). Don't pop--rivet aluminum rails to the canoe as is commonly done on

*You can buy self-sticking neoprene knee pads from the Blue Hole Canoe Company, Sunbright, Tenn. 37873.

flat-water racing canoes. You might shear off an exposed rivet in rapids or when the canoe smacks a boulder while lining.

Make the bow foot brace as suggested, or if your canoe has a sliding seat, simply move it forward until you can jam your feet against the bow flotation tank.

## EXTRA THWARTS IF YOU NEED THEM

A rough water canoe should have a thwart fore and aft of the yoke to brace the hull and tie in gear. But many of the best tripping canoes don't--possibly because the manufacturers want to save a few ounces or a few dollars. The rubber rope/chute cord security system mentioned in chapter 9 depends on three cross bars to work properly.

But it's no big deal--you can always add thwarts if you need them. Bolt the front thwart directly behind the bow seat and the rear thwart 23 inches in front of the forward edge of the stern seat. This spacing should give you barely enough room to squeeze two big Duluth packs in front of the yoke and three behind it in a typical 17-18 foot canoe.

No sense making the thwarts stronger than necessary. A piece of "one by two" ash or oak cut to a modified hourglass shape is adequate. I'd rather have thwarts break out than my canoe break up if it pins against a boulder in a rough water upset.

## SITTING PAD

When the temperature drops into the forties and the rains come, you'll wish you had some insulation between your duff and your canoe seat. Aluminum seats get impossibly cold, cane ones are only a little better, and every seat becomes uncomfortable after many hours afloat. The solution is to line seats with waterproof foam. You can buy commercial sitting pads or simply duct tape rectangles of foam to the seats. I prefer to make my own pads--it's less expensive, lighter, and I get a custom fit.

It's easy to make a seat pad. Just cut a piece of Volarafoam or EVA (Ethyl Vinyl Acetate) foam (don't use Ensolite; it deforms badly) to the shape of the seat. Sew a canvas* cover and attach nylon straps with Velcro tabs. Now you can quickly remove the pad from the seat and use it around camp.

Everything on a canoe trip should be multi-functional, and the seat pad is no exception. My seat pad becomes part of my sleeping system at night--it extends my short foam pad.

---

*Canvas provides a better non-slip surface than nylon and is more pleasant to sit on.

## CANOE POCKETS

Where to store small items like eye glasses, sun-tan lotion, mosquito repellent, etc., is always a problem on a canoe trip. Of course you can keep these small items in packsacks, but getting in and out of a waterproof pack everytime you want to daub on some bug dope is a hassle. So why not install pockets in your canoe?

An early pioneer of canoe pockets was Verlen Kruger, whose 7000 mile canoe trip from Montreal to the Bearing Sea made canoeing history in 1971. Verlen simply attached plastic bicycle baskets to his canoe thwarts. The baskets provided a convenient--though not loss-proof--place to store small articles of equipment.

Figure 6-5
**THE OTTER BAG**

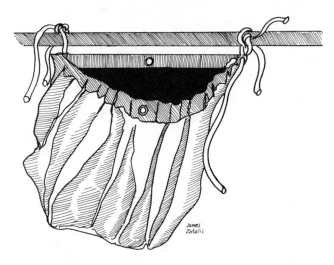

An alternative to bicycle pockets is the OTTER BAG, by Dragonfly Designs*--a 15 inch by 12 inch nylon envelope that ties to a canoe thwart or seat. Big enough for a sweater or lunch, the Otter Bag is elasticised at its mouth and secured with Velcro to prevent the loss of articles in upsets or on portages.

Best place to install Otter Bags is  on the rear thwart and back of the rear seat. Don't put one on the front thwart--it will obscure visibility when you portage.

*Drangonfly Designs Otter Bags are available from California Rivers, P.O. Box 468, Geyserville, CA 95441.

# THWART OR SEAT MOUNTED COMPASS

Like it or not, canoeing northern rivers requires frequent travel on large sprawling lakes. With the possible exception of Minnesota's Rainy Lake and Lake of the Woods, there is no American waterway that compares in complexity with the bigger lakes you'll find in Canada. For example, Great Slave Lake in the Northwest Territories is over 250 miles long, while Reindeer Lake in Saskatchewan is half that length. But that's only part of the story: Once I tried to count the islands on Reindeer Lake--I quit at 200 which was perhaps one-third of the total number!

You need more than good maps to thread your way through the maze of islands on a giant lake. You must also have two (always carry a spare) reliable compasses. But it's a hassle to stop paddling and fetch your compass from a pocket everytime you want to take a bearing. Better to install a "running" compass in the canoe. That way you'll always have accurate directions instantly.

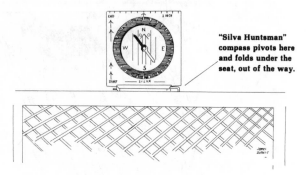

**Figure 6-6**
A "Silva Huntsman" compass mounted beneath the front edge of a canoe seat provides instant directions. The folding mechanism on the compass must be altered (reversed) so the instrument will fold *downward.*

**"Silva Huntsman" compass pivots here and folds under the seat, out of the way.**

I carry three compasses--a Silva Ranger which I keep in my shirt pocket; a Silva wrist compass, and a tiny Silva Huntsman. I mount the wrist compass on the aft thwart when I paddle stern and strap it to a front seat brace when I'm in the bow. The Huntsman, with it's hinged aluminum base, is permanently attached to the bottom front edge of the stern seat. It folds out from under the seat with a flip of the finger.

Two "running compasses" may seem like over-kill, but I've found them quite useful. Once I set a pack with a folding saw inside, against the back thwart. The wrist compass needle went crazy! A quick glance at the seat-mounted Huntsman solved the mystery.

You can make a nice fold-out compass to fit beneath your seat by attaching a brass hinge to any Silva or Suunto flat base Orienteering compass.

All Silva and Suunto Orienteering compasses are liquid-filled so their needles will come to rest quickly (within three seconds!) for a fast reading. Early liquid "damped" compasses would leak fluid if they were left in the sun for long periods. But new models are better sealed so this is no longer a problem.

## SPONGE

You'll use a sponge for bailing and cleaning your canoe, for soaking up water which has invaded a leaky tent, and for dozens of other camp chores. But not all sponges are good. The inexpensive plastic ones sold in discount stores don't absorb much water and aren't tough enough to withstand the rigors of a long canoe trip.

The early voyageurs carried a sponge that was large enough to absorb more than a quart of water with a single swoop! If you want a sponge like this you'll have to buy the "real thing" from an industrial cleaning supplier.

Natural sponges are classified by their texture: a "wool" sponge is stronger and rougher than a "grass" sponge and so will best take the abuse of cleaning canoes. A good natural wool sponge will absorb much more water than a similarily sized plastic sponge and last many times longer. But be prepared to pay a substantial sum--big natural sponges are very expensive.

You'll find some small natural sponges at wallpaper stores. Bigger and better ones are available from the Chicago Sponge Company, 512 North State St., Chicago, IL 60610.

Store your sponge in your "Otter Bag" or under a shock-corded thwart when you're not using it.

## BAILER

When there's too much water sloshing in your canoe to sponge out, use a bailer! White water folks make bailers from cut off bleach bottles but that's not versatile enough for use in a wilderness canoe. A graduated plastic two-quart pitcher works as well. You'll find many uses for the pitcher in camp--measuring water for freeze-dried meals, mixing powdered drinks and instant pudding, etc. Keep the pitcher tied to a canoe thwart until you need it.

# 7

# Covers Aren't Just For Whitewater

"Spray covers are helpful in both wind and whitewater. They allow you to run some whitewater that you'd otherwise have to walk around. They also permit you to venture into bigger waves when the wind is up. I heartily recommend them!" (Jill Bubier)*

"A cover would smother the children! I'll put a cover on my canoe about the same time I feel impelled to add a roll bar to my car." (Carl Shepardson)**

Canoe covers aren't absolutely essential, but they are nice--not just for paddling whitewater but to block the wind and keep you dry when it rains. I'm pretty conservative about running rapids in the wilds: If I don't think I can negotiate a drop without my cover, I'll portage! But occasionally I mis-judge the river--the height of waves, a safe passage around obstacles, a hidden ledge, etc. And sometimes I must choose between a long back-breaking portage and a short run through escalator-like waves which would swamp an open canoe but not a covered one.

At these times I'm grateful for my canoe cover!

But canoe covers can be a hazard, Larry Jamfeson of Easy Rider Canoe Company recently said, "...fabric covers are dangerous; some because they will not release paddlers easily, and others because they either do or do not come off canoes! Over the last eight years, I've rescued six paddlers who were entrapped in fabric canoe covers.

*Jill Bubier has paddled the Hanbury/Thelon and Kazan Rivers in the Northwest Territories as well as many ambitious routes within the timberline.

**Carl Shepardson has paddled more than 10,000 miles with his family since 1966. Routes have included--Kenora to Fort Smith (1800 miles); Marlborough to Kenora (2000 miles); Moise River in Labrador; The Pas to York Factory, and more.

In each case their canoes were turned over, and in two cases the cover's remained attached to the canoe but paddlers were unable to get out. In the third case the paddlers were still in a full cover which had come off their canoe...they and the cover became entangled in rocks. Tragedy was avoided in each case only because someone was immediately available to rescue them. All of the covers were commercially produced and recommended by the canoe manufacturer!"

Pretty strong criticism to be sure. But the fact is *not one* commercially produced fabric cover carries a safety warranty. The dangers of entrapment are real enough to discourage some very skilled paddlers from covering up. Real enough that cover makers are carefully deleting the words "for whitewater use" from their advertising literature.

Okay, now that you have these facts, with all their sinister implications, here are the realities: Most marathon racing canoes occasionally wear covers, as do *nearly all* wilderness boats that challenge the far north's turbulent waters. And performance minded paddlers are discovering that a low-sided USCA cruiser is a formidable big water tripper if covered.

**Figure 7-1**
"Three piece canoe cover: Cockpit sleeve of forward section is rolled and reefed, belly snapped down tight. Rear cover is rolled and tied on the stern deck."

If you select or make a cover that securely attaches to the canoe and has a quick and easy exit system, like the one suggested in this chapter, you should have no problems with entanglement if you capsize.

My own experience suggests that a three-piece cover--one with quickly removable bow and stern sections and an elasticised belly which expands or contracts as the load height and placement changes--is best. I've been perfecting this design for ten years and have found it to be extremely versatile. For example: when rains come, button up forward, center, and aft. In whitewater, omit the tail section (so the stern paddler can exit quickly if the canoe grounds on a rock or upsets). And when tacking across wind-tossed lakes, remove the end caps and use only the cargo section. That's all you need to keep out wave splash which invariably comes in near the waist of the canoe--the place of lowest freeboard.

## SOLO CANOE CONSIDERATIONS

Covers for solo canoes aren't just for whitewater. Try paddling an open solo canoe across a wind-lashed lake and you'll work much harder than your tandem friends. Now attach the cover. Magic! You've cut your wind resistance by half!

A cover will keep your solo canoe drier in calm seas too. When you "hut" (change paddle sides), the water which drips off your paddle will spill harmlessly on to the cover rather than into the canoe's bottom. Commercial covers for solo canoes are virtually nonexistent. But you can easily build one yourself.

**Figure 7-2**
"Two piece cover for a solo canoe. Front section overlaps and snaps to rear cover. Note stern line coiled and secured under Velcro Tab."

A *two piece* cover with a tail section that terminates just behind the seat and a forward section that overlaps and snaps to the rear section, works best for solo canoes. This design allows you to get at packs and loose gear without removing the whole cover.*

Distribute your gear in two packs: camping and cooking items go into a large capacity pack placed in the forward end of the canoe, while frequently used essentials (rain and wind gear, sweater, etc.) are kept in a medium sized day pack behind the seat. To get at the small pack, simply reach behind the seat and unsnap the two covers.

*See Chapter 15 "The Joy of Soloing."

In fair weather reef the front cover just in front of the cockpit. This produces a spacious opening with plenty of room to move about yet effectively catches paddle drips.

To portage, roll the front cover all the way to the bow and tie it in place (see "Making The Cover") so the fabric deck won't restrict visibility under the yoke. This eliminates the time consuming practice of removing the entire cover, essential with a one piece design.

## FABRICS FIRST

Recently, I completed a very nice cover of my own design for my Old Town Ranger from what was "advertised" as a very substantial four-ounce per square yard waterproof nylon. I barely finished the cover when I discovered the waterproof coating had abraided at every place the material wrapped a tight curve (gunnels, deck plates, etc.) on the canoe. Closer inspection revealed dozens of minute pinholes throughout the fabric that would easily pass water. I'd spent 22 hours laboring at a hot sewing machine to make a beautiful cover that *wasn't* waterproof! I flew into a rage and sulked for two weeks. Then I got it back together and began anew. This time I used the best material I could find--a seven ounce per square yard neoprene coated nylon twill from Lands' End, Inc.*--the same folks who made my unquestionably watertight rain suit. The new cover turned out much better than the old!

A cover fabric must be absolutely watertight and rugged enough to stay that way even after it has been folded, stuffed, and abraided hundreds of times. It should be lightweight, flexible in cold weather, resistant to the degrading effects of sunlight, and have extremely high tear strength. The perfect material for making splash covers has not yet been invented.

Technically, materials must withstand at least 25 pounds per square inch of water pressure to be considered "waterproof". Extruded products like plastics easily pass this test but woven fabrics like nylon must be coated with chemical compounds (polyurethane, neoprene, or vinyl) to make them waterproof. There are dozens of coating formulations and each type has its advantages. Generally, fabrics coated with polyurethane are more abrasion resistant but less waterproof than those sealed with vinyl or neoprene. And the thicker the waterproof coating, the more watertight the fabric.

It's easier to waterproof tightly woven fabrics than loosely wov-

*Lands' End, Inc., Lands' End Lane, Dodgeville, WI 53533, no longer carries this particular material.

en ones, so high count nylon taffeta and rip-stop would usually resist water better than heavier and more durable "Pack Cloth" and "Cordura". Even though the chemistry of fabrics and coatings is complex, you can eliminate much hocus-pocus in selecting a cover material if you perform these simple tests: 1) Hold the fabric to a strong light. Do you see any pinholes? If so, reject the fabric because it's not waterproof. 2) Coatings which are improperly applied may flake off when abraded. Roll a sample of the material over a sharp table edge. If the coating comes off, shop elsewhere. 3) Gather a piece of scrap fabric into a loose sack and pour water into it. Reject the material if even the slightest leakage occurs.

There's nothing you can do to improve the waterproof quality of a fabric, but you can solve the abrasion problem by lining high wear areas with a more rugged material.

There's general agreement among fabric-covered boaters that for extreme waterproofness and downright durability, vinyl-coated nylon scrim can't be beat. The stuff is so tough it seldom tears even when dragged through a rock garden on a capsized canoe. And it's much more dimensionally stable, stretches less when wet, shrinks less when dry, than polyurethane coated nylon. And all that means is it won't sag and pool water or shrink and pop snaps as readily.

But vinyl-coated nylon has disadvantages. It's heavy; at 10 to 17 ounces per square yard, a finished cover may weigh five or six pounds. And it isn't very flexible in cold weather, an important consideration if your trips take you into the high arctic. Finally, vinyl-coated materials emit a distinctive "new car" odor which some people find objectionable.

Here are my fabric preferences: For trips into the arctic where the premium is on durability, I'll stick with four ounce per square yard nylon twill with a three ounce neoprene coating, or six ounce nylon pack cloth (Super K-Kote), lined with additional material at all wear and stress points.

For less ambitious trips within the timberline, a well reinforced two to three ounce per square yard coated nylon taffeta or ripstop works fine.

Running a small rapid on the Hood River are David and Bob Dannert (left to right). Note three piece splash cover of the author's design.

## FASTENING THE COVER

Snaps are the most versatile and practical fastener for a cover that has removeable sections. But snaps are ugly and they don't fit properly if the cover shrinks. Some cover makers are experimenting with Velcro because it has a wider range of adjustment than snaps. However, snaps are more reliable than Velcro in wet freezing weather, and for that reason I prefer them.

Since there are no commercially available three piece covers, you'll have to make your own according to my plans--easy even if you can barely sew a straight seam. Over the past five years I designed and constructed ten covers--white water models secured with stainless steel cable*; three-piece cruising styles like the one shown previously in Figure 7-1, and versatile two piece designs for solo touring (see Figure 7-2). They have all been built on a portable sewing machine in five to twenty hours. And because fabric covers are built on the canoe, not from a pattern, anyone can assure a perfect fit even without much sewing experience.

## MAKING THE COVER

At best, I'm a mediocre seamster, so I've developed a method that doesn't require fancy paper patterns or precise measurements. Nevertheless, I think you'll find my simplistic way a good one. Add your own patience and ingenuity and you'll produce a splash cover that's much better than anything you can buy.

First determine the amount of material you'll need. Allow plenty for generous seam allowances, and add in an 80 inch by 25 inch piece of fabric for each cockpit sleeve you'll make.

Next, buy about 70 heavyduty glove snaps like the ones used on pistol holsters. If you can't find these snaps at a fabric store, try your local shoe repair man. Pop-rivet snaps through the canoe hull (use an aluminum back-up washer inside the boat) about two inches below the gunnels at eight inch intervals. Cut the interval in half--to four inches--for the first few snaps near the bow and just behind the cockpit.**

*See my book, "Wilderness Canoeing & Camping", E.P. Dutton Co., 1977 for a description of this cover.

**The closer spacing is to prevent the cover from being torn loose when the bow plunges in waves.

**Figure 7-3    Mid-Section (Belly) Cover**

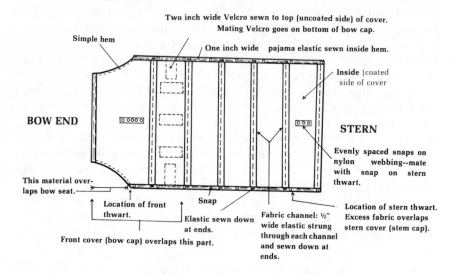

Two inch wide Velcro sewn to top (uncoated side) of cover.
Mating Velcro goes on bottom of bow cap.

Simple hem

One inch wide    pajama elastic sewn inside hem.

Inside (coated side of cover

**BOW END**

**STERN**

Evenly spaced snaps on nylon    webbing--mate with    snap    on    stern thwart.

This material over-laps bow seat.

Location of front thwart.

Snap

Elastic sewn down at ends.

Fabric channel: ½" wide elastic strung through each channel and sewn down at ends.

Location of stern thwart. Excess fabric overlaps stern cover (stem cap).

Front cover (bow cap) overlaps this part.

To construct the belly section (see figure 7-3): Cut a rectangular piece of fabric that reaches from the front of the bow seat to eight inches behind the rear thwart and is 18 inches wider than the widest part of the canoe.

Hem the bow and stern ends, leaving enough room in the stern hem for a length of half-inch wide elastic. Next, hem the long sides and sew in one-inch wide elastic webbing (pajama elastic) along the inside (coated) edge of each side.

Set snaps into the elastic webbing spaced to mate with those on the canoe. Nylon fabrics stretch when wet and shrink when dry, so mounting snaps in elastic eliminates the problems of poor fit when the material changes dimensions.

Sew two inch wide strips (channels) of fabric from edge to edge across the inside of the cover at approximate 18 inch intervals (figure 7-3). String lengths of half-inch wide elastic through these fabric channels and the stern hem. Tighten the elastic substantially and sew down the ends.

Install a snap (use a small flat-head brass screw) in the top center of the forward and aft canoe thwarts. Then attach the cover to the canoe and note where it touches these snaps. Mark the location on the surface of the cover.

Remove the cover from the canoe and sew a foot-long strip of nylon webbing to the underside of the material at each end as shown in figure 7-3. Then install some evenly spaced snaps in the webbing to mate with those on the thwarts. When the cover is in place on the canoe, it will snap to the thwarts at each end. The snaps spaced along the webbing allow you to keep the cover tight at the ends, regardless of the load height.

The belly section is now complete. And since it's rectangular, and not form-fitted to the canoe, it should fit any other canoe of roughly similar proportions without modification. In fact, I've found that the belly cover I built for my 17 foot Old Town Ranger works just as nicely on my 18 1/2 foot Mad River TW Special.

## MAKING THE END CAPS

The end caps are fitted to the shape of the canoe and so are more exacting to make than the mid-section. We'll start with the bow cap (the stern cap is constructed the same way).

Drape material from the apex of the deck plate to about two feet behind the front thwart across the gunnels of the canoe, with the coated side in. Duct tape the fabric to the sides of the canoe below the snap line. Make sure the material fits drum tight back to the front thwart. Leave some slack behind the front thwart where it overlaps the belly cover.

Now, mark the exact location of each snap on the fabric with tailors chalk. Remove the fabric from the canoe and sew pajama elastic to the inside, coated side of the material along the marked snap line. I put a straight pin through each snap's location to make sure the elastic will be accurately positioned. Set snaps into the fabric through the elastic. With all snaps in place, the bow cover (except for that part behind the bow thwart) should fit tightly on the canoe.

Now construct a cockpit sleeve for the bow cover. First snap the bow cover on the canoe. Next, draw the cockpit location on the material and cut the "porthole". You'll find that a sharp jack knife works better for this than scissors. I begin by cutting a small hole, then enlarge it a bit at a time until the size is right. When sizing the cockpit, remember you need to have room to both sit and kneel. And if your canoe has a sliding seat, be sure to provide for its range of adjustment.

Measure the circumference of the cockpit and add three inches. This is the length of material you'll need to make the sleeve. Next decide how tall you want the sleeve to be. A piece of fabric about 80 inches by 26 inches is usually a good starting size.

Sew the short ends of this material together to make the sleeve.

**Figure 7-4**

# Sleeve — Top View

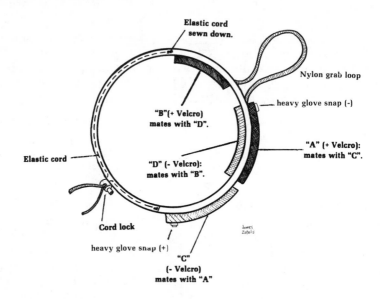

Elastic cord
sewn down.

Nylon grab loop

heavy glove snap (-)

"B"(+ Velcro)
mates with "D".

"A" (+ Velcro):
mates with "C".

Elastic cord

"D" (- Velcro):
mates with "B".

Cord lock

heavy glove snap (+)

"C"
(- Velcro)
mates with "A"

## QUICK RELEASE GUSSET

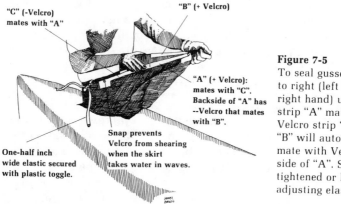

"C" (-Velcro)
mates with "A"

"B" (+ Velcro)

"A" (+ Velcro):
mates with "C".
Backside of "A" has
--Velcro that mates
with "B".

Snap prevents
Velcro from shearing
when the skirt
takes water in waves.

One-half inch
wide elastic secured
with plastic toggle.

**Figure 7-5**
To seal gusset, fold sleeve
to right (left hand over
right hand) until Velcro
strip "A" mates with
Velcro strip "C". Velcro at
"B" will automatically
mate with Velcro on back-
side of "A". Sleeve may be
tightened or loosened by
adjusting elastic hem cord.

Then sew the sleeve to the cockpit. Hem the other end and make the
quick-release gusset shown in figure 7-4 & 7-5. Your sleeve is now
adjustable for a tight waterproof fit. A pull on the Velcro secured tab
will release the sleeve from your waist--an important safety feature
which enables you to get out of the canoe quickly if you capsize.

Don't tie the free ends of the elastic waist cord together. An unsecured loop of elastic is dangerous in a capsize.

The last step on the bow cover is to sew two-inch wide Velcro strips to both the underside of the bow cover's trailing edge and the top side of the belly cover just behind the seat. This gives a snug, reasonably watertight fit between the two covers which can be adjusted to accomodate different load heights.

The procedure for making the stern cap is the same as for the bow piece except you don't need the Velcro tabs. Make the stern cap long enough so the belly section will overlap it by about eight inches.* If you want a better seal between the two covers, sew a few strips of Velcro along their leading edges.

Some nice final touches: Sew ties around each cockpit so you can roll and reef the sleeves in fair weather or when conditions require quick exit and entry.

Also install ties for the end caps so you can roll and reef them near the extreme ends of the canoe when portaging.

Sew Velcro or elastic to the extreme forward end of each fabric deck so you'll have a place to store your coiled lines.

Making a two piece solo cover is similar to constructing a three-piece model. The only difference is that you want a tight fit along the full length of the canoe with no expandable belly. Taping the fabric to the canoe, marking the snap line, sewing the pajama elastic, etc., is the same as outlined.

*The belly section must be unsnapped from the rear thwart to overlap the stern cap. I only snap the belly to the thwart when I'm running whitewater (no tail cap) and want a taut cover that won't pool water.

# LAST MINUTE TIPS

You can save considerable weight in a three-piece cover by constructing the stern section from ultra-lightweight coated nylon. Since the stern cap is used only for rain protection, never in whitewater, it doesn't need to be as rugged and heavy as the other cover sections.

Using the belly cover as a sail

You can also use the mid-section of your three-piece cover as a squaw sail or to cover packs or wood in camp.

**Figure 7-6 (a)**
A well fitted three piece
canoe cover on the
author's Old Town Ran-
ger canoe. Tail section
has been omitted. Marc
Hebert paddles bow and
demonstrates the gusset
on the Hood River, NWT.

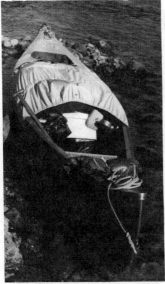

**Figure 7-6 (b)**
Three piece canoe covers add wind
and rain protection; however, they
are not always accepted by everyone
nor are they necessary in every
canoeing situation.

**Figure 7-6 (c)**
Three piece canoe cover.
Tail section is rolled and
reefed.

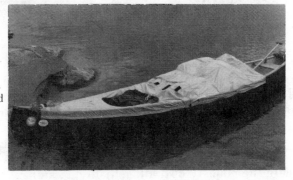

# 8

# Gearing Up

It was ten p.m. and the sky was gentle gray--about as dark as it gets near timberline in mid-July. Not too late to fry another round of fish and make some popcorn.

I pumped some air into the cold brass tank of the Optimus 111B. A flick of my butane lighter brought the stove to life. Momentarily I sat there mesmerized by the flickering yellow/blue flame and stunned by the piercing jet-roar of its tiny engine.

**Figure 8-1**
"I moved within arm's reach of the falls--close enough so that I could feel the penetrating mist rising from the dancing waters below."

I picked up the stove and moved it within arms reach of the falls--close enough so I could feel the penetrating mist rising from the dancing waters below. Overhead, a barely visible streak of luminous green flashed high across the sky. Northern lights?

I felt vibrantly alive, part of a vast greatness that was far beyond my comprehension. Here we were, the four of us--all good friends to share the majesty of it all, selfishly. . . alone.

Then I heard the clanking of their canoes, the voices. Damn! I called loudly at this intrusion to my privacy. I was hopping mad. The spell had been broken.

My anger subsided and I regained composure. Less than enthusiastically I welcomed them aboard and watched as one by one they filed into the light and warmth of our small fire.

My God, they're soaking wet! I thought as I stretched out my hand in reluctant friendship. One man took the gesture and shivering, asked politely, "May we use your fire?" Suddenly, I understood and my crew leaped into action. We piled the fire high, prepared tea and honey, and served them course after course of fresh fried fish, biscuits with jam, and good will.

We learned they'd run a drop we portaged. Both canoes had swamped--one capsized, the other pinned against a rock. It had taken them the better part of the day to free it. Otherwise they'd have made the falls in daylight. They were "Government men"--mapping the river for canoe travel. All were experienced canoeists, though from their looks you'd never guess it.

Later we helped the four of them unpack their gear and set up camp. Everything--from the leather boots on their feet to their sleeping bags and food--was wet. Their tent--a candy-striped canvas affair with a hard wax finish, oozed water and weighed at least 90 pounds.

They had no canvas Duluth packs or waterproof liners--only discount store aluminum frame packs which leaked like sieves. A less than watertight hand-built wanigan box contained some canned goods, eggs, and margarine. There was no stove or rainfly.

They were amiable fellows but we were not impressed by their gear or professed expertise.

Next morning they had the opportunity to see our equipment and methods. They stood in awe as we dropped and stuffed our tent in less than 90 seconds, prepared a gourmet breakfast of freeze-dried eggs and pancakes on our two gasoline stoves, filled Thermos bottles with coffee and soup, and packed and loaded our canoes--all in barely 60 minutes.

For the most part, they couldn't comprehend our equipment or our ways. We were warm, dry, and well-organized. They were not. They poked fun at our Royalex canoes--"Tupperware Tubs", they called them. But secretly we knew they were impressed. They were ordinary Fords and Chevy's; we were the sports cars that just blew past.

In retrospect, it's tempting to say, "they couldn't afford better." But I would question that--not for the sake of dollars spent, but for the choice of gear. There is, for example, no excuse for wearing leather boots on any northern river, or for using packs which are better suited to the alpine trail than to the way of the canoe. And to omit waterproof liners for packs and sleeping bags is unthinkable. And about those canned goods. . .

If your skills are very very good, and you're very very careful, you can get by quite well with pretty shoddy equipment. But if you're the least bit careless or have a run of bad luck, bad weather, bad rapids, or just bad judgement, watch out! You may find yourself in the same boat as the "map-makers" you just read about.

Professing your expertise won't keep you warm and dry. Good equipment and the knowledge of how to use it will. Here's what you need:

# PERSONAL GEAR
## LIFE JACKET

*Always* wear your life jacket whenever you're canoeing or working around water. This is especially important on arctic rivers where water temperatures are very low and a dunking may bring on rapid immobilization and hypothermia.

Canoeing isn't the only place where "accidents" happen. I know of two near drownings that resulted when canoeists slipped and fell into a bad rapid while they were lining their canoes around it. Fortunately, both men were wearing life vests and had good hold of the lines.

A decade ago it was almost impossible to find a really comfortable life jacket that was Coast Guard approved. Now we're deluged with choices. But not all models are suitable for wilderness canoeing: Orange horse collar styles chafe the neck, are terribly uncomfortable, and do not provide any protection against hypothermia. Panel types feel great when you're canoeing but they ride up over your head when you have to swim. And "high flotation" white water vests which boast up to 21 pounds of buoyancy* are wonderful for keeping you above the foamy white, but they're bulky and hot to wear.

My preference is a standard buoyancy (15 1/2 pounds) ribbed whitewater jacket like those made by Omega, Seda, and Stearns. This type is comfortable in and out of the water and it provides better protection against hypothermia than other styles. Though experienced canoeists occasionally upset in rapids during spring practice runs, they almost never capsize in the wilds. A dunking on a remote northern river is "dead serious", so every effort is made to avoid it. The standard rule in the north is "if in doubt, portage", so your life jacket is simply a last ditch safety precaution which you should never need.

---

*The minimum flotation requirement for "Type III" Coast Guard approved Personal Flotation Devices (PFD's) is 15 1/2 pounds.

**Figure 8-2**
Ribbed whitewater life vests
like those made by Omega,
Seda, and Stearns, are comfortable in or out of the water and
provide better protection
against hypothermia than other
styles. Author at left wears a
Seda vest; friend Chic Sheridan
at right wears a Stearns.

It's therefore important to choose a life vest that you can wear comfortably for long periods of time, day in and day out. A good life vest is more than just a buoyancy aid: it's a warm garment, a sitting pad, and an extension for a short length sleeping mat. Get a vest that's long enough to cover your kidneys. You'll appreciate the extra protection when an icy wind comes up from behind.

## TWO PADDLES PER PERSON

Each person should have an extra paddle in case they lose or break one. Four paddles per canoe is not over-kill--it's common sense. I use a lightweight laminated wood paddle in deep water and switch to a more indestructible model with a fiberglass covered blade and stainless steel tip, in shallows and rapids.

Paddle length is determined by the height of your canoe seat and length of your upper body not by some arbitrary "nose to toes" formula. Fifty-two to 54 inches is about right for most high volume fast cruisers, while 54 to 58 is a reasonable length for the big Grummans, Alumacrafts, and Old Towns. Give the matter of length serious thought: A paddle that's too long is unwieldy, while one that is too short won't reach the water when your canoe peaks on the waves of a running sea.

Some canoeists prefer paddles that have their blades set at 10 to 17 degree angles to the shaft (those with 14 degree bends are most popular). "Bent paddles" as they're called, offer a distinct performance edge when paddling flat water, but they're a bit awkward in rapids. Nevertheless, they'll do anything a straight paddle will do once you learn to use them. Their biggest drawback for wilderness use is that they stow poorly in a loaded canoe. It's also hard to find bent paddles that are longer than 54 inches.

Blade width: The trend is to 7 1/2 to 8-inch wide blades. Those wider than this are only more efficient in very shallow water (where you can't immerse the whole blade) and in highly aerated water. The rest of the time wide blades are simply heavy, awkward and noisy.

Blades wider than about 7 1/2 inches produce an unpleasant gurgling sound when they're pulled through the water. The sound is particularly annoying when you're trolling for fish or approaching wildlife. Blades that have vertical ribs along one or both faces also tend to be quite noisy as do those with metal reinforced tips.

Paddles, like canoes, are designed for specific purposes. What works best in rocky whitewater is often a poor choice on the flats, and vice versa. No rule says both your paddles must be the same length and style!

**Figure 8-3**
"Tip your paddle with metal or fiberglass. Stainless-steel tip is from Perception, Inc. Liberty, South Carolina.

Tip your paddle with fiberglass or metal* so the edge won't break out when it hits rocks. The secret to wrapping fiberglass in a tight curve, as around a paddle tip, is to lay it on the bias--weave of cloth at a 45 degree angle to the blade edge (see Chapter 21, "Mending the Tears"). Two layers of four ounce per square yard fiberglass cloth, epoxied in place is adequate and doesn't add too much weight. There are dozens of formulations of epoxies, so make sure the one you choose is highly resistant to abrasion. Most of the quick setting "glues" are too elastic to provide much protection.

Paddles with square-tipped blades (90 degree corners) tend to twist in your hands if you don't set them into the water dead vertical. Square corners are also food for rocks, so round them off on a wide radius and glass the bare wood so it won't splinter.

---

*Stainless-steel paddle tip kits are available from "Perception, Inc.", Box 64, Liberty, South Carolina 29657.

# CLOTHING

## HATS

You need a hat for sun, a hat for rain, and a hat for cold. It's doubtful you'll find a single chapeau that does it all well.

One solution is to carry a wool-felt crusher hat and a wool-knitted stocking cap. The former works marginally well for sun and rain, while the latter keeps your head warm when temperatures plunge.

Though it may seem extravigant, I carry three hats--a lightweight "Lands' End" canvas hat with a wide brim and grommeted crown for hot sunny days; a wool stocking cap for cold; and a comical looking but highly effective neoprene-coated Souwester for rain. I dislike hoods on rain gear: they restrict visibility, snap around my neck in the wind, and don't protect my eye glasses from rain. The Souwester is the logical choice. If folds compactly and weighs almost nothing. When It's *really* wet and cold, I wear my stocking cap under my Souwester!

## WINDBREAKER JACKET

A good windbreaker is a versatile canoeing garment. Wear it over a wool sweater or jac-shirt to cut the fierce wind, or alone on a hot day to keep the bugs from biting through your wool shirt.

Some authorities dismiss wind gear as superfluous and suggest that a rain jacket will suffice to block both wind and rain. It won't, for two reasons: 1) You'll broil in your own juices if you wear a non-porous garment and work hard; 2) Rain gear won't stay waterproof for very long if you wear it every day for wind protection.

This last point is extremely important. Everytime you lean against a rock you slightly abraid the material of the rain coat; and whenever you turn your head or move your arms, you scrape off a microscopic amount of chemical waterproofing from the inside of the fabric. And don't forget the spark holes you'll accumulate when you get too near the fire. In no time, pin-holes will develop and the garment will be useless for it's intended purpose. And it doesn't make much difference whether your jacket is made from polyurethane-coated nylon or nylon-laminated Gore-Tex. Gore-Tex may be waterproof and breatheable when spanking new, but wear it day in and day out for a month on a wilderness canoe trip and see how well it keeps you dry. If you use Gore-Tex, *decide when you purchase it,* which function--wind or rain resistance--you want it to perform, then treat it accordingly!

Some canoeists wear a lightweight Gore-Tex jacket for wind and light rain and add a polyurethane-coated nylon rain shell over it when the occasion demands. This was the combination preferred by Verlen Kruger and Steve Landick on their 28,000 mile cross-continent solo canoe trip.

It makes no difference whether your windbreaker is constructed of nylon, cotton, or dacron blends. What's important is that it is lightweight and sized large enough to fit over several layers of shirts and sweaters. Some expensive "mountain parkas" have stylishly cut sleeves and waists that won't accomodate layered clothing. The U.S. Army field jacket, available at most surplus stores, is a true mountain parka. It's rugged and quite inexpensive.

Invariably, you'll wear your life vest over your wind shell most of the time so there's little sense paying extra for sophisticated pockets you'll seldom use.

## SHIRTS

Two medium weight nearly pure wool shirts are enough for the longest canoe trip. Cotton shirts have no place on a northern river-- they provide little insulation   and are clammy when wet.

Best buy in wool shirts is the Marine Corps Officers Model shirt which can be purchased at many surplus stores. This shirt is woven from 100 percent fine wool and has extra long tails and button-down breast pockets. The last Officers wool shirt I bought in 1982 cost 10 dollars--a veritable steal. Sewing and tailoring on these shirts is equivalent to that found on shirts costing four times as much.

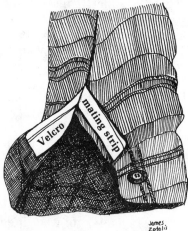

**Figure 8-4**
"Bug proof your shirt cuffs by sewing mating strips to them."

Bug-proof your shirt sleeves by sewing Velcro to the wrist openings just behind the cuffs. This will allow you to seal the shirt cuffs completely.

## LONG TROUSERS

Wool trousers are warm when wet but are not very mosquito-proof. Cotton-canvas pants are the opposite. In the end, your choice should depend on how cold it is, how buggy it is, and whether or not you plan to wear long johns.

I usually wear heavy canvas "Filson Tin Pants-- or army surplus "chino's" and pack a pair of medium weight surplus wool trousers as a spare and for really cold weather. But I wear nearly pure wool long underwear in all but the warmest weather.

Another solution is to team polypropylene or wool fish-net underwear bottoms with medium weight wool trousers. This combination isn't as good for stopping wind and bugs as the canvas/wool blend, but it sheds rain better and is cooler.

Trouser bottoms should hang straight (no cuffs) and be short enough so they barely cover the ankle. Long pant legs catch on brush and absorb water everytime you step in and out of the canoe. Seal the bottom legs of your trousers around the outside tops of your boots with military "blousing bands", or sew Velcro closing tabs to the bottom of each pant leg.

## SWEATER OR WOOL JACKET

A heavyweight pure wool jac-shirt or knitted wool ski sweater will round out your cold weather wardrobe. Team long johns, wool shirt and pants, wool sweater and windbreaker together, and you're set for near zero temperatures. If you're still cold with all this on, put on your foam-filled life vest. And if that doesn't do the trick you'd best hang up your paddle and wax your skis!

## LONG JOHNS

Long underwear isn't absolutely essential, but it will add greatly to your comfort on cold rainy days. It's the insulation right next to your skin that does the trick.

For years the material for long johns was wool--and only wool! No other fabric kept you as warm and dry in damp cold weather. Now there's polypropylene,the rage in cross-country ski wear. At least one Arctic canoeist--Bob O'Hara--swears by polypropylene. Bob wore wool for many years before making the change. He says the new synthetic is very good indeed.

Frankly, I'm a wool freak and remain unconvinced. My wool longies work for me so I see no reason to change. But perhaps I'm just stubborn.

Only cotton underwear, in any blend, is unsuitable for use in the wilds. If you wear cotton next to your skin on a damp chilly day, you'll be colder than if you hadn't worn the garment at all!

You'll discover that long johns of any type reduce black fly bites and their accompanying welts. Black flies can't gnaw through clothing of any kind, which means they must get under your underwear to bite. And that's not easy if you seal your lower pant legs and shirt cuffs as I've recommended.

### ALERGIC TO WOOL?

Then try a wardrobe of 100 percent Orlon acrylic Verlen Kruger and Steve Landick chose acrylics for their 28,000 mile canoe trip. Almost every article of clothing they wore was made from this material. Both men claim that acrylics dry faster than wool, insulate about as well, are soft and comfortable to wear, and are non-allergenic.

You'll find all sorts of acrylic shirts and sweaters at local stores, but you won't find acrylic field pants. Steve and Verlen made their own.

### FOOTWEAR

Want to start an argument? Just profess your choices of footwear to a group of experienced canoeists. Everyone has their own idea what's best, and debates will rage far into the night. However, when the smoke clears, all will agree that you need *two* pairs of boots--one for use in the canoe and on the portage trail, another for general camp use.

For trips in the barren lands where frequent lining and therefore wading in bitter cold water is the rule, *good quality* rubber boots with steel shanks and 12-inch high tops can't be beat. Rubber boots are the only footgear that will keep your feet perfectly dry when you stand in water for long periods of time.

Another solution is the L.L. Bean* shoe-pac which teams a fully waterproof rubber bottom with a water-resistant leather top. Bean boots are almost as waterproof as rubber boots but they're much more comfortable to wear. A real advantage of these boots is that they can be re-soled when the bottoms wear out. And they come in sizes to fit women and children.

Bean boots are best worn with sheepskin-lined leather insoles-- available from L.L. Bean. The latex foam insoles sold in drug-stores are an abomination; they destruct after a few weeks of hard use.

There are some less durable copies of L.L. Bean boots on the market which can't be re-soled.

*L.L. Bean, Inc. Freeport, Maine 04032

Just about any comfortable boot--leather, canvas, or shoe-pac, is adequate for camp use. The important thing is to select footgear that packs small and dries quickly--which eliminates foam-lined hiking boots with Vibram soles. Unlined leather boots or lightweight shoe-pacs are the sensible choice.

Some canoeists who like cold feet wear nylon sneakers or canvas Vietnam boots. This footwear is wonderful for paddling the warm waterways of Southern Canada and the United States, but it's not practical for use in the cold northern rivers. If you must use sneakers combine them with five-buckle golashes. These, plus leather boots, were the footwear Clint Waddell chose for his 7000 mile canoe trip.

My own preference is two pairs of L.L. Bean Shoe-Pacs. One pair has 10 inch tops for everday use; the other has six inch tops for hiking and relaxing.

Don't forget to include some leather conditioner in your kit. A 35 mm film can filled with boot wax will last a month.

## GLOVES

Gloves are one of the most essential and forgotten items on a canoe trip. Buckskin gloves dry soft and are a logical choice for warm weather. Wool gloves with leather palms (so you can grip the paddle) are better in rain and cold. Neoprene gloves, like those used by skin-divers, provide the best protection of all when freezing rains come to stay.

I carry buckskin gloves and leather-faced wool gloves for trips within the timberline. In the barrens and everywhere in the north country during spring and fall, I use leather-faced woolens and neoprene wet-suit gloves. You can't paddle with your hands in your pockets--reason enough to give gloves serious consideration.

## RAIN GEAR

No item of clothing is more important than really good rain gear! Ponchos and below-the-knee rain shirts don't qualify. Ponchos don't provide adequate protection in a wind-blown rain, and neither garment is safe in a capsize.

A two piece rain suit is your best bet. Buy your rain jacket a full size larger than you think you need--large enough to wear over several layers of warm clothes and your life vest. It's very frustrating (and time-consuming) to alternately put on and take off a life-vest every time an intermittant shower necessitates a change in your wardrobe.*

*It's recommended that you never wear anything over your life jacket when running rapids. In the real wilderness, however, it's occasionally necessary to make a few compromises for the sake of comfort.

Pay particular attention to the neck/wrist closures and hood design of a rain garment. It's essential that the neck area seal tightly and as high up the throat as possible. Even the smallest gap here will permit wind-blown rain to slither down your neck--a chilling experience!

If you don't plan to wear a Souwester hat, be sure the hood is roomy enough to accomodate a wool or canvas broad-brimmed hat. Only a fully waterproof hat or a non-waterproof one worn beneath a rain hood will keep you dry in a downpour.

When rains begin you'll slip your rain jacket over your life vest. As the weather worsens, you'll add your rain pants . . . and reverse the procedure as rains let up. So don't buy rain pants that have integral bibs (suspenders)--you'll have to remove your life vest *and* rain jacket everytime you want to put on or take off your rain pants!

If your rain trousers have an elastic waist cord, tear it out and substitute parachute cord and a plastic toggle. Elastic stretches when it gets wet and rain pants keep falling down. The nylon cord and toggle arrangement is more secure and comfortable.

Trim rain pants short enough so they won't catch brush when you walk, and don't use the silly snap closures at the ankle--they restrict ventilation.

**Fabrics:** Your choice of fabrics depends on how light you want to travel and how dry you want to stay. Good quality ultra-light weight polyurethane-coated nylon will suffice if you, 1) carefully waterproof the seams at least once a year; 2) wear the garment only when it rains; 3) are careful to avoid holes and tears; 4) store the outfit in a nylon sack when you're not wearing it.

Even with that, don't expect any lightweight rain suit to keep you dry in a severe all-day rain. Only heavyweight foul weather sailing gear that's built to military specs will do that. Using foul weather sailing gear for canoe trips may seem like overkill, but when the chips are down, weight and bulk is secondary to warm and dry.

**Gore-Tex:** Many paddlers have found that a rain suit of waterproof/breatheable Gore-Tex, is the answer to their foul weather needs. Early Gore-Tex rainwear was a disaster: the stuff leaked unpredictably. Now there's "Second Generation Gore-Tex", which is much better. I've been wearing a second generation jacket for two years now and have found it to be *almost* as waterproof as my lightweight rain clothing. My personal experience with Gore-Tex suggests it is very adequate for the kind of canoeing most people do, and it's great for whitewater as it doubles as a waterproof paddling shirt. But frankly, I'm not ready to trust it on a major expedition where I expect a lot of heavy cold rains.

Again let me stress that no waterproof garment will last long if you wear it as an every day jacket. If you use your rain gear only for its intended purpose it won't fail you when you need it.

My preference? I wear a lightweight nylon "Kelty" parka for wind and light rain and switch to a nylon-lined, neoprene-coated foul weather sailing suit when the rains come to stay.

## CURING WHAT BUGS YOU

It's said that fully 95 percent of all the protoplasm in the far north is concentrated in the bodies of black flies and mosquitoes. I believe it. There've been times when I'd swear the entire mass of them was on me! I've never been on a canoe trip north of the 55th parallel where I didn't need my headnet and repellent on at least one occasion!

I once saw a cow moose crash wildly into a small clearing along a portage trail in Northern Ontario. A huge cloud of black flies hovered around her head. The flies were everywhere--in her nose and ears, around her eyes and mouth. She stood there dampled in the morning sunlight, wildeyed, snorting in pain, and repeatedly beat her head against the branches of a scrub birch tree nearby. We came within 20 feet of her yet she never sensed us. She was obviously quite disoriented. I don't know why she didn't jump into the river which was just a few hundred feet away.

**Figure 8-5**
"Blackflies by the thousands coat the leeward side of this tent in the Dubwant Canyon along the Dubwant River. This photo was taken by Staffan Svedberg on Fred Gaskin's 1974 epic adventure, "Retracing Tyrrell's Trip Into the Barren Lands" (see Chapter 19 for the full story).

**Repellent:** The best repellents have a high concentration of "DEET" (N-N Diethyl-metatoluamide). Ounce for ounce, "Muskol" is most effective; GI Jungle Juice--available at every surplus store--runs a close second. Figure on using one ounce per week. Avoid sprays and sticks; they're not very effective.

**Head net:** I always carry two headnets in case I lose one. Best is the military helmet style with face hoops and elastic bottom.

**Repellent Jacket:** The repellent jacket may be the greatest invention of our time. It's simply a fabric mesh jacket that's saturated with a powerful repellent. Wear it over a light shirt and I'll guarantee you won't get bit. It's lightweight and cool and has a hood to cover your neck and head. It's expensive but worth ten times the price when you need it. A bug jacket plus a headnet is sometimes overkill-- usually the jacket and face repellent is enough. Virtually every arctic canoeist I know uses one of these jackets and raves about them. I've had excellent results with the "Johnson Repellent Jacket"* but have also heard good things about the "Shoo Bug" jacket, a competitive product.**

## PADDLING SHIRT

A paddling shirt is a lightweight waterproof nylon shirt that has elastic at the neck, cuffs, and waist. Whitewater kayakers wear these shirts over a wet suit top or wool sweater to trap body heat and keep out water.

Few north country canoeists carry paddling shirts, yet I think they're a useful garment. They provide a measure of protection against hypothermia if you capsize in cold water.

I keep my paddling shirt (which rolls to fist size) in my Otter Bag and slip into it just before I descend a major rapids. I once upset in a powerful Class III drop during a spring whitewater run while wearing wool long johns, wool shirt and sweater, and nylon paddling shirt under my life vest. The water was only a few degrees above freezing so I abandoned the canoe and struck out for shore which was only a few canoe lengths away. Later when I stripped off my wet clothes, I discovered that my upper arms and chest were almost completely dry.

Paddling shirts don't cost much or weigh much. Every canoe shop has them.

## SLEEPING BAG

No mystery here: If it packs small and keeps you warm, that's enough. No need to buy an arctic bag. Canoe country temperatures even near the Arctic circle seldom go much below 25 degrees, and for that any three season sleeping bag is adequate.

Bulk is much more critical on a canoe trip than weight, so get a bag that packs as compactly as possible. If it won't compress into a 9-

---

*Johnson Repellent Jackets are presently sold only in Canada and are manufactured by Johnson Diversified, Canada, Inc., Yorkbury Square, 3345 Service Road, Burlington, Ontario L7N3G2.

**You'll find the "Shoo Bug" jacket in many American sporting goods stores or write Cole Outdoor Product of America, 6801 P St., Lincoln, Nebraska 68508.

inch by 18-inch round bottom stuff sack, shop elsewhere. And don't believe that down bags are unsuitable for canoeing because "they won't keep you warm if they get wet". Really now, have you ever slept in a wet polyester bag? Or tried to dry one under typical field conditions? I doubt you'll find that either experience is to your liking.

If you get your down sleeping bag--or anything else wet--on a canoe trip, you need to learn some basic packing and camping skills! I've never gotten my sleeping bag wet. If you pack as I suggest in the next chapter, you won't either!

In case you're wondering, I prefer down sleeping bags. They're warmer, lighter, more compact, more luxurious, and longer-lived than any of the synthetics.

## TRAIL MATTRESS

The emphasis here is on comfort, reliability, and reasonable size when rolled. For my money, this means a three-quarter length (48 to 60 inches long) high density polyurethane foam trail pad with a breatheable cotton or dacron cover. Closed-cell foam pads--ideal for snow camping--just aren't comfortable enough for my ageing bones.

Air mattresses and air/foam pads? There's no such thing as a bomb-proof air mattress! If it's got air in it, it will fail...sooner or later. And the time of reckoning will invariably come on the bumpiest campsite of your trip.

Any air product will serve you well if you're willing to replace it every few years.* However, if cost and/or extreme reliability is a major consideration, best stick with fabric covered polyurethane foam. And don't be concerned that poly-foam absorbs water. As I've repeatedly stated, if you pack properly your gear will remain dry even in the worst upset.

---

*Air mattresses are downright cold to sleep on when the temperature drops below freezing. A simple solution is to team them with a quarter-inch thick closed cell foam pad. Put the pad on top, next to your body.

# MISCELLANEOUS EQUIPMENT

### POCKET KNIFE

The rage today is the "Swiss Army Knife"--a sophisticated version of the old Boy Scout pocket knife. Frankly, I'm not a fan of these red-handled tool shops. If you've got to whittle the center out of a wet birch log to get at the dry wood inside so you can start a fire on a rainy day, a Swiss knife won't cut it. You need something much more substantial--either a thin-bladed sheath knife, or (my preference), a big single-blade folding knife.

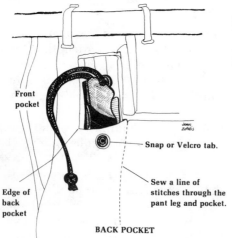

**Front pocket**

Snap or Velcro tab.

Sew a line of stitches through the pant leg and pocket.

**Edge of back pocket**

**BACK POCKET**

**Figure 8-6**
The best way to carry a big folding knife is in a pocket sewn into the back pocket of your field trousers.

Big folding knives are emminently practical on canoe trips. They'll do everything a sheath knife will do but won't catch in your life jacket or canoe seat. And they're safe too: there's no way you can accidently cut yourself with a folded "folder".

The best canoe knives have stainless steel blades that lock in place when they're open. The lock feature isn't to prevent accidental closing of the knife blade but rather to permit effortless--one hand if need be--opening. Lockblade knives don't have pressure springs like conventional jack knives, so they open and close easily. You can pull out the blade on a lockknife while wearing mittens in the dead of winter. Try that with a common pocket knife!

The best way to carry a big folder is in a pocket sewn into the back pocket of your field trousers. Just sew a line of stitches through the pant leg and pocket as indicated in the diagram and attach a snapflap or Velcro tab at the top. Equip your knife with a lanyard so you can pull it out with one hand.

I carry my favorite knife (a hefty Puma Plainsman) this way on all my canoe trips. It's secure, always available, and never a nuisance. If I want to open a tin can, punch a hole in leather, or snip a bandage, I'll use the appropriate tool for the job, which I carry in my repair kit, where it belongs.!

## FOLDING SAW

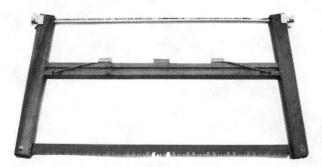

**Figure 8-7**
The "FAST BUCKSAW" is constructed of hard maple and is absolutely rigid when assembled.

This is your most useful fire-making tool. Aluminum-framed folding saws are flimsy and their triangular shapes don't permit you to cut big logs. Best camp saw I've ever used is a full stroke retangular model called the FAST BUCKSAW*. The FAST BUCKSAW is constructed of solid hard maple and has a quickly replaceable 21 inch blade. The saw locks up absolutely rigid when assembled and packs shorter than any folding saw with equivalent length blade (it fits nicely in a Duluth pack). It's almost impossible to bend or break this saw when it's packed or assembled. The FAST BUCKSAW is a fairly expensive unit, but worth it. It'll last a lifetime.

**Figure 8-7(b)**
"The FAST BUCKSAW is a reliable tool for firemaking. The sturdy 21 inch blade locks in place securely."

*FAST BUCKSAW, 110 East Fifth St., Hastings, MN 55033 or available from Indiana Camp Supply, P.O. Box 344 Pittsboro, IN 46167.

**Figure 8-8**
An all steel hand axe is an in-
despensible tool. The sheath
should be made of heavy
leather, secured with solid
copper rivets.

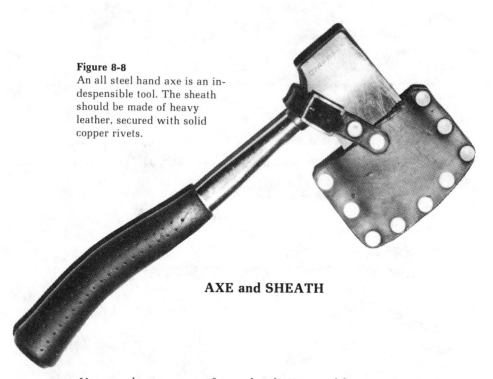

**AXE and SHEATH**

You need some sort of wood-splitting and hammering tool on a
canoe trip. My choice is an all steel hand axe. If you saw your wood
into 12 inch lengths you'll have no trouble splitting them with a small
hand-axe. The back-side of a hand-axe is useful for setting rivets in
torn pack-straps, straightening bent metal hardware on canoes, and
for a variety of other tasks. You don't need a full-size or three-quarter
axe as is recommended by some authorities. A big axe won't fit in a
Duluth pack and is only practical if you want to produce a week's
supply of firewood. If you can't start and maintain a small campfire
with a hand axe, pocket-knife, and folding saw, you'd best stay home
by your TV and oil furnace!

Make a sturdy sheath for your hand axe by riveting together two
pieces of sole leather. Sheaths that come with edged tools are
generally worthless.

## SHARPENING TOOLS

Include a flat mill file, a soft Arkansas or Wachita stone, and
some honing oil in your kit. Or if you don't want to mess with oil and
stones, carry one of the expensive but efficient "diamond
hones"which you can buy at most camp shops.

## SHOVEL

It's nice to have a tool for digging shallow latrines and to bury fish remains. You could use the axe, of course, but it gunks up the blade. A foot-long length of one-inch diameter aluminum tube with one end flattened, makes a moderately efficient lightweight shovel and emergency pancake turner.

## ROPE

Each canoe should carry *at least* 50 feet of three-eighths inch diameter nylon rope in addition to their two 25 foot lining ropes. You can never have too much rope on a canoe trip! Coil your ropes so you can use them for throwing lines in an emergency.

## MEDICAL KITS

If your trips take you far beyond the last road, you'll need a full *medical kit* in addition to a standard first-aid kit (the two should be packed in separate canoes).

The most complete mail order source of medical equipment and advice is "Indiana Camp Supply"* and the most useful outdoor medical text is "Wilderness Medicine", by Dr. Bill Forgey.

The items listed in Appendix "D" (THE MEDICAL KIT) are those suggested in Dr. Forgey's book.

You should realize that having the right medical gear is meaningless if you don't know how to use it. So read and re-read Dr. Forgey's book. And take as many first-aid courses as you can. You can never know too much first-aid!

On a very positive note, I should say that while I travel with a very extensive medical kit, I've never had to use much more than anti-biotcs, tape, and Steri-Strips (which are much better than butterflies). It's amazing how careful you are when you know there's no one around to help you!

## CAMERA

If you want good photos, get a good camera, and don't be afraid to keep it handy. We go armed to the hilt with camera gear--all sorts of lenses, filters, a tripod...the works! Don't worry about getting your camera wet. I'll show you how to pack it in the next chapter.

I bring enough film to shoot 18 color slides per day. "Real" photographers don't consider this nearly enough!

If you develop many rolls of film and find you can't remember the order in which you shot the rolls, try this: Write the number of each roll on a slip of paper and photograph it--first picture on each roll.

*Indiana Camp Supply, Inc. PO Box 344, Pittsboro, IN 46167

When the slides are developed, one slide in each box will indicate the roll number.

## BINOCULARS

Binoculars aren't just for viewing wildlife. They're essential for navigation and to check rapids. Use them to locate a campsite on a distant shore and to find the mouth of an obscure stream or portage trail. They'll tell you if a rapid is safe to run and precisely where to run it. A monocular is not an effective substitute for binoculars because you don't have good depth perception with one eye.

## COMPASS

A compass is essential equipment on every wilderness canoe trip. The Orienteering style instruments by Silva and Suunto are, in my judgement, the only ones suitable for serious navigation. Orienteering compasses have built-in protractors which enable you to plot courses accurately and quickly, even in a bobbing canoe. My two favorite compasses are the Silva Ranger--because it can be adjusted for magnetic declination; and the Silva Huntsman--because it's so tiny you can carry it comfortably in a shirt pocket. Every canoeist should have their own compass!

## LIGHTING UNITS

The farther north you go, the less light you need. At the height of the canoeing season, parts of Northern Canada and Alaska have more than 22 hours of daylight. Of course, farther South, you'll need a lighting unit of some sort.

A small flashlight which takes one or two C-cells is adequate for most wilderness canoeing. I've come to favor the "Moonlight--a very light, compact unit distributed by Early Winters, Ltd.* The Moonlight has a waterproof plastic case and a single Lithium C-cell. The Lithium battery outlasts a dozen standard batteries under typical field conditions, and it maintains full power in the coldest weather.

I often carry a small telescoping candle lantern in addition to my Moonlight. The candle warms my tent and provides a cheery atmosphere.

## MATCHES AND FIRE—STARTERS

I carry three waterproof plastic jars filled with about 150 matches each. Matches are packed with a foam plug on top so the heads won't be damaged. I glue coarse sandpaper inside each jar lid for a striker.

Two butane lighters and a tube of chemical "Fire-Ribbon" round

*Early Winters, Ltd., 110 Prefontaine Place South, Seattle, WA 98104.

out my fire-making materials. I consider myself a rabid environmentalist and so am reluctant to recommend disposable butane lighters. But they are much handier than matches and are completely waterproof. My butane lighters are the only concession I make to our "throw-away" society.

## WHISTLE

We gave each of our two pre-school children a whistle when we took them on their first canoe trip. The instructions were clear: "Blow the whistle *only* in an emergency!" In the early years the kids were very cooperative. But now that they're older they've developed a broader view of "emergencies". When, on a recent trip, nine year old Peggy Anne called her ten year old Sister a name because she "wasn't paddling right", a major brawl erupted. The pair responded with a continuous volley of whistles which brought my wife Sharon and I instantly to the scene. Needless to say, a stern lecture followed.

Whistles have only limited value on a noisy river. If you want to signal the canoe behind to portage some whitewater you've just run, you won't do it by whistling. The sound just won't carry far enough. The real value of a whistle is on land--if you get confused along a portage trail, for example. Portages in the far north aren't always evident; often you have to make your own trails.

A small plastic or brass whistle is sufficient. Keep it pinned inside a shirt or trouser pocket.

## THERMOS BOTTLE

I carry a two pint glass Thermos bottle on all my canoe trips. Sometimes I fill the Thermos with hot coffee, tea, soup, or water before I retire so I won't have to start the stove the next morning to prepare a hot drink or meal. Or I fill the Thermos at breakfast so there'll be something hot for lunch or in the event someone becomes chilled.

Later in camp, boiling water for tea or dishwater goes into the Thermos--saves gas because I don't have to re-start the stove so often to re-heat water.

A glass vacuum bottle is lighter and more efficient than a stainless steel one. If you're careful you won't break it. I keep my Thermos inside my pack-basket or protected by clothing near the top of my Duluth pack.

## RAIN TARP

Canoeing in foul weather without a rain tarp borders on insanity. Chapter 12 (Gearing Up) goes into the specifics of this essential and often under-rated item.

## LIP BALM AND HAND CREME

Don't underestimate the importance of these products. Your hands and lips will crack and bleed if you don't treat them frequently with medications. I use hand creme and lip balm almost every day on rigorous canoe trips. Carry plenty! You'll use much more than you think.

## STOVE AND COOKING GEAR

See Chapter 11 **(Edibles)** for a discussion of stoves and cooking gear.

## TENT

The tent is so important that I've devoted an entire chapter to it (Chapter 10 -- CANOE TENTS ARE DIFFERENT).

## PACKSACKS

You'll find everything you want to know about packs and packing in the next chapter.

Perhaps the best advice I can give you when choosing equipment for canoe travel is to carefully examine everything before you buy. If a zipper looks weak, it probably is; if there's a knob which can break, it most likely will; if there's an unsecured part that can be lost, bet on it. Go on the assumption that if something can fail, it will, and you'll get real value for your money and be well prepared for the unexpected.

Most important, be aware that some of the most highly touted products which work flawlessly over the short haul, fail miserably when the weeks turn to years. So be wary of advertising claims and the testimonials of individuals whose experience is limited to a single expedition. Instead, heed the advice of those who canoe the wild rivers of the far north year after year after year. These are the "real" experts, even though their opinions and methods are seldom seen in print!

# 9

# The Art of Packing

For close-to-home river floats where there are few portages, you can simply throw your gear into a couple of nested plastic bags. Or you can pack it in a big ice chest or small trash can that has a tightly-fitted lid. I once met two youths carrying a galvanized garbage can over a portage trail in Quetico Provincial Park. They'd chained the can lid shut to make a "bear-proof" cache. I couldn't suppress a wry smile when I walked past the contraption, for I knew a big black bear could demolish it with a single pounce.

Plastic bags and garbage cans are all right for local trips where equipment failure isn't critical. But for canoeing a wild river, you need the toughest packs you can get. Surprisingly, canoeing is much harder on packs than backpacking, probably because canoeists carry heavier loads than backpackers. A 50 pound pack is the rule on a canoe trip; an 80 pound one is not uncommon. Heavy packs must be built tough enough to withstand the abuse of being tossed into canoes and rocks.

That's a major reason why Duluth packs--which are the toughest packs of all--are preferred by seasoned canoeists everywhere.

Duluth packs are unsophisticated and uncomfortable to carry. Nonetheless, they're better adapted to canoeing than any other style pack. Here's why:

1. They're big! A number three Duluth pack (the most popular size) has a volume of more than 4000 cubic inches. You can stuff two sleeping bags, two foam pads, and a months supply of clothing for two in a pack this size.

2. Duluth packs utilize space in a canoe more efficiently than those with frames or rigid construction.

3. Pack frames can bend or break--Duluth packs can't!

4. It's easier to waterproof the single compartment of a Duluth pack than the many pockets of a frame-style hiking pack.

5. Duluth packs sit upright in a canoe (two packs can be stood back to back) whereas frame packs must be laid flat on the canoe's floor--in contact with accumulated water and mud.

Some canoeists who use frame packs set them up against a thwart, but this procedure raises the center of gravity of the canoe too high. And your splash cover may not fit over the load.

The best Duluth packs are made from heavy water-proof canvas and have riveted leather straps. Duluth Tent and Awning Company* is the most complete source of high quality Duluth packs. This company will ship direct to any part of the country and they'll custom make tarps or packs to your specifications.

Advertising claims to the contrary, good canvas Duluth packs will outlast nylon ones by many years and they can be easily rewaterproofed by painting on chemical compounds which are available at most hardware stores.**

# RIGID PACKS

If you have fragile or difficult-to-pack items like Thermos bottles, stoves, gasoline liter bottles, etc., you'll want one or more rigid packs. The woven ash pack-basket which is available by mail only from L.L. Bean, has for centuries been the traditional hard pack, and it's still my favorite. I nest my pack-basket *inside* a heavy rubberized army clothes bag and set this combo inside a number two Duluth Tent and Awning Co. "cruiser" pack. A loop of shock-cord seals the mouth of the rubberized bag. This is a very sturdy waterproof unit, and it packs well in a canoe. Order an 18 inch high basket from L.L. Bean, and ask Duluth Tent and Awning Company to extend the closing flap on your number two "cruiser" by eight inches so it will close nicely over the wide mouth of the pack-basket.

There are some rigid plastic packs available which seem to work well over the short haul. How they'll hold up year after year on major trips is anybody's guess. Personally, I'll take varnished wood and treated canvas over thin plastic anytime.

# WANIGAN BOXES

Trappers and fur traders commonly transported tools and equipment in heavy wooden boxes called "wanigans". Wanigans were quite popular in the early part of this century, though you seldom see them today. A few companies make very nice modern versions of these boxes from a sturdy ABS plastic. One model has detachable table legs and converts to a car-top carrier.

---

*Duluth Tent and Awning Company, Box 6024, Duluth, MN 55806.

**A new product from Johnson Camping, called "K-Kote RECOAT" will restore the worn coating on nylon and synthetic blend fabrics. You brush-on the material for a clear, flexible, waterproof finish.

I used wanigans a lot when I was much younger but now consider them more hassle than they're worth. They're great for carrying canned goods and other bulky items but   they take up an awful lot of room in the canoe. Even with a portage harness, they don't carry very well.

## THE SCIENCE OF WATERPROOFING

All food and equipment should be sealed in watertight containers. Unfortunately, attaining *complete* waterproofing isn't as easy as it sounds. Simply stuffing sleeping bags and clothing into packs or bags that are constructed of waterproof material isn't enough. The weakest part of any waterproof bag is its closure, not its stitching or fabric. Stitching is easily waterproofed with paint-on chemical compounds or tape, and fabrics are either waterproof or they aren't. But there's not much you can do with a "waterproof" bag whose mouth won't seal.

I've found that only bags which have these types of closures are really rapids-proof: 1) Sliding tubes like those pioneered by Voyageur Enterprises;* 2) Roll-down snap flaps like those used on Phoenix camera bags** and military amphibias assault gas-mask bags; 3) Zipperless sliding closures like those used on Zip-lock plastic bags.

## SLIDING TUBE CLOSURES

Bags with sliding tube closures are *absolutely* waterproof. They won't fail when the bag is compressed under the weight of a heavy object. However, tube closures are slow and awkward to seal, especially when your hands are cold or the weather is uncooperative. The plastic tubes also tend to cut through the plastic bags after they've been sealed and unsealed many times. Perhaps the main disadvantage of these bags is that they're not sized to fit standard Duluth packs. This is a wonderful system for infrequent whitewater runs but it's not practical for extended wilderness canoe trips.

## BAGS WITH ROLL-DOWN SNAP CLOSURES
### (Best protection for your camera and binoculars)

These are the fastest and easiest of all waterproof bags to use. And they're *absolutely* waterproof!

*Voyageur Enterprises, PO Box 512, Shawnee Mission, Kansas 66201.

**Phoenix Products, Inc., U.S. Rte. 421, Tyner, KY 40486.

Best buy is the military surplus amphibias assault gas mask bag which is constructed from very heavy canvas-covered rubber. Gas-mask bags cost under five dollars (1983 prices) at most surplus stores and are by far the best protection for your camera and binoculars that you can buy. They hold enough air when sealed so they'll float, and their snaps are so strong they can't possibly pop loose. Paint your camera bag "white" so it will reflect heat.

## ZIPPERLESS BAGS WITH SLIDING CLOSURES

Bags with zipperless locks (like Zip-lock bags) are waterproof as long as they're not over-filled and their locks are kept free of foreign matter.

## BAGS WITH OTHER CLOSURES

Other bags which are easy to use but of questionable dependability in keeping out water include those with "pleat and tie" closures, "standard zippers", and "U-roll 'em" tops.

The reliability of bags which pleat and tie depends entirely on how skillful the user is in gathering and tying the fabric. Zippers are fast and easy to use but they don't seal completely, and they eventually fail.

Leaf and lawn size plastic bags with U-roll 'em tops are too small and fragile for canoe tripping.

If you assume that the ideal waterproof bag hasn't been invented, you're dead right. Waterproof bags tend to be either dependable and awkward to use, or undependable and easy to use. And they almost never come in the sizes you need.

It's easy to find small waterproof bags, but almost impossible to locate serviceable ones big enough to fit a big Duluth pack. You may have to make your own.

Heading the list of commercially available bags are the giant 36 inch by 48 inch, *six*-mil thick plastic bags which are distributed by Recreational Equipment, Inc., in Bloomington, Minnesota, Hoigaards, in Minneapolis, and "Indiana Camp Supply".* These bags are large enough to fit a giant number four Duluth pack with room to spare. And they're much stronger than anything you can buy in local stores. Cost of these bags at this writing is three dollars each. Both Indiana Camp Supply and Hoigaards will mail bags out-of state if you pay for the packing and shipping.

*Recreational Equipment, Inc., 710 W. 98th St., Bloomington, MN 55420.
Hoigaards, Inc., 3550 South Highway 100, Minneapolis, MN 55416.
Indiana Camp Supply, P.O. Box 344, Pittsboro, IN 46167.

You can also make very serviceable plastic liners for Duluth packs by taping (use Silver Duct tape) up bags of six-mil plastic sheeting which you can buy at every lumber yard and hardware store. I've found from long experience that plastic pack liners thinner than six mils just don't hold up on a wilderness canoe trip.

**Now some principles of waterproofing:**

1. No waterproof bag will remain watertight forever. Eventually it will develop pin-holes and abrasions and you'll have to repair or replace it. So it makes little sense to spend a lot of money for fancy waterproof packsacks. Instead, use an inexpensive waterproof liner inside your conventional canvas packs.

2. Holes almost always develop from *within* a plastic bag, not from without. Everytime you stuff a sleeping bag or pair of boots into a packsack you stretch or abraid the plastic pack liner. In no time there's a hole. And it makes no difference whether the bag is a six-mil thick plastic Duluth pack liner or the PVC-coated walls of a fully waterproof packsack!

The answer? Nest a tough "abrasion liner" *inside* each waterproof pack liner. The abrasion liner may be standard six-mil plastic, a woven polypropylene bag (better) or a sack you've sewn from heavy nylon or cotton. It need not be waterproof.

The abrasion liner will protect the waterproof plastic bag from being punctured by your gear inside, and the canvas packsack will eliminate tears from the outside.

When you've filled your pack with equipment, roll down the top of the abrasion liner, then twist, fold over, and seal the outer plastic bag with a loop of shock-cord or band cut from an inner tube. Hint: be sure the abrasion liner and waterproof bag liner are long enough so you can roll or twist them to provide a good seal. Bags should be *twice* the length of the pack!

If you have a pack with zippered compartments, you'll have to waterproof each compartment by the double-bag method recommended. This is a major reason why experienced canoeists scorn packs with exterior pockets. Besides, zippers are often the first things to fail on a rugged canoe trip.

## PACKING THE SLEEPING BAG

If there's one thing you must keep absolutely dry, it's your sleeping bag. The recommended procedure for waterproofing the sleeping bag is to stuff it into a nylon sack that has first been lined with a plastic bag. This is foolish advice! If you re-read the second principle of waterproofing, you'll see why.

My method: Stuff your sleeping bag into a nylon stuff sack (which need not be waterproof) then put the sack into a six-mil thick plastic bag. Seal the plastic bag with a loop of shock-cord and set this unit into an oversize waterproof nylon stuff sack. Note that the puncture-prone plastic bag is where it should be--sandwiched between two protective layers of tough nylon!

## PUTTING IT ALL TOGETHER

You'll need three to five Duluth packs per canoe, and one pack-basket for the crew, for an extended trip. I usually allow slightly less than one number three Duluth pack for each person's clothing and sleeping gear.

Each individual packs their personal gear in a separate pack. If a packsack is lost, as in a capsize, at least there'll be some extra clothing and sleeping bags to share.

Food is distributed among as many packs as possible, both for the reason above and to equalize weight.

The tent and rain tarp are packed last. These items go at the very top of a Duluth pack--between the rolled abrasion liner and sealed waterproof pack liner. I set my rain gear on top of the waterproof pack liner just under the canvas pack flap. This system keeps wet rain gear, tent and tarp, separate from dry pack contents and it lets you get at these items with a minimum of fuss. The waterproof pack liner also protects your tent from getting wet if you capsize.

## CARRYING FIREARMS

As I pointed out in Chapter four, there's no reason to carry a gun on any canoe trip. Nevertheless, grizzlies and polar bears can be unpredictable: they may not respect your "live and let live" philosophy. For this reason, many canoe expeditions choose to go armed. To my knowledge, no shots have been fired, and hopefully, none ever will.

If you decide to go armed, here's a good way to pack your weapon: Load the magazine but not the chamber and place the gun into an unlined canvas case* which has been tightly tied to one gunnel of the canoe. A gun that's packed this way is hidden from view, secure if you capsize, out of the way of packs, instantly available, and out of contact with the wet bottom of the canoe.

When it's time to portage, just unzip the back of the case, remove the gun and sling it, and take off down the trail. There's no need to remove the gun case from the canoe.

Northern Indians and Eskimos usually set their rifles in the canoe with no security or protection from the elements. That's okay for hunting, but it's not the best way to treat a fine gun.

*If you get a padded gun case wet you've got a mess on your hands.

# SOME FINAL SUGGESTIONS FOR PACKING

1. You may need your wind-jacket, first-aid kit, or a roll of film sometime during the day, so plan ahead. Pack frequently used essentials near the top of your pack, or carry a small day pack just for these items.

2. You could lose a canoe in a rapid, so don't put all your eggs in one basket. Distribute food, matches, cooking gear, and other necessities, among the two or more boats in your party.

3. Equipment may have to be carried over some pretty grueling portages, so don't overload your packs. You may be able to muscle a 90 pound Duluth pack two miles down a groomed trail, but can you carry it 30 feet up the side of a canyon wall?

4. Keep your extra paddle, map and compass within easy reach. And wear--don't pack--survival items (knife, matches, bug dope).

Packing for an expedition requires careful attention to details. You can't afford to omit anything. For example, did you test your waterproof bags and hard packs to be sure they're really waterproof? Have you checked the straps and fittings of your packs to be sure that threads are secure, rivets tight? Did you remember to pack the extra compass, insect head net, or canoe repair kit? Use an itemized check list like the one shown in Appendix "C" so you won't forget anything.

# SECURE YOUR GEAR

Everything should be secured so tightly in your canoe that it can't possibly fall out if you capsize. And running a packstrap around a canoe thwart isn't good enough: A pack which "bobs out" of an overturned or swamped canoe may be sheared off between passing rocks--or worse, snag the canoe and cause it to "wrap up".

Small items can be placed under shock-corded thwarts or in the Otter bags mentioned in Chapter six. But packsacks must be locked tightly in the canoe with rubber ropes and nylon cords as shown in photo 6-2.

I run two heavy rubber ropes with adjustable steel hooks over each packsack and secure them to holes or loops of parachute cord in the gunnels (See Chapter 6--TANDEM RIGGING). As an extra precaution I string one or two lengths of parachute cord fore and aft from the yoke to each thwart. Cords are tied with a quick-release "power-cinch" knot explained in Chapter 16--HAZARDS AND RESCUE. The final touch is to snap the belly section of my nylon splash cover over the load.

This entire procedure takes only a minute and produces a compact buoyant mass that will function as a giant life preserver if the canoe swamps or over-turns.

When it's time to portage I stuff the belly cover under a pack flap, snap the rubber-ropes to the gunnels, and tie the parachute cords to the thwarts. This eliminates loose cords which might snag on brush along the trail.

# 10

# Canoe Tents Are Different

Take a mid-morning paddle along a popular canoe route after a major storm. You'll see wet clothes, sleeping bags, boots--all strung from a network of lines which seemingly run everywhere. Look closely at the tent(s) in each camp as you paddle by. A thoughtfully designed tent, properly pitched, is the key to "storm survival".

Note that some campers have well-designed badly pitched tents, while others have badly designed well-pitched ones. In between these extremes are scores of moderately experienced trippers who've weathered the rains with a modicum of comfort, a sprinkling of know-how, and an array of equippage.

Let's get one thing straight. You don't "need" a sophisticated tent for canoe camping. A knowledge of basic outdoor skills will do more to ensure your comfort than the most eye-popping supershelter. But the "right" tent plus the right skills will keep you on the canoe trails in weather that sours all but the most committed paddlers.

The least satisfactory tents for canoeing are those advertised as "canoe" or "portage" tents. Simple A-frames, lean-to's and open front "Baker" tents, are the usual bearers of these titles. Though adequate for canoe tripping, the designs of these tents date to the last century BNE (before the nylon era) and are not well-suited to the camping style of modern paddlers. Tents good enough for Grandpa still work today, but they're heavier, less wind-stable, more time-consuming to pitch, and more cumbersome to carry than sophisticated models of modern design.

Good backpacking tents usually are good canoe tents, but not always. The requirements of canoeists are much different from those of backpackers. For example, hikers are free to travel to an ideal camp spot (scrambling up a rock face to reach a flat grassy area is par for the sport). Canoeists are less mobile as our sites are limited by the often unforgiving terrain which lines our waterways. Consequently, canoe tents are frequently pitched on solid rock, loose pebbles, or sand.

It follows that a canoe tent should pitch quickly and easily on any terrain, be small enough to fit on the skimpiest sites, yet large enough to assure a measure of sanity when bad weather or hordes of insects confine you to its fabric walls. It should also be lightweight, compact when packed, able to withstand a minor hurricane, *absolutely* weatherproof and bugproof, quick to dry after a rain, comfortable in warm and cold weather alike...and affordable!

# TENT REQUIREMENTS

**Weight:** Most canoe portages are less than two miles long, so canoeists can afford to carry more gear (and weight) than backpackers. A *few* extra pounds won't affect how a canoe handles and will hardly be noticed when the outfit is carried over land. An item's bulk is usually much more important than its weight. For example, a 10-pound tent that rolls compactly enough to fit *crossways* in a number three Duluth pack is better for canoeing than a 7-pound model that won't fit. The villain is usually the length of the pole sections. Twenty-three inches is about maximum for a good fit in a number three Duluth pack: Tents longer than this may have to be stood lengthwise in the pack which fouls up the whole packing system. You're therefore better off with a heavy tent that has short poles than a light one with long poles!

Figure on a maximum tent weight *per person* of about six pounds. Good canoe tents are available which weigh much less than that.

**Size:** A tent 6 or 7 feet wide, by about 8 feet long is ideal for two people. Larger tents are awkward to pitch on small wilderness sites, while smaller ones may be too confining. For ease of dressing, peak height should be around 5 feet. This is high enough for comfort, low enough for stability in high winds. In a pinch, four people can sleep crossways in a tent this size--important in the event a tent is lost in a capsize or destroyed by wind.

Some tents are put out of commission quite easily. For example, the Eureka Timberline (which is a fine tent!) has three critical components--the center ridge-pole section, and a pair of pole junction tubes. Lose any one of these and the tent won't go up! A few years ago on a conoe trip in Minnesota, some friends lost the ridge pole from their Timberline tent. They packed the tent under the flap of a Duluth pack (which I advised you *not* to do in the last chapter) and the pole slid out of the tent bag into the lake. Fortunately, there was enough room in my Cannondale Aroostook to sleep the crew. It was crowded, but we survived.

# FABRICS

**Nylon:** Best is a two-layer nylon tent--one which has a waterproof fly suspended over a non-waterproof inner canopy. Body-produced moisture passes out through the inner tent and condenses on the inside of the cooler fly where it slithers harmlessly to the ground.

Avoid tents that are constructed of one layer of waterproof nylon (single-walled tents). They drip condensed water from their inner walls and leak through their many exposed seams, which are almost impossible to waterproof.

To keep condensed water from contacting the inner tent, the fly should rig drum-tight and be separated from the porous canopy by several inches. This construction also provides a dead-air space which maintains the interior of the tent at a fairly uniform temperature--a modified Thermos bottle effect.

It's interesting to note that Bedouin tribes have used doublewalled tents for thousands of years. Bedouin tents traditionally are constructed of two layers of dense wool (usually black-colored to reduce the sun's glare) to provide a cool (or at least cooler) respite from the hot desert sun.

The size and method of attachment of the fly is important. To save weight and cost, and to provide good ventilation, many tents have short (cap) flies. A cap fly will protect a tent in a vertical rain but wind-whipped water will blow up under it and, if there's enough force, will tear the fly right off the tent. For this reason, flies should be generous in size--*long enough to touch the ground on each side of the tent*. The extra length adds a few ounces of weight to the fly, but it makes the tent much more wind-stable and watertight.

The space between the fly and tent at ground level can also be used to store muddy boots and damp gear. Boots have no place in a tent. They take up valuable space and dirty sleeping quarters.

A few of the early double-walled tents had their flies attached at the ridge (the old Gerry "Fireside" models). This design was once bad-mouthed on the guise that the tent could not be pitched without the fly (invalid criticism because you almost never use a tent without a fly). But now, both hikers and canoeists are re-discovering that it's a hassle to install a fly on a tent, especially in a high wind. As a result, tents with permanently attached flies--like the intelligently designed Cannondale models--are making a comeback.

Most tent flies require eight or more stakes and lines to keep them secure. Unfortunately, it's not always possible to find good staking points on the sand and rock of canoe country camps. For this reason it's best to avoid any tent whose fly requires more than about four stakes to anchor. The best flies attach to the tent corners with shock cords and metal clips and can be installed or removed in less than a minute.

**Cotton:** Some canoeists still prefer cotton tents. But *good* cotton tents are hard to find--mainly because recent fire-retardant legislation has boosted the weight of cotton fabrics too high. An advantage of cotton over nylon is its greater resistance to abrasion. Nylon fabrics whose waterproof coatings have become abraded cannot be easily repaired by home remedies wheras canvas can easily be "re-waterproofed" with brush-on chemicals that are available at every hardware store. However, cotton tents are heavy when dry, heavier when wet, and they mildew. For these reasons, nylon tents are better for canoeing.

**Gore-Tex:** Gore-Tex is used in a limited number of highly sophisticated and expensive backpacking tents. Gore-Tex tents, however, tend to be rather small for canoeing (only two person models are presently available) and they don't have a fly to protect their exposed seams from rain. Moreover, I'm not convinced that Gore-Tex is reliable enough for use in an expedition canoe tent.

**Dacron:** Theoretically, dacron is used in tent construction because it is more resistant than nylon to the degrading effects of the sun. But all dacron tents have sun-degradable nylon flies which cover the dacron tent body and therefore negate its value on this score.

The *real reason* manufacturers use dacron in tents is its lack of stretch. Some tents (domes, especially) depend upon uniformly stressed construction to retain their form. Dacron stretches much less than nylon when it gets wet and so assures fabric tightness.

## GEOMETRY

There are A-frames, teepees, wedges, boxes, domes, lean-to's, and sophisticated geometric shapes.

As far as space is concerned, domes are the most efficient of all tent designs. The high, gradually sloping sidewalls of a dome tent provide a pleasant spacious atmosphere, and the hexagon (or octagon) shaped floor permits occupants to sleep in any direction--a real advantage if the tent is pitched "wrong" or on a sloping site.

Though domes are highly efficient at shedding rain, they're badly ventilated (the fly covers the windows and door) and they perform badly in high winds. Getting into and out of a dome tent in a driving rain calls for quick-footed skill: Whenever you unzip the fly, rain pours into the tent!

Manufacturers have attempted to rectify these shortcomings by providing tunnel entrances and through-the-fly guy points on the vertical poles. But no matter how you rig them, domes blow down when winds blow up--reason enough to eliminate them from consideration as expedition canoe tents.*

Teepee style tents share the same wet-weather inadequacies as domes but offer one important advantage--rigidity! The best teepees

*__Geodesic__ domes are very wind-stable but they're time-consuming to pitch. And they're no better in rain than conventional domes.

are supported by three rigid aluminum poles (domes use a network of flexible thin-walled fiberglass or aluminum poles) and so remain rock-solid in winds that would flatten conventional tents of equal height. The American Indian knew what he was doing when he designed the teepee!

The main disadvantage of teepees is that their flies are slow and awkward to install. These tents have guylines which run everywhere!

Tunnel-shaped tents with low profiles are excellent for use in wind but they're much too confining for canoeing.

The best canoe tents have modified A-frames (an A-frame consists of two angled poles joined at the ridge) and are almost completely self-supporting. Tents like the Eureka Timberline and all the Moss and Cannondale models, go up fast on any terrain. "U-stake 'em" tents take time, especially if you have to search for rocks or logs to hold stakes in uncooperative ground. A conventional style tent will usually flatten in a wind if one or more of its stakes pull out, but an unanchored free-standing tent may become air-born if it isn't tied down. The *real* advantage of a completely or semi-self-supporting tent is that it can be anchored securely with four to eight stakes, or about half the number required to pitch a conventionally supported tent.

Besides a relatively free-standing A-frame design, four other features distinguish a good canoe tent. First, is a "bathtub" or wrapup floor. In this construction, the waterproof floor is sewn to the porous tent body a few inches above the ground. This eliminates seams at ground level. It's next to impossible to prevent ground level seams--or indeed *any* exposed seams from leaking if they're in contact with water for long periods of time, no matter how carefully you've coated them with seam sealant.

Second, the door panel should be *inside* the mosquito net rather than outside it as is usually the case. This way you won't have to unzip the bug-screen everytime you need to adjust the door for ventilation or to see outside. This feature is extremely important in black-fly country.

Third, if you'll be tripping where "no-see-ums" (tiny biting gnats) are a persistent problem, specify fine-mesh no-see-um net. Common mosquito netting will not stop no-see-ums. You can use standard mosquito netting in no-see-um country if you spray it with insect repellent.

Finally, the tent should have a vestibule (an add-on extension that secures to the front of the tent). Vestibules provide a protected place to store gear, out of the main sleeping compartment. Equally important, they waterproof the door end of the tent by sealing off zippers, eaves, and seams. And they improve the aerodynamics of the tent by presenting a sharp wedge-shape to the wind.

Some tents have "niceties" like lantern loops and inside pockets for the storage of small items. These features, which require only a few minutes at a home sewing machine to make and install, add considerable cost to a tent without significantly increasing its utility. Some of the best canoe tents have a minimum of interior niceties.

Constuction features are overrated. All that hullabaloo about number of stitches per inch and reinforcement of zipper ends and such, proudly touted by tent makers, takes a back seat to good design. I've experienced bent poles and torn stake loops, and I've seen flies ripped loose and carried away by high winds, but I've never seen a *well-designed* tent come apart at its seams, or a zipper tear out of its stitching. Zippers jam and break; their seams rarely pull loose. A well-sewn, badly designed tent is more apt to blow apart in a high wind than a badly-sewn well-designed one. Quality of construction is not always an indication of quality of design!

In summary, the best canoe tents have semi-self-supporting modified A-frames, bathtub floors, fine mesh mosquito or no-see-um netting, and a vestibule. They weigh less than 6 pounds per person and measure about 6 feet by 8 feet, with a 5 foot ridge. They have flies which stake right to the ground, and their longest pole section is no more than 23 inches.

## TIPS FOR GETTING THE MOST OUT OF YOUR TENT

**1.** Waterproof the seams of a new tent. I prefer to use "Thompson's Water Seal" rather than a "glue". Glues eventually crack and peel and absorb dirt; they get soft and sticky in hot weather, brittle in cold weather. For best results apply the compound *twice* to each side of the seam. Allow a couple hours of drying time between applications.

**2.** Attach loops of shock-cord or bands cut from inner tubes to all guy lines. Shock-cords take up the wind stress normally reserved for seams and fittings. Even a badly sewn, poorly reinforced tent can be used in severe weather if it's rigged with shock-cords.

**3.** Tents which are completely self-supporting (like the Eureka Timberline) will blow down in a gale if you don't run one or more guylines off the peak at each end.

**4.** Use a ground cloth or aluminized space blanket *inside* your tent. If your tent springs a leak, water will be trapped beneath the ground sheet and you'll stay dry. *Don't* place the ground cloth under the tent(exception--for winter use to prevent the tent floor from freezing to the ground). Surface water may become trapped between the ground sheet and floor and wick through the floor seams.

Contrary to the claims of tent-makers, you don't need a ground cloth under your tent floor to protect it from abrasion. Surprisingly, holes in tent floors usually develop from *inside* the tent, not from outside. If you don't believe that, begin a trip with a new plastic ground-sheet inside your tent, then count the holes it accumulates with each day of travel. Old belief's die hard!

**5.** Reinforce stress points with heavy carpet thread and nylon webbing.

**6.** Color-code non shock-corded poles for easy assembly. It's frustrating to look for a "center ridge section," an "apex pole" or a "spreader bar" in failing light. Colored plastic tape sticks to poles better than paint which eventually rubs off.

**7.** Tents should have at least three stakes along each side to ensure adequate security in high winds. If there aren't enough anchor points, sew loops of nylon webbing to the hem of the tent and use them whenever severe weather threatens. For additional security in big winds, attach *two* separately staked guylines to each end of the tent.

**8.** Shock-cord all tent poles. Shock-corded poles are more rigid than those whose sections are held together by friction alone. Shockcording kits are available at most camp shops.

**9.** You can make tents with "cap" flies suitable for use in rough weather if you extend the sides of the fly (they should touch the ground). Matching material can be obtained from the tent manufacturer and many outdoor stores. Sewing can be done on a light duty sewing machine.

**10.** Tents with self-supporting frameworks depend heavily on brass hooks, pins and spring clips for attachment to the poles. Be careful that this hardware doesn't abrade the nylon fabric when you roll these tents. Whenever possible, pull hooks and pins to the edges of the roll where they won't bear on adjacent material. And don't roll these tents too tightly!

**11.** If your tent doesn't come with an oversize stuff sack, make one. A snug fitting sack looks nice in the store, but the tent won't fit when it's watersoaked and mud-caked. For long-term storage use a porous stuff sack. Waterproof sacks encourage condensation--and mildew. (Nylon tents are slow to mildew but their cotton/polyester stitching isn't.)

It's possible to pay hundreds of dollars for a good tent, especially if you want bomb-shelter design, hurricane stability, a profusion of interior niceties and extra-light weight. These things are nice, of course, but they're not essential--even for trips above the timberline.

Fortunately, many of the best canoe tents are relatively inexpensive--about what you'd expect to pay for moderately sophisticated two person mountaineering tents. To be sure, a medium-priced canoe tent will lack refinements: You may need to reinforce seams, shock-cord poles, construct a larger stuff sack, and perhaps even lengthen the fly. But the end product, if carefully pitched and well maintained, will deliver a lifetime of good service and reflect your special canoe tripping needs.

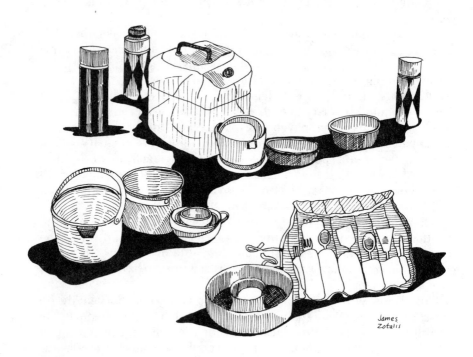

James
Zotalis

## THE RECIPE

One high ledge overlooking a misty falls.
A crisp clear evening.
A sprinkling of sunset.
A small bright fire.
One or two well-blackened pots, dented with memories.
Generous servings of camp-brewed coffee.
Appetites honed by the passage of a long tough day
One full bottle of comraderie.

      Stir well until mixed and simmer with a dash of inspiring conversation. Serve as needed to experience the flavor of the North Country.

# The Recipe

It's heartening to know that when the daily problems of machines, poverty, inflation and the space program become overwhelming you can always go canoeing. Canoeing is one sport everyone can enjoy without becoming involved in science, mechanics, or debate. Well almost.

On every canoe trip there's at least one person who wiles away the grandest moments of each day with scientific talk about the best canoe design, most weatherproof tent, most efficient trail stove, etc. Sometimes, this individual even gets scientific about foods. That a food tastes good, looks appetizing and provides plently of energy for a strenuous expedition isn't enough. He or she wants to know how its nutritional value and caloric content compares with **"U.S. recommended daily allowances."**

That a balanced diet is important--in the woods or at home--is a forgone fact. But how scientific do you have to be when selecting foods for a wilderness canoe trip? Not very-- as long as you use good sense and plan reasonably well balanced meals.

What works at home will work in the wilds--with one exception. Calories! You need lots of 'em--4000 or more per day if you're really working hard. By comparison, a typical homemaker expends about 1400 calories a day, an office worker about 2500 calories, and a factory worker approximately 3000 calories.*

An average canoeist will burn about five calories per minute (300 per hour, 2400 per eight-hour day); a racer or serious wilderness traveler may use twice that amount. Since a pound of body fat contains approximately 3500 calories, you can easily plan biologically correct meals that will retain your body weight if you have a calorie chart and some knowledge of the nutritional value of each food you select. (This information is available in every basic nutrition text.)

Fortunately, you don't need to be too scientific in determining "nutritional value," as your body's natural craving for variety will

*From "Biology of Work," by O.G. Edholm, McGraw Hill, 1967.

help you make good food choices. It's important, however, to understand to which food group each edible belongs (carbohydrates, fats, proteins) and to "weight" your daily intake of foods so that they correspond roughly to the following formula:

# CARBOHYDRATES

Carbohydrates provide quick energy and should supply at least 50 percent of your daily calorie requirement. Trail foods which contain carbohydrates include breads, cereals, honey (honey and tea is the traditional North Country drink), jam, dehydrated fruits, and of course, candy.

# FAT

Fats contain about twice as many calories per pound as carbohydrates and are the body's major source of stored energy. Generally speaking, fats should provide about 20 to 25 percent of your daily intake of calories, though for a really tough trip that amount should be increased five or ten percent. Twenty-five percent is a good ball-park figure, however. It's hard to carry more fatty foods than this on the average wilderness canoe trip without significantly increasing pack weight and bulk. Examples of foods which contain fats, are margarine, cooking oil, nuts, peanut butter, cheese, bacon, and sausage.

# PROTEIN

The recommended daily minimum intake of protein is 70 grams (two-and one-half ounces). Wilderness canoeing is a strenuous activity so you'll need more protein than that. A hearty breakfast of oat or wheat cereal and reconstituted non-fat dry milk; a lunch which includes cheese, beef jerky, peanut butter or sausage; and a supper which contains freeze-dried meat (or if you're really enterprising, fresh fish) will provide all the protein you need.

In short, when working up a wilderness menu, select foods that contain enough calories to keep your body operating at peak efficiency when you're working hard. Carbohydrates and fats should supply the vast majority of these calories. Proteins are essential for cell repair but are an inefficient source of calories. Even without planning, you'll probably have plenty of proteins in your diet.

# VITAMINS AND MINERALS

It's only on extended (several months) trips that you need to be concerned about vitamins and minerals. Even then, don't lose any sleep over providing enough of them, as a properly balanced diet almost always contains all the vitamins and minerals you need. Only the water soluble vitamins (the B and C group) that are lost from your body need to be replenished daily. And that's no problem since you probably already carry vitamin C fortified fruit drinks and vitamin B rich cereals on your canoe trips. (Incidently, high doses of vitamin B complex make you smell bad to mosquitoes—that's something to remember when tripping in buggy country.)

If you're worried about vitamin or mineral deficiencies, carry a bottle (plastic, of course) of chemical supplements on lengthy trips.

## FOODS THAT WORK

If you want to keep weight to a respectable limit, omit canned goods from your menu. Certainly there's nothing wrong with packing a can or three of peaches, pineapple, or bacon for "special occasions;"* but by and large you'll want to depend on lightweight dried foods for most of your needs. If you plan your meals carefully, you should be able to keep your crew well fed and working on one and one-half to two pounds (uncooked weight) of food per day.** That figure includes extras like popcorn, peanuts, and special treats.

As important as dried foods are to the success of a canoe expedition, they alone don't supply enough energy to keep bodies humming happily. As mentioned, you need lots of calories on a tough canoe trip and that means extra amounts of breadstuffs, peanut butter, margarine, nuts, cereals, and cheese. Important in all wilderness foods is that they be lightweight, slow to spoil, easy to prepare, and stable in hot weather. These requirements alone necessarily eliminate many otherwise excellent food products from your canoe trip shopping list.

You'll also want to know which foods REALLY work to keep you working and which don't. And you won't find that information on a calorie chart or from nutritionists who don't canoe. That's because a food can look good on paper and be completely worthless on the canoe trails. A good example is "Moose Juice".

Moose Juice was a product of the mind of Verlen Kruger and the 1966 Atikoken Ontario to Ely, Minnesota canoe race. The Atikoken to Ely run was once touted as the toughest canoe race on the continent. And with good reason. Equipped with only the bare essentials of a canoe, map and compass, rain gear and food, competitors would paddle non-stop to Ely 55 miles away. After a rest they'd run back again at top speed. The 110 mile route included 28 grueling portages,

---

*PLEASE don't bury tin cans. *Pack them out!*

**At least half of the foods you select should need no cooking (cheese, peanut butter, crackers or pilot biscuits, energy bars, jerky, etc.)

several huge lakes and an occasional bog. Navigating in the dark called for a high degree of resourcefulness; most canoe teams never finished the race; many canoeists became lost. (Evidently the Ely to Atikoken race ultimately proved too tough as it has since been discontinued for lack of competitors.)

To supply his body with the energy necessary to maintain the quickened 60 stroke per minute cadence used in canoe racing, Verlen developed a "complete nutritional liquid supplement" which he affectionately named "Moose Juice". When Clint Waddell, Verlen's racing partner, learned of the nutrient concoction, he objected strongly. But Verlen, a soft spoken man of infinite patience, pointed out that Moose Juice was a product of modern science. It met every nutritional requirement, didn't need to be unwrapped or cooked, and could be consumed on the run.

Clint wasn't convinced so he hid away a few sticks of beef jerky "just in case." Good thing, too: "Just in case" came about four hours into the race when Clint became violently ill from the effects of the home-made brew. The beef jerky helped some, but not enough. In the end, the Moose Juice won and Clint and Verlen lost the race.

That episode points out an obvious but often ignored food fact: *the physical makeup of foods must not be so unusual  that they disagree with your system.* And since one person's system rejects what another's relishes, you'd best stay away from fancy or unusual edibles until you've first tried them under fire--that is, under the fire of your own kitchen stove!

You may also find that your body dislikes "sameness" in foods. A continuous diet of oatmeal, dried milk, dehydrated fruit and peanut butter may be scientifically acceptable fare, but your stomach may refuse it anyway. No need to prepare gourmet delights to please your system on a wilderness canoe trip, but you may want to give it a few simple food options to choose from.

The old Northwest Company did a lot of research on foods during the fur trade days of the 17th and 18th centuries. They found that pemmican* was the only food which a man could tolerate for long periods of time. Even today, pemmican is considered an excellent trail food, though most modern voyageurs never learn to develop a taste for it.

If you want to learn which of today's canoe trip suitable foods work to keep your body working and which don't, ask a professional canoe racer. Racers push their canoes unbelievable distances for unbelievable hours, and in the process they burn tremendous

---

*Seventeenth century pemmican usually consisted of pressed buffalo meat with a generous amount of buffalo grease added. The voyageurs often mixed the pemmican with flour and water and cooked up a substantial soup called "rubbaboo," which they heartily devoured daily for weeks or months at a time.

numbers of calories.

On their 7,000 mile canoe odyssey to the Bering Sea (1971), Verlen Kruger and Clint Waddell discovered that pancakes provided the greatest amount of energy of all foods they carried. "We found we could paddle about five miles per pancake," said Verlen. "So whenever we anticipated a tough day (or night), we filled up on cornmeal-spiked pancakes smothered in syrup." Clint and Verlen also learned that canned "pork and beans" was an excellent fuel for traveling, wheras fish and meat were almost worthless. All of which supports our original suggestion that canoe tripping foods should be high in carbohydrates and fat.

Now that you know why some trail foods work and some don't, you'll want to run out and buy a text on nutrition so you can plan biologically correct meals for your next canoe trip, right? Wrong! Experienced canoeists don't plan their meals that way and neither should you. What works at home will work on the canoe trails, provided you consider the basic nutritional and physical (light weight, low bulk, etc.) parameters mentioned earlier.

Men who do hard physical labor for a living have about the same food requirements as those who take strenuous canoe trips. And seldom do they, their families, or the restaurants they frequent use calorie charts and nutritional guides to prepare their meals. These men simply suit their foods to the demanding needs of their bodies-- and so should we.

The same foods you eat at home--only in increased amounts- should be injested on the canoe trails. The only difference is that at home the products you choose will be picked from the fresh food section of your grocery store, wheras in the wilds, they'll be taken from aluminum foil, plastic wrappers, or to a limited extent, tin cans.

## WORKING MENUS WITHOUT A LOT OF WORK

I prefer to keep foods simple. If it takes longer than 30 minutes to prepare, forget it! Sure, I'll occasionally fry fish, make popcorn or bake blueberry rightside-up cake well into the night. But these are "special occasions". It's unrealistic to expect to make time on the water if you spend half your waking hours cooking and washing dishes. I'm generally on the water at dawn, lunched by 11 a.m. and camped by four. This routine enables me to enjoy the early morning solitude, cover plently of distance, and select a decent campsite before sunset. To keep this schedule, my meals necessarily look like this:
BREAKFASTS:

About three-sevenths of our breakfasts require only boiling water to prepare; two-sevenths are "cold meals" (no cooking whatsoever) and the rest can be made on my gasoline stove in less than 30 minutes. The menu for a given morning is programmed by what lies ahead that day.* For example, if we've just got to make time before the wind blows up, we'll eat our Granola bars, Jerky, and run. But if the weather's cold or we've got more time, we'll crank up the stove and boil water for oatmeal or hot Granola cereal. If the day is short and predictable we'll lollygag and cook freeze-dried eggs or pancakes, stew fruit, etc. Nothing is cut and dried on a canoe trip. We take our cue from mother nature.

Here are three of my favorite breakfasts:

## SLOW COOK BREAKFAST

- Corn-bread flap-jacks with syrup and margarine or freeze-dried egg omlet with cheese.
- Canned bacon or fried Summer Sausage.
- Vitamin C-enriched beverage.
- Mocoa (cocoa mixed with coffee). Make hot chocolate according to the package directions only substitute hot coffee for the boiling water.

## BOILING WATER ONLY BREAKFAST

- Instant Oatmeal (Maple and brown sugar flavor is most popular) or Hot "Granola Plus" cereal. Pre-package the
  following ingredients:

    3/4 cup Granola cereal
    1/3 cup non-fat dry milk
    1 tsp. non-dairy creamer
    Handful of raisins
    Some chopped, sugared dates
    2 tsp. wheat germ
    2 tsp. Millers bran

  Re-hydrate with boiling water to make one very hearty serving.

- Pillsbury food sticks
- Beef jerky
- Beverages (coffee, mocoa, tea with honey)

## NO COOK BREAKFAST

- Breakfast bars or Granola bars
- Beef jerky
- Mixed evaporated fruit (eaten right out of the package)

*What *really* lies ahead, of course, can only be predicted from your maps and trip information.

- Coffee-flavored candies
- Vitamin-C drink

## LUNCHES:

It's a hassle to stop and cook lunch. Not only do you have to ferret out the pots and stove (or take time to build a fire) but you also have to clean up the mess when you're through eating. For this reason, experienced wilderness canoeists prefer a "no cook" lunch. The typical hot shore lunch is just too time-consuming to prepare.

A half dozen years ago, I guided a group of teenagers down the scenic Granite river which borders Minnesota and Ontario. A steady drizzle fell off and on for the first few days of our trip. Fire building required some determination but was no problem. Everyone was warm and dry; all were having a good time.

One evening about 10, the rains let up and a patch of blue appeared in the heavens. We rejoiced. "Anyone for a moon-light paddle? I offered. Soon the canoes were off into the moist stillness of the night. As we rounded a point we saw a man and woman sitting quietly on a ledge, several feet above the water. There was no campfire in sight.

After exchanging formalities, the man told us of his mis-fortunes. "This is my first trip", he said. "Cause of the rain, I ain't been able to get a fire goin' for two days now." We offered to help. "No thanks," was the reply. "I like it better this way." He explained that his outfitter had supplied slow cook foods for most meals: pancakes or French toast for breakfast, macaroni and cheese for lunch and the usual freeze-dried dehydrated fare for supper.

"We usually get up around 8," he said. "Build a fire, cook breakfast and pack up. It's 10 before we get on the water. We paddle a couple hours, then stop to cook lunch. That takes at least an hour. By the time we're done eatin', it's after 1. This gives us only a couple more hours to paddle before we make camp. We're only canoeing three or four hours a day!"

The man told us he'd rather go "fireless" and eat sandwiches, candy bars and crackers and have more time to "see the country".

You can build only so much variety into a "no-cook" lunch. After two weeks on the water, any instant lunch gets boring. However, variations on the entrees suggested below remain palatable (if not enjoyable) for weeks.

## LUNCH

- "Seasoned Rye Krisp", whole wheat flat bread, Pilot biscuits*, or Kosher bagels**.
- Processed cheese, peanut butter, jam, or deviled spread.
- Beef jerky, pepperoni sticks, hard sausage, or Spam.
- Granola bars, Instant Breakfast Bars, or peanut-rich candy bars.
- Mixed evaporated fruit or sugared fruit bars.
- Powdered drink.

## SUPPERS

After two boring meals, supper is a blessing. You can vary suppers as much as you wish--depending on how much money you want to spend and/or how much time you're willing to slave over a hot stove. If you're new to instant foods you'll develop your own ideas of what's good and blah quickly enough without my biased suggestions. And if you've "boiled and stirred" for years, your prejudices are too well rooted for my suggestions to overcome.

## SUPPER

- A pre-packaged freeze-dried meal. (Decrease the suggested number of servings by the amount necessary to obtain a 14 ounce re-hydrated serving per person. Most freeze-dried meals which "serve four" rehydrate to four 8 to 12 ounce servings--not enough for a hungry tripper.)
- Lipton, Maggi, or Knorr instant soup. You can eliminate the soup and instead increase the main meal portion. But soup adds variety and is a good "pick-me-up" that can be cooked quickly--important after a tough day.
- Bisquik biscuits with margarine and honey.
- Dessert of some sort (fruit bars, candy bars, fig newtons, etc.)
- Your favorite beverage.

*Pilot biscuits are hard to find South of the Canandian border.

**Bagels with cheese and sausage are a rare wilderness lunch treat. We buy the frozen kind which are available at most supermarkets. The onion and rye varieties keep longest (about nine days) and taste best on the trail.

MUNCHIES
- Mixed nuts, fruitcake, popcorn, canned fruit; hot tea spiked with brandy, cinnamon, honey, and a pat of margarine.

I prefer a three-course supper: soup, main dish, dessert. Canoeing is not backpacking; my cuisine need not suffer the bland effects of one pot meals.

## PACKING SUGGESTIONS

To eliminate confusion and shorten preparation times, package each meal for your crew as a complete unit. Remove all unnecessary cardboard and paper wrappers from foodstuffs to save as much weight and space as possible.

"Flowable solids," like sugar, baking mix, Tang, and so on, are best pre-measured in the amounts required, and placed into small plastic "Zip-lock" bags which are encased in sturdy nylon bags.

Breakable and crushable items like crackers, cheese and candy bars, should be packed inside rigid cardboard containers. I use cutdown milk cartons, which also make great fire-starters.

Liquids are best carried in plastic bottles that have screw-cap lids. I've found that genuine "Nalgene" bottles (available at most camp stores) are most reliable. Plastic bottles with flip tops and pop-up tops usually leak. I melt these tops shut in the flame of a gas stove or replace them with trustworthy metal screw caps.

"Gerry" style food tubes are okay for packing flowable solids but not liquids (for which they were designed). The first time a honeyfilled tube ruptures in your pack you'll understand why. If you use food-tubes pack them inside Zip-lock bags so you'll be well prepared for the inevitable.

When packaging each meal, carefully fold over the edges of all foodstuffs that are packed in aluminum foil. The sharp foil edges of "breakfast bars" and soup packets will cut through plastic bags. And never pack moist items in the same bag as dry products. I once packed beef jerky and Velveeta cheese together in heat-sealed plastic bags. The jerky absorbed moisture from the cheese and mildewed in just four days.

For additional protection place each plastic bagged meal into its own color-coded waterproof nylon sack. I traditionally pack breakfasts in green nylon bags, lunches in yellow or blue, and suppers in red. Since I don't like surprises I attach masking tape labels to the outside of each sack.

If you pack your food as I've suggested you'll have no trouble finding the specific meals you want even if they're at the bottom of your pack. And you'll never have to eat damp oatmeal!

## PREPARATION HINTS

BISCUITS AND CAKES: Ever watch a novice camper make biscuits? His or her hands and clothes are invariably covered with gluey batter. There's a messy pot to clean and scattered about is enough batter to furnish a feast for several curious animals.

I always mix batter in a plastic bag. Just pour the correct amount of mix into the bag, add water, and knead the bag with your hands. When the consistency of the mixture is correct, punch a hole in the bag bottom and force the gooey mess into your awaiting oven. Burn the plastic bag!

QUICK 'N EASY LOW-COST SUPPERS: You can make excellent low-cost main dishes by adding dumplings, rice, or instant mashed potatoes to a heavy-bodied soup mix. Mix dumpling batter in a plastic bag as suggested. For a gourmet treat, drop chunks of raw fish into boiling soup. It tastes much better than it sounds.

MAKING POPCORN: If you're tired of trying to season popcorn in a pot that's too small, try this: Carry some large paper grocery sacks on your next trip. As you complete each batch of popcorn, pour the corn into the paper bag (don't use a plastic bag--hot popcorn will melt right through it). Season the corn and shake the bag to mix it. When the popcorn's gone, burn the bag. Or fold it and store it in a Ziplock bag for future use.

## HOW TO PREPARE FREEZE-DRIED FOODS SO THEY ALWAYS TASTE GOOD

Freeze-dried foods are fickle. Prepare 'em according to directions one day and they're great. Repeat the procedure another time and...ugh!

Take heart. Here's a foolproof cooking method that works regardless of the weather, the Zodiac, or a cranky stove.

### STEP ONE

Read the cooking directions, but don't take them too seriously. What works at home on the range often fails on a flat rock in a norwester.

### STEP TWO

Separate the component parts of the food. There are usually two parts: 1) a meat portion, 2) a noodle, rice or vegetable portion. Sometimes, there's a third "spice packet". (See Note #1 at the end of this procedure for the specifics of preparing "cook-in-the-bag" type meals like those made by "Mountain House".)

Typical directions say: "Add contents of all packets to X cups of boiling water. Reduce heat, simmer 15-20 minutes or until noodles (or whatever) are tender."

## STEP THREE

Put 20 percent *more* water in your cooking pot than the directions call for, and add the *meat portion only* to the water. Bring the water to a boil and add a healthy dash of "All-Spice" (see suggested recipe below).

Mix approximately equal amounts of the following spices:

Oregano                    Dash of onion powder
Marjoram                   Dash of thyme
Seasoned salt and
    pepper mixture (I buy a commercial blend)

## STEP FOUR

When the water is a rolling boil, add contents of the spice packet (if there is one). Reduce heat to slow boil and let spices and meat stew together for a full five minutes. If there is no spice packet allow meat to stew for five minutes before you proceed to step five.

## STEP FIVE

Add contents of noodle, rice or vegetable packet to the boiling water. Reduce heat, cover, simmer and stir occasionally for the amount of time indicated in the directions (15-20 minutes, for example).

## STEP SIX

Eat and enjoy. All portions of the meal are thoroughly cooked and the taste has been fully developed.

## NOTES: WHY SOME MEALS FAIL

**1.** You haven't cooked the meat long enough. Half-cooked reconstituted meat spoils the whole stew. Except in very warm weather, "cook-in-the-bag" foods just don't get done. It's best to place the cooking bag in a covered pot of near boiling water for 10 minutes. Add about 10 percent more water to the cooking bag than the directions call for.

**2.** You burned the pasta. This is easy to do on a one-burner trail stove, especially if you plop the contents of all food packets into the boiling water simultaneously. If your stove's turned on high, you may burn your meal quicker than you can say "turn the heat down Jack!"

**3.** Insufficient water. Remember, you can always boil out too much water but there's not much you can do with a stew that's so thick it's burned and glued to the pot bottom.

**4.** Not enough spices. Don't underestimate the value of spices when preparing freeze-dried/dehydrated foods. Most quick-cook products are unacceptably bland unless they're well spiced. The suggested "All Spice" works wonders on everything from Spaghetti to Shrimp Creole. The recipe is fast and easy to make; add what you like. Two weeks supply will fit nicely into a 35mm film can.

**5.** Spoilage: Dehydrated foods usually come packed in plastic and so have a shelf life of about a year. This is because plastic is very slightly permeable to the passage of water molecules. If the food contains bacteria of the right kind, enough moisture may eventually pass through the plastic wrapper to cause spoilage.

Freeze-dried foods, however, come packaged in aluminum foil, which is an absolute vapor barrier. Consequently these products have an unlimited shelf life; they may be used safely even when they're many years old.

This should tell you something about end-of-season food sales. Don't buy dehydrated foods in September if you plan to use them the following July. Your autumn "bargain" may turn out to be summer indigestion.

It's important to realize that many products contain both freeze-dried and dehydrated components (for example, "Spaghetti with freeze-dried meatballs"). While the foil-wrapped meatballs won't spoil, the plastic-wrapped spaghetti and/or spices might. Only foods which are *completely* sealed in aluminum foil are immune to spoilage. Unfortunately, you almost never see these products offered at sale prices.

**6.** Introduction of bacteria and/or water vapor during repackaging: Don't handle dried foods or expose them to air any longer than necessary when you re-package them. This will reduce the chance of bacteria and water vapor getting into the food.

Slice meat and cheese with a knife that's been dipped in boiling water for a full minute. (The boiling water treatment does not kill *all* bacteria. If you want to really sterilize the knife, place it in a pressure cooker at 15 pounds pressure for 15 minutes.) And never re-package foil wrapped products--like instant soups--in plastic.

## COOKING PARAPHERNALIA

My cooking outfit consists of three nesting pots, the largest of which has a capacity of 3½ quarts. I also include a 10-inch diameter teflon-lined skillet with detachable wire handle, a 6-cup coffee pot, and a compact "Bendonn"* aluminum dutch oven. After years of scoffing at fabric utensil rolls, I decided to make one. A fabric roll is more than just a utensil organizer; it simplifies the preparation of rainy day meals as you'll see in Chapter 12. I also carry a 1-1½ quart large ring Jello mold for those times when I want to bake on my stove.

**Figure 11-2**
Using the Bendonn Oven. This unique tote oven can also be used for frying or boiling.

## USING THE BENDONN DUTCH OVEN

Grease the shallow pan and put your bake-stuff inside. Slip on the cover and build a small hot fire in the ring. Provide some heat from below with a number of coals. Cooking time depends on the amount of heat your fire provides.

You can also make a simple dutch oven from any pot and lid by following the above procedure.**

## TO USE THE JELLO MOLD OVEN

**1.** Grease the mold and pour your bake stuff into the outside ring. (Decrease the suggested amount of water by up to one-fourth for faster baking.)

*Bendonn Co., 4920 Thomas Ave. South, Minneapolis, MN 55410.

**If weight is no object and you depend heavily on fires for all your meals, consider a "Woody" Dutch oven (available from Indiana Camp Supply). These ovens are made of heavy cast aluminum and come in two sizes--6½ inches by 9 inches (3 pounds), and 9 inches by 9 inches (6 pounds). Each oven section may be used separately as a griddle. These are sturdy high quality units.

**2.** Bring the stove to its normal operating temperature, then turn down the heat until you have the lowest possible "blue flame" setting. Center the Jello mold over the burner head, top it with a high cover (necessary to provide sufficient room for the bake good to rise)...and relax. Cooking times are nearly identical to those suggested in the baking directions.

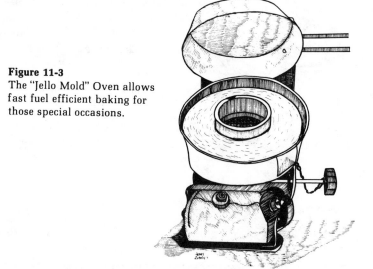

**Figure 11-3**
The "Jello Mold" Oven allows fast fuel efficient baking for those special occasions.

**3.** Cool the mold by setting it in a shallow pan of water for a few moments.

You can also fire your Jello mold with a *small* (2-⅝ ounce) can of Sterno. Don't use the large size can; it puts out too much heat. To ensure ample draft, use a pair of sticks to prop up the ring about one half inch above the Sterno. Vent the lid with a match stick.

Sterno is useful for those times when you want to use your stove for cooking but don't want to build a fire for baking. However, Sterno is temperamental; the slightest breeze will blow out the flame, so be sure to keep your oven well protected from the wind. Obviously, Sterno isn't suited to use on lengthy expeditions.

You'll note the conspicuous omission of the reflector oven. Reflectors are heavy and awkward to carry and they require a highly polished surface to work properly. They also have a voracious appetite for wood. Both dutch ovens and Jello-mold ovens are much better suited to modern canoe tripping.

# THE STOVE

A lot of canoeists, even those who regularly trip above the timberline, travel without a stove.* To each his own. As for myself, I wouldn't consider undertaking a canoe trip of much significance without my trusty Optimus 111B. There are just too many times when rough weather and a tight schedule precludes making a fire.

If a stove is essential in the northern wilds, it's even more important on well-traveled routes where all the "good" wood has been picked clean. And if you've driven many miles to a favorite wilderness and found a fire ban in effect, you'll wish you'd brought a stove!

## A REVIEW OF STOVE TYPES

There are gasoline, kerosine, butane and propane stoves. Only gasoline and kerosine stoves make much sense for wilderness canoeing.

## GASOLINE

Gasoline stoves are the most reliable of all trail stoves, especially in difficult weather. And gasoline has the highest heat output of all stove fuels.

Generally, gasoline stoves accept only "white gas" or Coleman or Blazo fuel (highly refined forms of naptha). It's not safe to burn leaded gasoline in them. An important distinction must be made between additive-free white gasoline--which is difficult to obtain in most areas, and additive-packed automotive "unleaded gasoline" which is available at every gas station. Unleaded gas is more volatile than white gas and may produce excessive pressures in stoves designed for white gas only.

## KEROSINE

Kerosine has about the same BTU rating as gasoline but it's less volatile. Where a gasoline stove will explode, a kerosine one will burn. Unfortunately, kerosine stoves don't start unless they're first primed with alcohol or gasoline--a hassle. Nonetheless, kerosine stoves are very reliable, and kerosine is available everywhere. White gas isn't! If you can get a good deal on a kerosine stove, buy it!

---

*There's usually enough scrub willow or driftwood along tundra rivers to permit making fires.

# BUTANE

Butane stoves are popular because they don't have to be primed, pumped, or filled with gas. You just turn the adjuster knob and light the escaping fumes. Re-fueling takes seconds and consists merely of replacing the exhausted gas cylinder with a new one. And because butane is so clean burning, there are no clogged fuel jets to clean. Sound great? It isn't! The efficiency of bottled butane is directly proportional to the temperature. Butane stoves quit working altogether when the temperature drops below freezing. And they're not very wind-proof. Equally important, unthoughtful campers leave the empty gas cylinders in the woods for those of us who care to "pack them out"! Avoid butane stoves!

# PROPANE

Forget it! Propane stoves are too heavy and cumbersome for canoeing.

# STOVE FEATURES

*Stability:* The stability of a stove is really important if you're cooking for large groups. There's nothing more frustrating than cooking a big pot of spaghetti on a precarious little beast that wobbles with every stir of the spoon. Before you buy a canoe stove, be sure it will *comfortably* accomodate your largest pot.

**Wind-screen:** The first time you've got to build a rock wall around your stove to keep it perking you'll understand the value of a good wind-screen. Avoid stoves with thin aluminum windscreens that burn up, and detachable ones which can be lost.

**Pump:** Pumps are necessary on kerosine stoves but not on gasoline ones. Some of the best little backpacking stoves are "selfpriming", which means they generate their own heat. But pumps increase the efficiency of any gasoline stove and so are highly desirable. An expedition stove should have a pump.

**Roarer or Silent Burner:** As the name implies, "roarer" burners make noise--lot's of it! The gas feeds through a single hole in the vaporizer tube and strikes a flat plate on the burner head where it dissipates. Simple, efficient, and always reliable. If you spill pancake syrup on the burner head, a single counter-clockwise turn of the adjuster knob--which is connected to a geared cleaning needle-- cleans the jet, and you're back in business.

Silent burners are more refined. They have a network of tiny holes around the head and look almost exactly like the burner on a modern gas range. These have two drawbacks: 1) They're not very wind-proof--you need an exceptional wind-screen to keep them humming in a gale; 2) They're a hassle to clean if you spill food into the burner head (the cleaning needle clears only the generator tube, not the burner holes). I once inadvertently set a plastic bowl on top of a hot Coleman Peak I (yeah, I know it was dumb!). The plastic melted all over everything and sealed many of the tiny burner holes. It took me two hours to clean the stove! A roarer burner would have been much easier to clean.

As I pointed out in Chapter 8 (GEARING UP), some of the most highly touted products which work flawlessly over the short haul, fail miserably in the long run. The adage couldn't be more true for stoves. Some stoves have steel tanks which rust, plastic knobs which burn off or break, parts to fit together, and wires that bend. Nonethless, any gasoline or kerosine stove can be made to perform reliably providing you maintain it rigorously, keep it protected in some sort of rigid container, and learn to cope with its eccentricities.

**Figure 11-4**

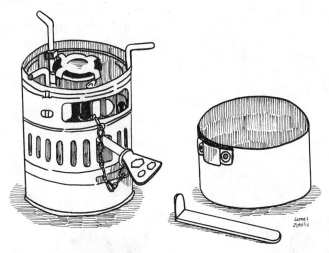

For example, the **SVEA 123** is a tippy affair--you'll spill a lot of soup until you learn to stabilize this stove before you start cooking. You'll also discover that the stove isn't very wind-proof, and that an eyedropper filled with gas works as well for priming as the optional (and expensive) mini-pump. In all, the SVEA is a fine little stove for one or two people, but it's not stable enough, wind-proof enough, or powerful enough, for expeditions.

**Figure 11-5**

**Optimus 8R:** Except for its front-mounted fuel tank, the 8R is the same stove as the SVEA 123. Its main advantage is stability--reason enough to prefer it over the SVEA. But it doesn't burn as hot as the SVEA or start quite as well. And like the SVEA, it's not very windproof. The optional "mini-pump" works much better with the 8R than its upright cousin.

**Figure 11-6**

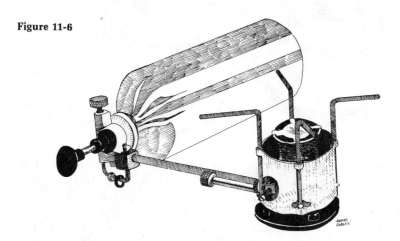

**MSR (Mountain Safety Research, Inc.):** The MSR is a wonderful stove for winter use and anytime you want a full fledged blow-torch. But you're instantly out of commission if you bend, break, or lose, any of its parts, or if foreign matter (blowing sand!) gets into the open hole of the burner unit when the stove is disassembled. And since the MSR has two speeds--*hot and hotter* (it's the hottest of all the stoves), you'll need to carry a can lid to place on the burner to dissipate heat so you can fry pancakes. You'll also need to rig up a different windscreen: The aluminum foil one supplied with the stove won't accept a frying pan handle. The MSR does not have a built-in jet-cleaning needle. However, the stove can be disasembled in the field for cleaning.

The MSR is a highly specialized and very reliable stove. But it's much better adapted to backpacking and winter moutaineering than canoeing.

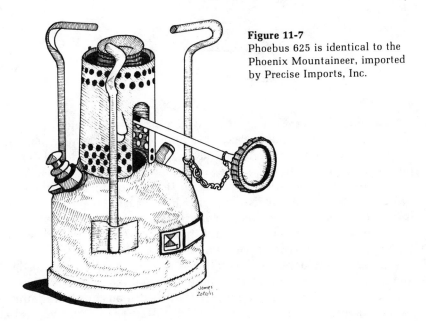

**Figure 11-7**
Phoebus 625 is identical to the Phoenix Mountaineer, imported by Precise Imports, Inc.

If you own an old *Phoebus 625* (no longer imported into this country but copied and sold by Precise Imports* under the PHOENIX tradename) you'll discover that it carbons up and "starves out" if you prime and start it with gasoline instead of the recommended alcohol. However, you can start the stove on gas if you remove the vaporizer cap (the burner part with the holes in it) during the priming process. You'll also need to carry a wrench to keep stove parts tight so they don't leak gas. Despite these shortcomings, the Phoebus, with its powerful silent burner, runs very hot and quiet. Its wind-screen is a bit awkward but effective. This is a proven expedition stove.

*PRECISE, Inc., 3 Chestnut St. Suffern, NY 10901

Figure 11-8

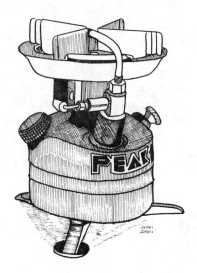

**Coleman Peak I:** Keeping the leather pump washer oiled is a major inconvenience as are all the exposed dials and wires which can bend or break. And contrary to manufacturers claims, the PEAK I doesn't perform flawlessly in wind. The stove runs (it's almost impossible to blow out!), but not efficiently: One of its four quadrants which are protected by a unique X-shaped wind-screen blows out which increases cooking times. And in cold weather you've got to pump and pump and pump the tiny Coleman to make it fire. Nonetheless, the PEAK I is a good little stove at a very attractive price.

**Coleman twin burner:** You'll see one of these stoves wedged among piles of gear in every Indian and Eskimo watercraft in the North country. That should be sufficient testimony to the reliability of this venerable war horse. Dollar for dollar, the *small* two burner Coleman is your best stove buy. Two burner Coleman's run forever, always start, and they work in wind. Granted, they're heavy, bulky, and burn a lot of gas, but they're reliable and inexpensive. If you can't afford a good one-burner trail stove for canoeing, then get a two-burner Coleman. You won't be disappointed.

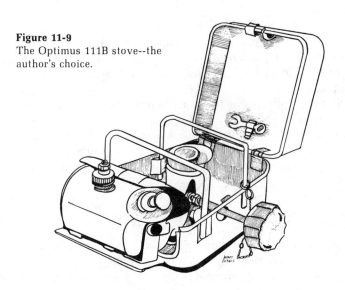

**Figure 11-9**
The Optimus 111B stove--the
author's choice.

**Optimus 111B:** This is *the* expedition stove. It is preferred by
serious canoeists hands down over all other types, and for good
reason. The 111B is powerful, stable, wind-proof, and it always
works! The 111B is terribly expensive (about one-third the price of a
modern gas range!) but it outperforms every other stove under rugged
field conditions. Drop it in water, spill food on it, pitch it off a cliff,
and the 111B comes back for more. Its only bad habit is minor: you
must keep its leather pump washer well-oiled--a bi-weekly chore.

As you can see, every stove has good and bad points. As much as I
favor the 111B, it's a very heavy unit, not one I'd choose for
backpacking or ski-touring. But I own four stoves so I can select
what's best for each sport. If you can afford only one stove, you'll need
to be more selective. If expedition canoeing is your first love, then
look hard at stoves which are powerful, reliable and rugged--Optimus
111B, Phoebus 625, Coleman 2-burner, and to a lesser extent, the
Coleman Peak I. If you backpack as much as you canoe, consider an
MSR, Peak I, or one of the small Optimus or Svea stoves. And if cost is
a major factor then go out now and buy the two burner Coleman
before the price gets any higher.

The important thing is to know the shortcomings of your stove
and how to correct them. After you've used a certain stove for awhile,
you'll develop such efficient ways of dealing with its problems that
they'll cease to exist. Ask any SVEA owner how he or she keeps their
cranky little stove running in rain, wind, and even snow. It is being
done...efficiently!

# STOVES...DO'S AND DON'TS

## DO'S

**DO** carry fuel only in recommended containers. Gasoline and kerosine is best transported in aluminum liter bottles, in the original steel can, or in gallon size plastic jugs designed especially for carrying volatile liquids.

**DO** frequently check the temperature of your stove's fuel tank by feeling it with your hand. If the tank is too hot to hold, reduce the stove's heat and/or pour cold water on the tank.

**DO** carry extra stove parts and tools. An extra pressure cap and leather pump washer is usually enough. Bring a small screwdriver and pliers.

**DO** filter white gas (the felt-lined Coleman funnel is ideal) to remove impurities (not necessary with prefiltered Coleman and Blazo fuels).

**DO** empty the fuel in your stove at least once each season. Impurities in fuel left in stoves can cause malfunctions.

**DO** keep your stove protected in a rigid container when it's not in use. (Some stoves are thoughtfully protected by built-in metal boxes)

## DON'TS

**DON'T** loosen or remove the filler cap of a gasoline stove when the stove is burning. This could result in an explosion!

**DON'T** re-fuel a stove that is hot. There may be sufficient heat still available to ignite the gas fumes.

**DON'T** set over-size pots on stoves. Large pots reflect excessive heat back to the fuel tank, which may cause overheating of the stove. Run stove at three-fourths of maximum heat output if you use over-size pots.

**DON'T** use automotive gasoline (regular or unleaded) in a stove designed to burn white gas.

**DON'T** start a stove inside a tent or confined area; the resulting flare-up can be dangerous.

**DON'T** operate any stove where there is insufficient ventilation. A closed tent is not sufficiently ventilated!

**DON'T** set stoves on sleeping bags, nylon tent floors, or plastic or wooden canoes. There's enough heat generated at the base of some stoves to melt or warp these items.

**DON'T** run stoves at full power for extended periods of time. The tank may overheat and cause the safety valve to blow.

**DON'T** poke wire cleaning tools into burner jets from the outside. This pushes foreign matter into the vaporization barrel and clogs the stove. Always remove jets (most unscrew) and clean them from the inside.

**DON'T** enclose a stove with aluminum foil to increase its heat output. The stove may overheat and explode.

**DON'T** fill gasoline or kerosine stoves more than three-fourths full. Fuel won't vaporize if there's insufficient room for it to expand.

The procedures I've offered are those of a wilderness tripper who prefers to spend his time with a paddle in hand instead of a roaring fire in view. Admittedly, I occasionally find more joy in the warmth of a crackling bonfire than in the T-grip of my laminated paddle. At these times, I mourn the passing of my iron skillet, fire-grate and reflector oven. And as I look deep into the flickering coals, I question if modern ways have enriched my wilderness experience or simply made it easier.

# 12

# The Experts' Edge

The great arctic explorer Vilhjalmur Steffanson on return from one of his many expeditions, was once asked if he had had any adventures. After some thought, Steffanson curtly replied: "Nope...no adventures, just experiences!"

There's a notion that exploration--whether by canoe, foot, or dogsled--is fraught with dangers. A major falls at every river bend, a fierce gale each morning, impossible portages, impassable rapids, unending hordes of insects, ravaging wild beasts, and dozens of death-defying encounters.

Nothing could be farther from the truth. If you've done your homework even the unexpected can be predicted and prepared for. As Steffanson pointed out, experts have "experiences" not adventures. Only incompetent fools suffer the latter!

I know "canoeists who've paddled and camped for 30 years and still can't start a fire in the rain or rig a snug camp. They tolerate the misery of being unprepared, mistakingly assuming that their years of experience will provide "all the answers". Their 30 years of experience is but a single year of continuous repetition.

Simply paddling and camping a lot won't teach you the right way to do things if you've never capsized, become lost, or encountered long stretches of bad weather, bugs, or determined hungry animals. Groups of inexperienced teenagers, led by only slightly more experienced leaders of college age are now regularly tripping the most remote northern rivers. That these people "survive" indicates perseverance not expertise. The human body is a tough machine; it'll take a lot of abuse before it flatly quits. *Experts are distinguished by the style in which they travel, not by the difficulty of the trips they take, the frequency of those trips, or the "number of days out".*

Contrary to popular belief, you don't have to trek to the Arctic to perfect your canoeing skills. You can learn almost all of what you need to know on challenging routes near your home if you go out in all kinds of weather and water conditions, and keep an open mind.

I won't pretend the procedures outlined in this chapter are the "best" or "only" way to do things. The wilderness is too varied a place to apply formula solutions. But hopefully, you'll get some useful ideas from these pages.

# RAIN

"Day and night, the drizzle did not cease for so much as an hour. With the rain, the water we shipped over the gunnels in the fast stretches, and the water that seeped through the many cuts in the bottom of the craft, our equipment sloshed about constantly, our clothing and food were soaked through, our blankets were equally soaked. The woods oozed with water, every leaf held a pond, every dead twig and log was rotten with wetness. In order to build a fire at night we would spend two or three hours whittling out chunks of heartwood. Not even birchbark would burn. In our wet clothes we slept, wrapped in wet blankets..."*

I once asked my friend Bob Dannert to define the word "expert". Bob thought awhile then replied..."details". A perfect answer, for an expert considers the most minute details when planning a trip; a beginner seldom gets down to details at all.

Canoeing in foul weather is largely a matter of details, like putting on your rain gear *before* you get wet; making sure the waterproof liner in you pack is *really* watertight; gathering dry kindling *in advance* of the coming storm; and knowing *when* the lake is too rough for traveling.

Of course there are other skills too. Making a fire in the midst of a major downpour is no easy task; threading your way through a maze of islands in a foggy drizzle requires navigation know-how; and keeping your craft upright when a sudden squall turns the lake on edge demands paddling competence.

Even experts don't profess to know everything about foul weather canoe tripping. They still get plenty scared when they're caught on open water in a lightening storm, very uneasy when they've used two matches and a carefully built rain-soaked fire won't start; and downright mad when their hat blows out to sea because they didn't have sense enough to tie its chin strap.

*From "Return To God's Country", by Eric Sevareid, Audubon Magazine, September, 1981, originally from Sevareid's wonderful book "Canoeing With The Cree", which should be required reading for every wilderness canoeist.

It takes practice to become a proficient rough weather paddler, but it only requires diligent studying to learn its procedural details. The continuing emergence of new equipment and materials suggest that there is no one right or wrong way to camp and canoe. If a method works for you stick with it, even if an expert says you're wrong! It's not unusual for some casual paddlers to have better tripping habits than many of the "big guns" in the sport.

## TRAVELING IN THE RAIN

If you dress in wool from head to toe, wear waterproof rain gear, boots, and gloves, as I've advised, you're off to a good start. To this add a fabric canoe cover, a shock-corded thwart to secure your map in its waterproof case, a thwart or seat-mounted "running compass", and a sponge for bailing the canoe,* and you're set for the worst rains. The only thing you really need to fear is storms!

## STORMS

The oft-quoted advice to "get off the water" when a storm brews up is sound. And when lightening strikes, getting to shore fast is even more important because a canoe on open water is a perfect lightening rod. Lightening strikes the highest thing on the water--and on a lake that's usually you! Along the shore line, there's a "cone of protection" which extends about 45 degrees from the top of the trees. If you must paddle in a storm, stay within this "cone of protection" but don't get so close to the tree trunks that lightening may jump from them to you. Where possible, follow this same procedure when making camp: pitch your tent away from the highest points of land, not too close to the trunks of taller trees.

There's a common misconception that canoes built of wood, fiberglass and Royalex are safer in a lightening storm than those built of aluminum. No way! A bolt of lightening can generate millions of volts--enough to thoroughly fry any canoe (regardless of the material) and its paddlers.

The most difficult thing about paddling in a storm is keeping your canoe upright and free of water in big waves. Virtually every canoeing text recommends "quartering" waves (paddling into them at an angle of about 30 degrees) rather than knifing straight into them. Quartering exposes more of the canoe's hull to the water and gives it more buoyancy, which translates into a drier ride.

*See Chapter 6--TANDEM RIGGING, for the procedures of outfitting your canoe.

Quartering is sound practice provided: **1)** you and your partner are sufficiently skilled to prevent the canoe from broaching (turning broadside to the waves) and; **2)** your canoe has a very straight keel line, is very heavily loaded, or has extremely narrow ends.

Lightly loaded blunt-nosed canoes, unless equipped with deep keels for stability, are very difficult to keep on a quartering course in heavy seas. And the shorter the canoe, the more difficult it is to control. If the wind isn't too strong, a good canoe team can usually maintain a 30-degree angle by simply paddling on the same side (the downwind side) of the canoe. But if the wind is really severe, even the strongest paddlers may not be able to keep the canoe on a tack for very long. Since the penalty for failure in maintaining the proper quartering angle is broaching--and possibly dumping--the best thing to do when conditions get scary is to tighten the quartering angle 10 to 20 degrees or lighten the bow (move the bow person behind the front seat) and paddle aggressively into the waves. Most novices will be safer in a rough sea if they forget about quartering waves and instead follow the "head-on" procedure.

Obviously a canoe cover eliminates all chances of swamping!

You might think that running downwind in a heavy blow is the reverse of running upwind. It isn't. You don't have to lighten the stern in a following sea if your canoe has good forward speed. As long as you *keep paddling*, you'll maintain directional control and have enough buoyancy at the tail to keep the biggest waves from rolling in.

The only thing you need worry about when running down wind is surfing on big waves. Once you get stuck on a giant roller it's not always easy to get off without swamping. Fortunately, heavily loaded canoes don't usually remain on waves for very long; if you can "go with the flow" for a short time, the wave will ordinarily pass harmlessly by. The alternative is to get up enough forward speed to break the surf--a maneuver which requires a very fast canoe and powerful paddlers. Generally, surfing only poses a threat if you're headed towards a rocky shore. Under these conditions you may have to break the surf by broaching the canoe--a procedure that's almost guaranteed to swamp you (unless, of course, you have a canoe cover).

To summarize: Don't quarter into man-eating rollers unless *both* you and your partner are highly skilled in handling the canoe. Instead, lighten the bow (or attach your spray cover) and paddle aggressively into the waves. For down wind travel, maintain your positions on the seats and *keep paddling!*

## SNUG CAMP

Campcraft books are rich with advice on "choosing the right campsite", But most commentary is a waste of space since even a rank

novice knows better than to pitch his tent in a depression, on unlevel
ground, or in a bog. Since it's unethical (and often illegal) to clear trees
and brush to improve a camp spot, you usually have to take what's
available and use your ingenuity and wet weather skills to make your
stay comfortable. Shorelines along northern rivers are frequently
very unforgiving; most of the time I'm overjoyed just to find a level
place to set my tent. After that I worry about other creature comforts
like a South facing slope, proximity to good water, effective drainage,
shade, wind protection, a nice view, etc. Nonetheless, here's one bit of
advice worth repeating: "Don't camp in a meadow or flat mossy area."
Cold damp air settles in meadows, and the effect is much like sleeping
in a refrigerated greenhouse! Moss also acts like a giant sponge--it
traps water for miles around. If it rains while you're camped on moss,
you'll be elbow deep in water by morning. Even the most water-tight
groundcloth won't save you under those conditions!

**Figure 12-2**
Customize your rain fly as shown.

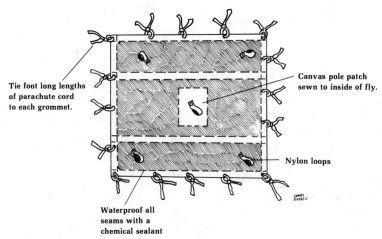

Tie foot long lengths
of parachute cord
to each grommet.

Canvas pole patch
sewn to inside of fly.

Nylon loops

Waterproof all
seams with a
chemical sealant

## A DRY PLACE TO WORK AND COOK OUTSIDE YOUR TENT

A large nylon tarp pitched between trees or suspended from
guyed poles provides a dry place to cook and relax. Tie foot long
lengths of parachute cord to each grommet and sew *five* equally
spaced nylon loops to the outside face (back each loop with heavy
material). Also sew a canvas "pole patch" to the inside center as
indicated in figure 12-2. These improvements will enable you to pitch
your tarp in a variety of geometric configurations with a minimum of
fuss.

**Figure 12-3**
Rigging the rain fly for rough weather.


### Rigging the tarp (if trees are available):

String a tight line about six feet high between two trees and tie one edge of the fly to the line. This will distribute the wind load among several points along the fly. Wrap the corner ties around the line a few times before you tie them. This will produce sufficient friction to prevent the fly from sliding inward along the line when it's buffetted by wind.

Stake or guy out the back end of the fly. Then guy the center to an overhanging tree limb or to a rope strung overhead. If this is impossible, prop up the center from the inside with a pole or your longest paddle. Don't try this unless you've sewn a protective "pole patch" to the fly as I've recommended. Without one, you'll stretch the fly out of shape or tear it.

Complete all knots and hitches with "quick-release" loops (see the KNOTS section at the end of this chapter)* so you can change or drop the outfit at a moments notice. When severe winds threaten, simply lower one or both ends of the ridge rope.

---

*Except where absolute security is desired (as when lining a canoe) it's always best to complete all knots and hitches with a quick-release loop. The first time you have to pick apart a "gobber" knot to drop a clothes line or change the orientation of a rain fly, you'll understand how important this feature is.

**If there are no trees:**

Prop up two canoes on paddles as shown in figure 12-4. Space the canoes about six feet apart, parallel to one another, and cover them with your rain tarp. Stake and guy the fly and push out the center with a pole or paddle so it won't pool water. *Don't trust this set-up in a strong wind!*

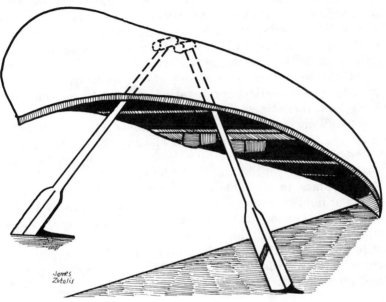

**Figure 12-4**
Use this method to prop-up two canoes side by side. One canoe can provide instant shelter with the use of a tarp.

If it's perfectly calm you can prop up the back ends of the canoes as well as the front, to produce a non-sloping shelter with more interior space.

I don't like the "canoe prop" method. It's hard on paddles and not very secure. But it's useful in light rain and handy when you need protection for a small fire.

**Packing Your Rain Tarp:**

Be sure to pack about 50 feet of nylon cord and a half dozen wire tent stakes along with your rain tarp so you won't have to cut wooden stakes or scrounge lengths of rope in a driving rain.

## PROTECT YOUR FOOD AND GEAR
## FROM RAIN AND DAMPNESS

You just can't leave things lying around in a rainy day camp. Everything must be secured under your rain tarp or in your tent. Even then, equipment and food may get wet if it's not protected by a waterproof covering. I make waterproof nylon bags for everything-- clothing, rain tarp, folding saw, trail stove, even my dirty clothes. (Hint: Pack a waterproof nylon sack *inside* your waterproof clothes bag to separate damp dirty clothes from clean dry ones.) And don't leave open packsacks scattered around camp! If you think this is needless advice, stroll through a typical "rainy day camp" sometime: You'll see wide open packs...and tent flaps, everywhere.

If flooding results from a heavy rain, anything placed on the ground beneath your rain tarp will get wet--another reason to store everything in waterproof bags. A convenient solution for keeping things off the wet ground is to simply string one or two lightweight clothes lines just beneath your rain tarp. Hang everything you want to keep dry from these lines.

I store all my cooking utensils and spices in a fabric roll that has snaps at the top edge. When it rains, I hang the open roll from a protected clothes line. Everything from spoons to spices is then instantly available yet immune from the weather.

**And a place to sit:** There's nothing more disconcerting than "standing around" because you can't find a dry place to sit. If you've outfitted your canoe with removeable sitting pads as I've recommended, you've got the problem solved. If not, carry a square of Ensolite or EVA (Ethyl-vinyl-acetate) foam. Wrap your glass Thermos bottle in the foam for extra protection when you're not using the pad for its primary purpose.

# CABIN FEVER

We were about 100 miles into the trip, pushing hard into the face of wind-whipped rain. My head was down, obscured in the hood of my rain parka. Only occasionally did I look up--directly into the icy drizzle--to check the course. This weather system had been with us for eight days now. Not once had the sun shone between the clouds of twisted gray. And the black flies..they seemed inexhaustible!

My partner and I said little. We just plodded methodically ahead, one stroke, then another and another. Occasionally we squinted towards shore in search of a level clearing to pitch our tents. But there was nothing--only endless tag alders punctuated by occasional bog.

"Sure wish we'd find a nice cabin," I mused aloud. I'd barely finished the words when my friend pointed to the right and said..."There!" Sure enough it was a cabin, incredible as it seemed.

We back ferried* to shore and eagerly scrambled up the mucky bank to the old cabin. The door was unlocked so we let ourselves in. There was a wood stove, four bunks with rotting mattresses, a

*See Chapter 17 (HAZARDS AND RESCUE) for a discussion of the ferry technique.

**Figure 12-5**
"Sometimes there's a cabin."

kerosine lantern (but no kerosine), some rusty tools and a profusion of whiskey bottles. A stench of musty rottenness pervaded everything. But it was dry and there were no bugs. For tonight, at least, we'd call it home.

We fired up the old tin stove then flipped a coin to see which four of the six of us would get to sleep on the bunks. I lost and reluctantly unrolled my foam pad on the drafty board floor.

A good supper, fresh coffee, a hit of brandy, and instantly to bed. We'd had it!

It was well into the night when I heard them scratching, cussing, scratching again. Bed bugs? I chuckled to myself...the floor wasn't so bad after all! About four a.m. someone turned on a flashlight and with much profanity, suggested we "get the hell out of here!" In 30 minutes we were gone, paddling into the teeth of an icy rain.

Over the next three weeks we passed at least a dozen winter trapping cabins like the one which "befriended" us that night. But we found only two that were free of bugs, drafts, and intolerable smells.

As you travel the northern rivers you'll come upon many unoccupied cabins, most of which are in bad need of repairs and are innundated by bugs and rodents. In all likelihood you'll find your tent a much more welcome home. However, if you do find a habitable dwelling, it's an unwritten law that you're welcome to use it. Just fill the stove box with wood and leave a note of thanks on the door.

## FIRE

The ability to make a fire is one of the most difficult (and important) of all campcraft skills. Yet it is one which few outdoors people have mastered.

"Aw c'mon," you say. "*Anyone* can build a fire; all you need is some birchbark or paper, dry wood and a match. In fact, fires often start *too* easily--they get out of hand and burn down forests!"

A convincing argument? Not really. Certainly anyone can set a bone dry forest ablaze on a breezeless summer day. But add a 30-mile per hour wind and a week long rain, and you may discover that where there's smoke there won't be fire!

Outdoor handbooks define dozens of campfire types: There's the "keyhole," "beanpot," "teepee," "log cabin," "leanto," "chimney rock" and more. And along with this information is usually a detailed comparison of the heat efficiency of various wood species. (Evidently the author thinks everyone can tell a stick of oak from that of hickory, or a splitting of pine from spruce.)

**Figure 12-6**
"An experienced woodsman
lights his match only when he is
reasonably certain of success!"

A discussion of fire types and heat production of woods makes interesting reading, but it won't help you get a fire going. What will, is a basic understanding of "what makes fires burn." (Don't laugh: the U.S. Forest Service Forest Fire Experiment Station at Missoula, Montana has been studying this question for years and it still doesn't have all the answers.)

If you've ever watched an experienced outdoorsperson make fire under difficult conditions, you'll find the presence of these variables:

**1.** A cool deliberateness--he or she knows exactly what to do.

**2.** Non-use of paper or gasoline, even when these materials are available.

**3.** Painstaking, almost scientific-like placement of each piece of tinder and kindling on the fire base.

**4.** The fire almost always starts with one match.

**5.** The fire burns brightly with a nearly smoke-free flame, even if the wood is damp.

Generally a good woodsman can make a cheery fire within five minutes, even on a wet or windy day. But not always. In severe conditions the process may take much longer. However, the extra time is spent in securing and splitting dry wood--not in wasting matches trying to ignite materials that won't burn. Herein lies the difference between the veteran fire maker and the novice. The former lights his match only when he is reasonably certain of success. The latter strikes away haphazardly, one match after another, until he is matchless..and frustrated.

The key to a successful one match fire is the "tinder," highly flammable material that ignites instantly and produces great heat.

Tinder is, of course, bone dry. But equally important (and seldom mentioned, it is thin in cross section--the rule being that *it must be no larger in diameter than the thickness of a match stick!* Attempting to ignite materials that are thicker than a match stick is generally a waste of time.

Some favored tinders include birch or cedar bark, very dry leaves and grasses, straw-thin dead twigs taken from the dead lower branches of evergreen trees, abandoned bird or insect nests, and long dead pine needles and cedar foliage.

You'll note the conspicuous absence of paper from the list of preferred tinders. Paper works fine in dry weather, but in damp conditions it absorbs moisture from the air and burns reluctantly.

Waxed paper is an exception: It burns efficiently in any weather and so makes an excellent fire starter. A flattened waxed milk carton can also help you get a fire going quickly. If you tear the carton into thin strips it will burn nicely for several minutes.

If you want to make more sophisticated fire starters, simply roll small pieces of newspaper into. miniature logs and soak them in melted paraffin. Or buy one of the excellent commercial fire starters (solid or paste) available at every camping shop.*

*One of the best natural fire starters is resin from the balsam fir tree. The outer bark of the Balsam Fir produces big resin blisters. Just break a few blisters and collect the resin, which is nearly as flammable as kerosine.

The trouble with natural tinder is that it often doesn't work when you need it most. For example, if it has rained for several days, those dry grasses, pine needles and even birch and cedar bark may be too wet to burn. It's then that the fire starters prove their worth.

Okay, fire-starters are great. But what do you do if you don't have them? Where do you get suitable tinder on a wet day?

The answer is to split the driest log you can find--which on the outside may not be very dry at all--and to cut wafer thin shavings (tinder) from the heartwood with your pocket knife. The center of a four-inch diameter or larger log is almost always dry enough to burn, even if the log has been exposed to a week long rain.

In fact, a demonstration I regularly perform when I teach fire building for the Minnesota Outdoor School, is to fish a small floating log out of a waterway; split it, and secure tinder-fine shavings from its heart. A single match almost always produces a slow but reliable blaze.

You'll find some of the best fire starting materials in old beaver houses and dams along lake shores. The de-barked aspen sticks left by the beaver make excellent kindling and shavings for tinder. The heart of beaver wood is bone dry, even after it has been exposed to weeks of rain. But for the sake of the beaver, please take only a *few* sticks.

Dead and downed trees that are not in contact with the ground also provide exceptional fire wood. You'll find these "blowdowns" along lake shores, river fronts, and in open areas where constant exposure to sunlight has killed off the bacteria and fungi which would otherwise rot the wood and make it unsuitable to burn. The wood of these trees is frequently wet to the touch after a rain, but like "beaver wood," it is usually dry in the center.

Don't begin to build your fire until you have a good supply of shavings and kindling. A handful of shavings is enough, but you'll need three times that much kindling. Kindling should grade in size from pencil-thin, to no thicker than your thumb.

Though there are dozens of fire styles, a real expert will usually avoid them all. He or she will simply set a ball of fine shavings or natural tinder on the ground, light a match to it, then carefully feed, one at a time, shavings or tiny sticks of increasing size into the tiny blaze.

As the flame picks up, the fire maker will add thin kindling, taking care to place each stick a *half diameter's width* away from the next (for example, two one-half inch thick sticks should be separated from each other by one-fourth of an inch). Substantial separation of sticks insures a rich oxygen supply for the young flame. Lack of oxygen is the major reason why most young fires fail. For this reason, novice fire makers are routinely taught to be sure they "see light" between every shaving, stick, or log, placed on a fire.

Let's summarize why fires don't start or burn properly:

**1.** The wood is damp or wet. Even here, wet wood will burn *if you cut it thin enough!*

**2.** Not enough oxygen. Are pieces of wood placed so you can "see light" between them?

**3.** The tinder is too thick or balled up too tightly.

Unfortunately, I can only share with you the "techniques" of fire making. The mechanical skills you need to implement these techniques must be acquired through diligent practice. So don't wait until the first rainy or windy day of a trip to try these procedures. Get out and practice them now while they're fresh in your mind.

Keep the campfires burning. And don't forget to put them out when you leave!

# BEARS

"When we saw the grizzly he was walking toward us along the river bank about 300 yards from where we were standing. He wasn't aware of us; he just ambled along, stopping occasionally to dig for ground squirrels. His silvery coat shimmered with every step. We watched for several minutes, fascinated.  Ultimately, we decided he'd come close enough so we naively rang our bear bells to scare him away. He never changed course, never missed a step. In unison we yelled! Nothing. Then I remembered my tiny compressed air horn (the type used to call a yacht club launch). That did it. He stopped...ran back into the woods, then a moment later returned to "identify the problem". Finally he seemed satisfied that we posed no threat, and slowly, on his own terms, he ambled off. We hadn't scared him away: he chose to leave!"

Kay Henry, MAD RIVER Canoe Company
Along the Koyukuk river in Alaska

I've had two major encounters with bears in the years I've been canoeing and I've been forced to pack up and leave on both occasions. The recommended procedure for scaring off an intruding bruin is the one poignently described by Kay Henry in her anecdote. Sometimes it works, sometimes not. I've clanged pots, blown whistles, and even fired guns with no effect. If you've got a determined bear on your hands you'll have to make a very loud noise to scare him away. An air horn, cherry bomb, or stick of dynamite might do! If that fails you'd better retreat to the safety of your canoe.

Figure 12-7

### "Tundra Grizzly"

Grizzlies and polar bears are very unpredictable. Their interest in you is purely biological: it's your food they want. And in the case of Polar bears, you may be the food! There are numerous accounts of Polar bears that have stalked the hunter who was hunting them.

Grizzlies and black bears are less bold: if you stay out of their way and are very very careful with food, they'll leave you alone. Usually. Bears don't see very well--what most folks interpret as a charge is often just mild curiosity. Most bears have never learned to fear man. Ordinarily they just want to get close enough for a better look.

Being "charged" by a bear is a sobering experience, but one you'll probably come through okay if you *stay put, wave your arms frantically,* and make lots and lots of noise. The alternative is to play dead (assume the fetal position--hands behind your head). *Don't run!* Bears are *much* faster than you are, especially on the flats and uphill.

That's something to remember if you can keep your wits when the time comes.

The above is an oversimplification of the facts, of course. No two bears are alike; each must be judged on his own "suspected intent" and with full knowledge *he's boss,* not you! The science of "bear psychology" is still in its infancy--there are no "bear-proof formulas".

Actually you have little to fear from bears. My research indicated that not one canoeist has been mauled by a bear (grizzly, polar, or blackie) in the last two decades.

Black bears are much easier to frighten than polar bears or grizzlies. A loud yell or mock charge will usually send them scurrying. But not always. If you've got a hungry "camp bear" on your hands you may have no recourse but to pack up and leave. We encountered a nasty sow bear along the Fond du Lac some years ago. We tried everything to scare her away. Ultimately she came within three feet of our bonfire. When we smacked her solidly in the rump with a rock she yelped and scampered off, only to return shortly, teeth bared and clacking, head swaying, "woofing" loudly. We beat a hasty retreat to the canoes where we watched her glare at us from shore for several minutes before her anger passed and she wandered off. Ultimately, she allowed us to return to shore just long enough to tear down camp and move on. When we put to sea the second time she waddled confidently out on a high rock face to see us off, snapping, woofing, and re-affirming her unfriendliness.

Despite what you may have read or heard, black bears are not always timid. Or predictable!

In all my years of canoeing I've never been injured or suffered the slightest damage or loss of equipment to bears. I know of many other canoeists who have been much less fortunate, mostly because they've taken camping books and government publications too literally. For example, the common advice is to hang your food packs from a tree limb out of reach of a bear. "Even if he smells your food he won't get it," so they say. *Don't you believe it!"* Survey some campers who've been robbed by bears: I'll bet you'll discover the vast (and I mean vast!) majority hung their food in trees. Black bears are much better climbers than most people think (polar bears and grizzlies don't climb!). Young black bears can easily outclimb most humans. And bears of all ages are very adept at getting treed packs, regardless of how creative your system.

Here's my philosophy: *If a bear can't smell your food, he won't get it!* And if you pack as I've suggested in chapter 9 and 11, and are extremely careful with your food in camp, you'll eliminate almost all odors. Bears are creatures of habit; they're classically conditioned to respond positively to what pleases them. And what pleases them is food. They learn quickly that food comes in bottles, cans, and packs. And in places where there are humans! How else can you explain why they bite open tin cans or tear up packs which don't have an ounce of food or food smell in them?

Just what does this have to do with hanging food packs in trees? A lot, if you use the same trees as every other camper. Most campsites don't have a lot of good high "bear trees". There's often only one suitable tree--or a juryrigged horizontal pole set-up--that's used by everyone. Once a bear discovers his special tree he'll tear apart whatever you hang in it, be it food pack or football!

My system is more logical. I simply place food packs *on the ground** out of the main camp area. I space each pack at least *50 feet apart* for safekeeping. And I *seal* the plastic pack liners tightly. Sometimes I mask food smells with mosquito dope or insecticide (I hear moth balls work well). I've *never* had a problem. On one occasion, two hungry black bears walked through my campsite, nosed around awhile, and left. They hit another site down the lake, destroying everything, including a new packbasket which was hung in a "bearproof" tree!

I asked Lyn Rogers (*the* North American black bear authority) about my method. Lyn agreed the system makes sense.

I never put my food packs under my canoe or cover them with pots and pans as suggested by some old time woodsmen. A powerful bear can break the back of a wooden or fiberglass canoe with one swipe of his paw if he has a mind to. And topping your food pack with pots so you'll "hear the bear" when he comes suggests you've done something wrong in the first place. Pack your food securely in plastic, get it out of the immediate tent area when you leave camp or retire, clean up your meal time messes, and you won't have trouble with bears or any other animals.'

## MORNING

A "good" morning just doesn't happen; it's the result of good planning the night before! It's no fun fumbling through packs in twilight to locate food, cookware, or stove fuel. And if you've got to search for things in rain, your problems will be compounded.

So begin your morning the night before. Get fresh water, fill your largest pot and plastic water jug. Set these together in the middle of your cooking area or under your rain tarp or tent vestibule. Then clean and gas the stove and put it in a convenient place along with your dishes and eating utensils.

---

*On the barrens, where there are no trees you'll have to cache your food on the ground--safe enough if you follow the procedure I recommend.

Now comes a monumentous decision: "What's for breakfast?" When you've decided that, find the "right" meal and set it at the top of a food pack so you won't have to search for it when you arise. If you'll need cooking oil, coffee, etc., get these foods and pack them in the nylon breakfast bag. And while you're at it, ferret out the next day's lunch. Take some time now and organize this meal. Invariably, lunch will require foods like jam, peanut butter, or margarine which have been packed separately in large containers. Combine all your lunch foods into the nylon lunch bag so you'll have only one unit to pull out of your pack when it's time to eat. Rotating the peanut butter, jam bottle, etc. from lunch to lunch is a daily evening routine.

Put your lunch sack in the pack along with breakfast. Then seal the pack and "bear-proof" it by setting it out of the main camp area.

Next consult your "weather man (or woman)". Look like rain? Perhaps you should rig a low-slung rain fly "just in case". Or maybe just run a tight ridge line between two trees so you can set up the fly quickly if you have to. I'm pretty lazy about fly rigging: I consider a rain tarp just "one more thing" to take down in the morning. And I hate packing a dew-drenched sheet of nylon. So I usually opt for the ridge line and take my chances with the weather. Besides, I can always prepare a nice meal in the comfort of my tent vestibule.

Check the canoes. Are they tied to a tree or boulder, bellies facing upwind? What? No trees or boulders to tie to? No problem; tie the boats to each other--parallel, gunnel to gunnel. Tilt each paired canoe opposite the other so wind can't turn them into a kite.

Last thing before I retire is to pack everything I won't need when I arise--extra clothing, camp shoes, hand axe, saw, first-aid kit, etc. The more time you can save organizing things now, the less you'll have to do in the morning.

Now that you've got everything under control, you can settle down to the warmth of your sleeping bag and visions of what tomorrow will bring.

Here's the procedure upon awakening: Pack all personal gear--sleeping bag and foam pad, clothing, the works, before you exit your tent. When you make your grand entry to the newborn day--a matter or perhaps 10 minutes--take everything with you and set it in a pile under the vestibule or alongside the tent (unless it's raining, of course).

Though you're still bleary-eyed, ferret out the stove and fire it up. Put water on to boil.

That accomplished, stagger down to the river's edge and splash some chilled champagne-clear water on your face, neck, arms. Wow! Now you're ready to embrace the day.

Then to work. Pull the ground cloth out of your tent and fold it neatly. Pack your Duluth pack--sleeping bag and foam pad on the bottom, nylon clothes bag next, then camp shoes and sundries, finally your ground cloth. Next, drop your tent.

*Stuff* your tent, don't roll it! Rolling takes far too much time. So what if the tent's wet from an all night rain? It'll dry when you pitch it that evening. If not, you've got a *dry* groundsheet to put inside.

Check the stove. Water boiling? It should be. About 20 minutes have passed since you emerged from your tent--just about the time required to boil a gallon of water on a good stove.

Set out the breakfast bars and oatmeal, beef jerky, tea and honey. And shut off that mindless stove--the noise is driving everyone crazy! While the water's hot, charge your Thermos bottles with tea, soup, or whatever. Use what water is left in the pot for breakfast...and don't forget to save some to wash the dishes.

I pack insulated cups and bowls and a metal spoon for each person so there's not much to wash. Everyone washes their own breakfast dishes: They just swish some water in their bowls and cups and dry them with the four sheets of paper toweling I pack with each breakfast and supper meal. Trash goes in a plastic-lined nylon sack to be fished out and burned in the evening.

Bellies full and the sun's arisin'--everyone finishes packing and readies the canoes. The cook puts away the stove and cookset and places the day's lunch beneath the flap of the packbasket so he or she will know exactly where to find it when the pangs of hunger strike at high noon.

Obviously, more exotic breakfasts take more time, but the general procedure is still the same. "Getting out" in the morning should never take more than 90 minutes.

Let's summarize the time savers: Stuff sleeping bags, tents, and rain flies--don't roll them.

Use quick-release knots and hitches on all your tent lines and tarp.

Have a method to your madness: Know the exact order you plan to do things. Remember, it takes at least 15 minutes to produce boiling water for your crew, so fire up your stove first thing, not after you've completed half your packing.

If my procedures seem too "military" for a good time, consider this: If it takes you 60 minutes to "get out" in the morning under ideal conditions, it'll take twice that long when the weather is really bad. So unless you want to waste away the day doing camp chores, you'd best develop an efficient, orderly system. An early start means an early camp; time to fish, hike, photograph, and do all the things you planned. And there's no contesting that good morning habits set the tone for the day, if not the voyage. Have a good morning and you'll have a good day!

# KNOTS

Most canoeists never learn to use their ropes effectively. As a result, it takes them far longer than necessary to rig (or drop) a snug camp. Sophisticated canoe rescue procedures require a working knowledge of knots and hitches: An overhand knot just won't do for everything!

A superior knowledge of rope handling techniques is the experts' edge in camp or canoe.

Here are some of the most useful knots and hitches:

## QUICK-RELEASE DOUBLE HALF-HITCH

Figure 12-8

Use the quick-release double half-hitch whenever you want to secure a rope to a tree or boulder. It tightens under load yet releases instantly.

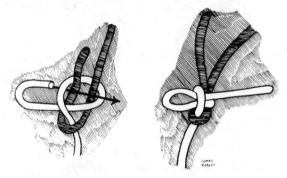

## QUICK-RELEASE SHEET-BEND

Figure 12-9

The quick-release sheet-bend is the best knot to use whenever you want to tie *two* ropes together. Be sure the free ends of the ropes are on the *same side* as illustrated or the knot may slip. This knot is handy for rigging rainflies, extending clothes lines and tent guylines, etc.

**Figure 12-10**

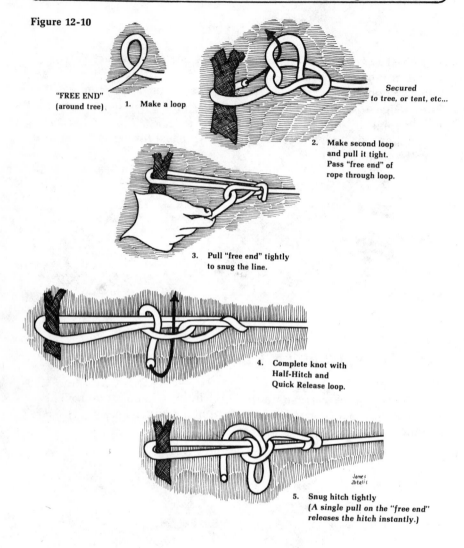

"FREE END"
(around tree)    1.   Make a loop

Secured
to tree, or tent, etc...

2.   Make second loop
     and pull it tight.
     Pass "free end" of
     rope through loop.

3.   Pull "free end" tightly
     to snug the line.

4.   Complete knot with
     Half-Hitch and
     Quick Release loop.

James
Zotalis

5.   Snug hitch tightly
     (A single pull on the "free end"
     releases the hitch instantly.)

## POWER-CINCH
(Quick-release, single pulley)

Figure 12-10

The power cinch (there is no recognized name for this widely used
hitch) is useful whenever you need a combination knot and pulley. I
use it for tying canoes on cars, tightening clothes lines, rigging rain
tarps, and to guy tents. Since it's a very powerful hitch it has wide
applications in canoe rescue work (see Chapter 17, HAZARDS AND
RESCUE).

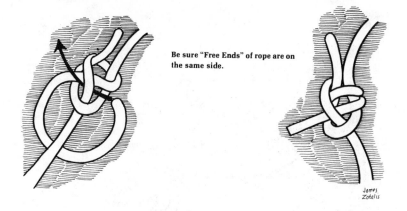

Be sure "Free Ends" of rope are on the same side.

James Zotalis

## DOUBLE SHEET-BEND

Figure 12-11

The double sheet-bend is more secure than the "single" sheet-bend shown above. Use it when ropes are very dissimiliar in size or will be subjected to a severe load. This is the knot to use when you want to extend the length of a tracking line. It absolutely, positively, *will not* slip!

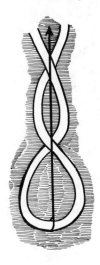

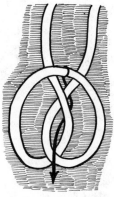

**Figure 12-12**
Twist the loop as indicated, fold it up, pull it down through the center.

James Zotalis

## BUTTERFLY NOOSE

Figure 12-12

Climbers use the BUTTERFLY NOOSE for the attachment of carabiners or wherever they need a non-slip loop in the middle of a rope. These loops are secure and will accomodate a load in any direction. Butterfly loops can be spaced along a line to provide purchase points for a winch line--essential in canoe rescue work.

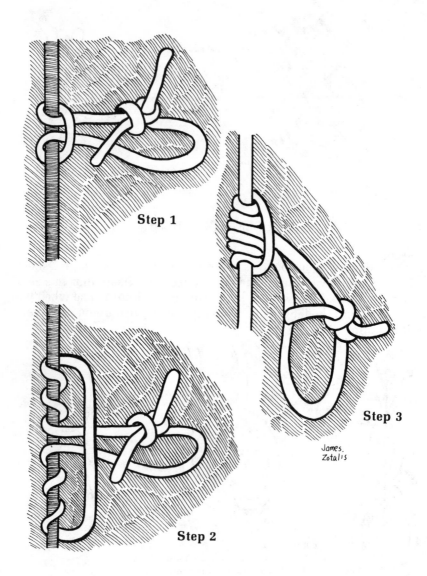

**Step 1**

**Step 3**

James.
Zotalis

**Step 2**

## PRUSSIK KNOT

Use the Prussik knot whenever you want an absolutely secure loop that won't slip along a tight line. Moutaineers use this knot to help them climb a vertical rope. I've found it's useful for rigging rainflies and for canoe rescue. Make the loop from a length of parachute cord, tied with a bowline.

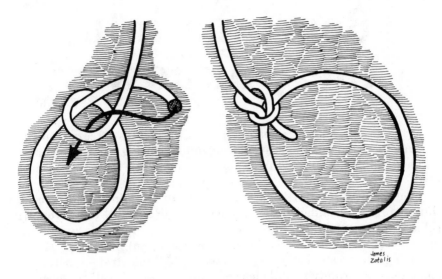

BOWLINE

Figure 12-14

Use the bowline whenever you want a non-slip loop. The bowline won't jam under the heaviest load, and it's absolutely secure. The bowline is the mountain climbers most essential knot.

# 13

# Bearings into the Unknown

The 40 mile lake was dead calm; not the faintest breeze rippled the water. An hour of aimless paddling failed to bring into perspective an identifiable ground feature. Sundown and subtle reality. We were lost!

Reluctantly we put ashore at the tip of a peninsula to "check things out". I unfolded the map sheet on the ground, went "round robin" for suggestions--anything that might help unravel the mystery. But it was no use. We could agree on nothing!

I dug out the stove. We were too weary to think straight; perhaps some tea and brandy would clear our minds. Later I walked out to a high rock point and began to shoot compass bearings to distant islands in hopes of triangulating our position.

An hour later we discovered the problem--a simple misinterpretation of the map. Evidently we'd paddled through a narrow opening in what was shown on the map to be a contiguous land mass. Had water levels been a foot lower when the camera shot the aerial photo from which the map was drawn, there'd be no channel--just a pile of boulders. Surely, that was the answer. Instead of canoeing around the big island as we supposed, we'd gone through it!

Pretty dumb, huh? Not really. Mistakes like this happen among the most experienced canoeists. The important thing is not to panic or keep trucking aimlessly down the lake in hopes that blind luck will see you through. Better to resort to sophisticated compass skills, confidence...and patience!

## EQUIPMENT FIRST

The map! Enough has been said about the importance of good maps that you're sure to have the best. The compass is another matter. A lot of canoeists still take to the wilds with antiquated dial or "hunter" style compasses when they should be carrying liquid-filled Orienteering compasses.

Crossing a complex lake often requires precise directions, and therefore an accurate instrument with a built-in protractor to compute them. Orienteering compasses, like those made by Silva and Suunto, score A+ in both categories. They permit computation of true directions from a map *without* orienting the map to North--a real advantage when you've got your hands full paddling a canoe. Don't sell the little plastic Orienteering compasses short: even the least expensive models are capable of consistent accuracy within two degrees of an optical transit!

**Figure 13-1**
"The Orienteering Compass" permits computations of true directions from a map
*without* orienting the map to North--a real advantage when you've got
your hands full paddling a canoe. This is a "Silva" Type 3.

For greatest accuracy when sighting (Orienteering compasses aren't "sighted"; they're held waist-high and pointed) and for computing map directions, select an instrument with a base plate at least three inches long. Long base compasses point more naturally than short base ones and are more efficient protractors.*

## DECLINATION

In Alaska and most parts of Canada, there's quite a discrepancy between *True* (geographic) North and *Magnetic* North (where the compass needle points.** This variation between the "two Norths" is called *declination* and it's something you'll need to consider if you

---

*The procedures suggested in this chapter, while quite elementary, assume you've mastered the basics of using a map and Orienteering compass. If you need a refresher course, see my book, "Wilderness Canoeing & Camping" (E.P. Dutton Co.) You may also want to read Bjorn Kjellstrom's fine book, "Be Expert With Map And Compass" (Charles Scribner's Sons Co.)

**The North magnetic pole is currently located about 1000 miles South of the True North pole--on Bathurst island (100 degrees West Longitude).

want to avoid serious navigational blunders when you use your compass.

A line of zero declination--called the *Agonic line*--runs roughly from the True North pole through Churchill, Manitoba, South to Thunder Bay, Ontario, and down through Indiana and Florida. If you're east of this line your compass will point west to compensate for the earth's magnetic field (west declination), and if you're west of the line, it will point east (east declination). Obviously, the farther you get from the Agonic line, the greater the declination. In the eastern and western regions of northern Canada, declinations may reach 40 degrees and more!

Failure to account for declination can lead to serious problems. For example, the declination on the Alymer map sheet (Figure 13-2B) as indicated in the rectangle below, is 32½ degrees east. Mathematically, one degree of compass error equals 92 feet per mile of ground error. Compound a 32½ degree variation over a one mile distance and you'll miss your objective by 2,990 feet (92 feet/mile × 32½°) or more than half a mile!

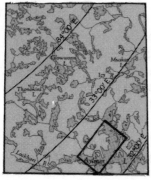

**Figure 13-2A**
Declination diagram for the Alymer Lake map on the facing page (figure 13-2B). The declination of the compass needle from the 1963 Alymer Lake quadrangle (figure 13-2B) is decreasing 7.5 minutes annually.

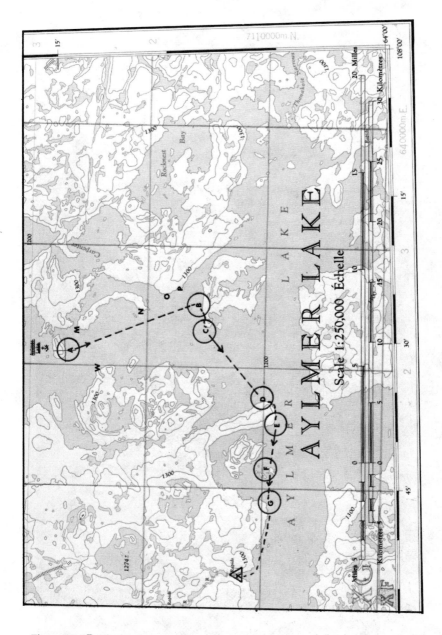

**Figure 13-2B**
Your true North/South reference line is the 108º00' east map border of
longitude (lower right hand corner). **Do not use the grid lines;** they point to
grid north, which in this case is three degrees to the east of true north.
Figure 13-2A gives the declination for this map sheet.

**"DETAILS"**

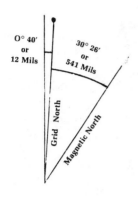

**Figure 13-3**
Standard Declination Diagram

KEY:

**The Star**--Direction of **TRUE NORTH**
**The Sphere**--Direction of **GRID NORTH**
**The flag**--Direction of **MAGNETIC NORTH**

Magnetic declination
indicated in this diagram is
31°06′ *East* (30°26′ + 0°40′ =
30°66′ or 31°06′). Information is
also indicated in *mils* for use by
the armed forces. There are 6400 mils
in the 360 degree compass rose
(circle).

# DEALING WITH DECLINATION

The numerical value of the declination is indicated in the margin of all topographic maps. It may be portrayed as a series of curved lines as on the Alymer map, or in a standard declination diagram like that in figure 13-3. Diagrams are ordinarily used only when the declination holds constant for the entire map sheet, which unfortunately isn't always the case. The five degree declination spread shown on the Alymer quadrangle is quite typical for maps of this latitude and longitude.

You'll understand declination much better if you learn these definitions:

**True North:** The actual direction of the geographic north pole. Lines of longitude--the values of which are indicated in the upper and lower map margins--indicate the direction of true north and south.

**Magnetic North:** The direction of the north magnetic pole. A compass doesn't actually "point" to magnetic north; it really lines up with the earth's north/south magnetic field.

**Grid North:** The direction of the grid lines on the map. Topographic maps *do not* have lines of longitude imprinted on their face, but they do have grid lines. The two are not the same! When you peel the skin off a globe (earth) and lay it flat, you distort the curved meridians. This distortion--or variation from true north, is reported in all declination diagrams (see figure 13-4).

**Azimuth:** An azimuth is a direction. More precisely, it's a *horizontal clockwise angle* measured from North (True, Grid, or Magnetic) to the direction of travel. If the measurement is taken from true north, it's a *true azimuth;* if made from magnetic north, it's a *magnetic azimuth*; and if determined from grid north--a *grid azimuth.** Diagrammatic comparisons are shown in figure 13-4.

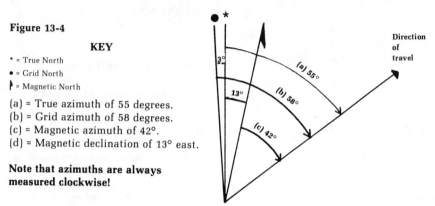

**Figure 13-4**

**KEY**

\* = True North
● = Grid North
⸙ = Magnetic North

(a) = True azimuth of 55 degrees.
(b) = Grid azimuth of 58 degrees.
(c) = Magnetic azimuth of 42°.
(d) = Magnetic declination of 13° east.

**Note that azimuths are always
measured clockwise!**

    "Bearing is a nautical term which relates the degree reading east or west of a north/south reference line. A "bearing" compass is divided into four quadrants of 90 degrees each. It is *not* numbered from 0 to 360 degrees as is the standard azimuth compass. Below is a comparison of some azimuths and their equivalent bearings:

| An Azimuth of | Equals a Bearing of |
|---|---|
| 45° | N45°E (North forty-five degrees east) |
| 225° | S45°W (South forty-five degrees west) |
| 350° | N10°W (North ten degrees west) |

    Bearings have an advantage when you compute reciprocal (back) directions. The "back azimuth" of 45° = 225° (180° + 45°). But the back *bearing* of N45°E is simply S45°W. Surveyors, foresters, and professional people prefer bearings over azimuths and choose compasses that are calibrated accordingly.

    When you use the protractor function (no magnetic needle) of your Orienteering compass to compute a direction from one point to another off a map, you'll have to use one of the "three Norths" as a reference. When working from standard topographic maps, the True *North* direction is preferred.

    If you're using military maps which have uniform UTM (Universal Transverse Mercator) grid lines, you'll want to use *Grid North.*

    *Magnetic North* may be used as a map reference *only* when the

---

*Azimuth and "bearing" are not the same though the terms are commonly used interchangeably. Azimuth always relates to the 360 degrees of the compass dial. A numerical reading of 20 degrees, etc., is technically a compass azimuth.

magnetic north/south meridians are over-printed on the map sheet--
which is never on standard topographic and military UTM maps.

## ESTABLISHING A TRUE
## NORTH/SOUTH REFERENCE LINE ON YOUR MAP

The east and west "neat" lines (lines of longitude at the east and
west map borders) are defined by geodetic meridians and therefore
give the direction of true north and south. If you use either of these
lines as a north/south reference when determining true azimuths from
your map, you'll be right on target. Almost.

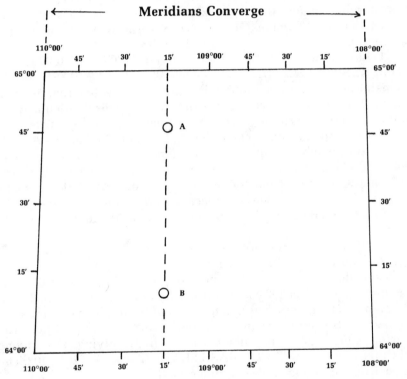

**Figure 13-5**
The actual TRUE NORTH direction is not constant across a given map but varies with
the direction of the true north meridian as shown above. Any two points, such as A and
B, selected on a common meridian, should be on a TRUE NORTH line within the limit of
map accuracy standards.

The direction of True North is not constant across a given map
because the meridians converge towards the north (see figure 13-5).
So if you want to know the precise direction of True North for a

specific area of the map sheet, you'll have to plot a line of longitude across it. That's easy enough--just connect the tick marks of equal longitude at the bottom and top map borders and you'll have a true north/south line.*

Invariably, the neat lines at the map borders are good enough. The error from map edges to center seldom amounts to more than two degrees. Don't make the mistake of assuming that the grid lines run true north and south. They almost never do! On the Alymer map they point three degrees to the east of true north (as defined by the direction of the 108°00' line of longitude).

Now that you have a True North/South reference line(s) you can use your Orienteering compass or a plastic protractor to compute true map azimuths. You may then use the declination information in the map margin to *change these true azimuths to magnetic ones which can be set on your compass.*There are several ways to make the conversion.

**1.** Easiest method is to apply the rhyme, DECLINATION EAST, COMPASS LEAST: DECLINATION WEST, COMPASS BEST. Translation: if the declination indicated in the diagram is *east*, subtract its value from your *true azimuth.* If the declination is west, add it. Reverse the rhyme to convert magnetic azimuths to true ones.

For example, assume you're located at point "A" on the Alymer quadrangle. You've computed a true map azimuth of 160 degrees to point "B". The declination is 32½ degrees *east* (we'll call it 33). Subtract 33 degrees from 160 degrees and you get 127 degrees--the value you should set on your compass and *follow on the ground (lake).*

Similarily, if the declination were west, you'd add it (160° + 33° = 193°).

**2.** By drawing a representative diagram, the mathematics of which simply reflect the rhyme.

Consider diagrams "A" and "B" below (figure 13-6). The declination of "A" is 20° east and the true azimuth (determined from the map) is 60 degrees. The magnetic azimuth equals the difference-- 40 degrees. Since the declination "flag" is to the right (east) of True North, you'd get the same answer by applying the rhyme DECLINATION EAST, COMPASS LEAST. Thus, 60° - 20° = 40°. The opposite situation is shown in diagram "B".

If you remember that azimuths are *always measured clockwise,* you'll have no trouble with your diagrams.

**3.** By mechanical means. I'm no math wizard and when faced with the complexities of big lake travel, I need all the help I can get. That's why I stubbornly cling to my Silva Ranger compass which has a built

---

*The direction of *True North,* as indicated in a standard declination diagram, is accurate *only* for the center of the map sheet.

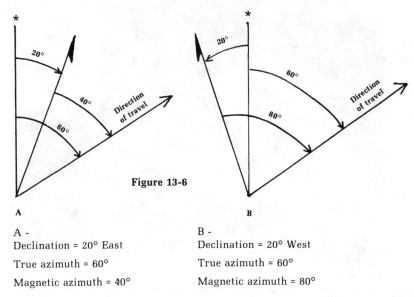

Figure 13-6

A

B

A -
Declination = 20° East

True azimuth = 60°

Magnetic azimuth = 40°

B -
Declination = 20° West

True azimuth = 60°

Magnetic azimuth = 80°

If you want to know the precise direction of TRUE NORTH for a specific portion of the map sheet, simply plot a line of longitude across the map.

in mechanical device for off-setting declination. I turn a tiny screw which takes only a second, and the declination for the area is locked into the compass. Voilá...problem solved!

**4.** By make-shift mechanical means: You can adjust any *Orienteering compass* for declination by sticking a narrow piece of tape across the face of the dial at an angle equal to the value of the declination.

For example, if the declination is 30 degrees east, set the tape so it passes through the 30 degree and 210 degree graduation on the compass dial. If the declination is 30 degrees west, apply the tape across the 330 degree and 150 degree lines.

Use the compass per instructions to compute *true* azimuths from the map then convert them to magnetic readings by aligning the compass needle with the tape rather than the printed arrow in the capsule (be sure you match the *north* end of the needle to the *north* end of the tape. Your compass will now point to your *magnetic* azimuth. If you have an Orienteering compass, try the procedure. It's much less complicated than it sounds.

**5.** Adjust the *map for declination. Easy enough--just draw lines across the map that are parallel to the direction of magnetic north.* Then use these lines as magnetic north/south reference lines when you determine map directions. This will enable you to compute **magnetic azimuths** directly from the map without doing any

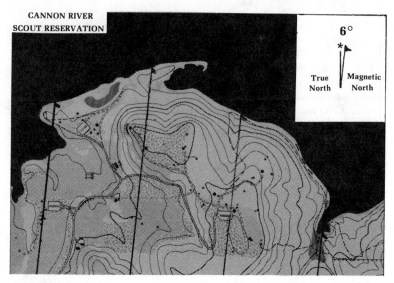

**Figure 13-7**
Competitive Orienteering map adjusted for a magnetic declination of six
*degrees east.* Note the angle of the declination lines in relation to True
North.

mathematical calculations. Consult Figure 13-7 for an example.

Declination lines are over-printed on all competitive
Orienteering maps.

My recommendation is that you buy a compass with a mechanical
declination adjustment, or learn the rhyme. Either way you can't go
wrong.

## UPDATING THE DECLINATION

The magnetic poles are constantly moving. Their location
changes from year to year (and minute to minute). Movements are
subtle, however--generally small enough that only surveyors
interested in extreme accuracy need worry about them.

The problem only surfaces when you're working off a very old
map, like the Alymer quadrangle shown in Figure 13-2B. Note that the
declination information given in Figure 13-2A is more than 20 years
old (1963) and its value is *decreasing* 7.5 minutes each year. To update
the data for 1983, multiply minutes by 20 years. Answer: 150 minutes
or 2.5 degrees. If you're canoeing in the "boxed" zone (declination 32½
degrees), adjust the value accordingly: 32½ minus 2½ equals *30
degrees).*

We're probably splitting hairs here as 2½ degrees isn't enough to get you lost...or even confused. But why add to your error if you don't have to?

There's a common misconception that due to the large declinations in the far north, magnetic compasses are generally worthless. Hogwash! It makes no difference if the variation* is three degrees or 30--as long as you know what it is and apply it correctly.

Granted, there's some inconvenience when values vary considerably across a single map sheet. Even so, the difference seldom amounts to more than five degrees--nothing to worry about if you keep your compass shots relatively short (less than a mile or two) and "aim off" to minimize errors.

## AIMING OFF

"Aiming off" is an Orienteering term. The idea is to introduce a calculated error in a known direction into your travels. For example: Assume you're located at point "A" on the Alymer map (Figure 13-2B). Your objective is "X"--the rapid-filled river.

Let's face it, best way to get around the horn to "X" is to proceed directly to "W" then follow the shoreline of the land mass south and west, jumping the wide bays.

But wait! You've heard the northwest tip of the island at "C" has a marvelous level campsite--room for a dozen tents! That's worth going a bit out of your way for. The lake is dead calm and the weather is foggy but stable so you plot a bee line to the middle of the island at "B". Why "B"? Shouldn't you strike a course directly to "C"?

Look at the map scale--the island is nearly eight miles away--too far to see from your location, fog or no fog. And the limited visibility definitely complicates matters; there's some likelihood you could pass the island without seeing it if your azimuth to "C" is even a few degrees in error to the west. To be safe, you "aim off" for the center of the island ("B") rather than its easy-to-miss northwest corner. When you reach the island just paddle west along the north shore until you come to "C". You can't go wrong!**

Aiming off is an important navigational procedure. It enables you to rely heavily on your watch. If you figure a travel speed of four miles per hour (reasonable for a loaded wilderness canoe) you should hit the island in very nearly two hours. If your "ETA" passes and there's no island in sight, put ashore immediately and try to determine where

---

*"Variation" is a seafaring synonym for declination.

**The example here is for illustrative purposes only. It would be much safer and almost as fast to proceed to "C" via M-N-O-P-B, then to cut straight across the lake as suggested. It's never a good idea to span large sections of open water in a canoe, even when the weather is favorable.

you goofed. If you continue to paddle down the lake you'll only compound your error.

Getting from "C" to "X" is academic. Simply plot a compass course from one recognizeable "attack" point (island, peninsula, bay, etc.) to another. Then follow your course religiously and keep accurate track of your time. Re-affirm your position at each attack point and you won't get lost!

You may want to check your own navigation skills by computing the magnetic azimuth and travel time to the alphabetical attack points on the map. Answers are given below.

| FROM | TRUE AZIMUTH | MAGNETIC AZIMUTH (1983 decl. equals 30°E) | DISTANCE (miles) | TRAVEL TIME/HOURS (Four miles per hour) |
|---|---|---|---|---|
| A to B | 161° | 131° | 8 | 2 hours |
| B to C | Follow shore line | - | - | - |
| C to D | 229° | 199° | 5 | 1 hour 15 minutes |
| D to E | Follow shore line | - | - | - |
| E to F | 278° | 248° | 2.5 | About 40 minutes |
| F to G | 275° | 245° | 2 | 30 minutes |
| G to H | Follow shore line | - | - | - |

## TRIANGULATION

Assume you're "lost" somewhere in Whigam Lake (Figure 13-8). To find your position by triangulation, shoot magnetic compass directions to two or more points which you can identify on both the map and ground (a hill top, channel, bay, the mouth of a river, end of an esker, fire tower, gravel bar, etc.) and plot the *reciprocal* azimuths of these points on your map. You're located where the lines cross.

In the example: Magnetic azimuth to island "A" with it's large identifiable hill equals *70 degrees*. Magnetic azimuth to the high hill at "B" equals 119 degrees.

First, convert these *magnetic* azimuths to *true* azimuths so you can plot them on the map. By *reverse* application of the rhyme

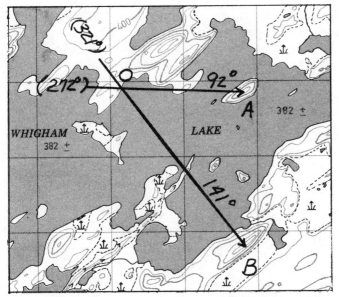

Magnetic declination = 22° East

**Figure 13-8        POSITION BY TRIANGULATION**

1.  Determine *magnetic* campass azimuths to two or more recognizable
    points.
2.  Convert the readings to *True* azimuths by reverse application of "the
    rhyme".
3.  Plot the *reciprocal* values of these True azimuths on the map.
4.  You're located where the lines cross.

(Declination east, compass least) you get:

> A:  70° + 22°(value of the declination) = 92°
> B:  119° + 22° = 141°

Now plot the *reciprocal* of these true azimuths on the map.
Reciprocal of 92° = 272° (180° plus 92°).
Reciprocal of 141° = 321° (180° plus 141°).
Draw the lines. You're located at "O".
For greatest accuracy choose triangulation points which are at
least 30 degrees apart. And the more points you can "shoot at", the
more precisely you'll pin-point your position.*

---

*Once you become skilled in using the Orienteering compass you'll discover you can
draw triangulation lines without making mathematical computations. See my book
"Wilderness Canoeing & Camping" for the mechanics of this procedure.

# FREE TRIANGULATION

Establishing your location along a river is easier than on a lake as the river provides a "free" triangulation line. For example, assume you want to determine your position along the river in figure 13-9. Your compass reveals that the large hill to your right is at a magnetic azimuth of 34 degrees.

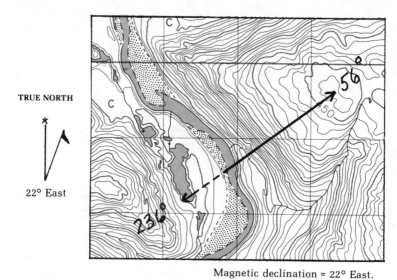

Magnetic declination = 22° East.

**Figure 13-9**
"FREE TRIANGULATION": You're located where the line crosses the river.

Convert this value to a *true* direction by adding the declination (34° + 22° = 56°). Then, determine the reciprocal (56° + 180° =236°) and plot it on the map. You're located where the line crosses the river.

Let's summarize what we've learned:

**1.** If you don't want to get lost on a complex lake, know exactly where you are at all times. Check your map and compass frequently; you can become confused easily in fog or by paddling around or between islands.

**2.** Don't expect to correctly interpret ground features that are very far away (a mile is about the limit of accurate perception even in good light).

**3.** Keep your compass shots as short as possible, and "aim off" to minimize the chance of error.

**4.**Believe your compass. It won't fail you if you use it correctly and apply the appropriate declination. Contrary to popular belief, a compass is reliable in the far north.

## BEAVER STREAMS AND MOOSE TRAILS

Finding your way through a maze of beaver streams and "moose trails" call for resourcefulness. Modern maps are made almost entirely from aerial photos. And if you can't see the sky because of a too dense tree canopy and/or tall grass, the plane-mounted camera certainly can't see the stream. Therefore, in these areas your map may be in error, though the general flow of the water course--minus the switchbacks--is usually accurate.

The heads and mouths of small streams are almost always plotted correctly, but deciphering the maze in between often calls for a ready compass. Moreover, stream beds are constantly changing and these changes will not be reflected on a topographic map that is many years old.

Some hints of navigating small meandering streams: 1) Where a stream forks, take the route with the strongest flow even if it looks more restrictive than a broader channel. If there is no discernible current, note which way the grass bends in the channel and follow. 2) Check your compass frequently; don't rely on your map, expecially if it is many years old. 3) If you come to a dead end and see a "portage" trail, scout it without your canoe and gear. Your "portage" may be an animal trail leading to a connecting tributary or dead-end pond.

It's beyond the scope of this chapter to provide a complete course in navigation. Even the "advanced basics" require more space than these pages provide. If you're really serious about canoeing complex waterways you'll study one of the excellent books listed below. Then you'll get out and practice!

As you gain experience and develop your map interpretation skills you'll become less dependent on your compass for precise directions and more confident of your own visual acuity. But you'll never dismiss the importance of your compass or diminish its value as a route finding aid.

Map...compass...perception...skill...confidence. These are the tools that ensure a confusion-free canoe trip.

# SUGGESTED READING

Be expert with Map & Compass, by Bjorn Kjellstrom (1976, Charles Scribner's Sons, New York.

The Wilderness Route Finder, by Calvin Rutstrum (1967) The Macmillan Company, New York.

Wilderness Canoeing & Camping, by Cliff Jacobson (1977), E.P. Dutton Company, New York. (Chapter 11).

---------------14---------------

# Portage
# Trails

"If a man can pack a heavy load across a portage, if he
can do whatever he has to do without complaint and with
good humor, it makes little difference what his background
has been. And if he can somehow keep alive a spark of
adventure and romance as the old time voyageurs seem to
have done, then any expedition becomes more than a
journey through wild country. It becomes a shining
challenge and an adventure of the spirit."

-- Sigurd Olson
From "The Lonely Land"
Alfred A Knopf. Inc. 1961

The axe-blazed spruce which juts from the river bank indicates
we have arrived at the portage. A two mile carry will see us safely
around the thundering cascades below. Dead tired, we haul the canoes
and gear up the steep muddy bank to the small clearing above. There
is no argument where to camp. This is the only level place around and
it's near sundown.

Rain. We rig a hasty tarp, stack the packs beneath it, then all
crowd in for a hit of schnapps and a hand in the decision making
process. The consensus is to carry the boats and food packs over the
portage and pitch camp when we return. Maybe by then the rain will
stop.

I pick up the canoe and take off down the trail. My friends follow
close behind with the other canoe and packs. It's easy going; we
should be there in 30 minutes. The path merges into a logging road
which a quarter mile later ends in a tangled web of other roads. I drop
one arm from the gunnel of my canoe and pull out my compass. The
map says to head east so I pick a road which runs roughly in that
direction. Thirty minutes pass and no sign of water. We continue on,
another 15 minutes. Still nothing. At 8:30 p.m. we stop and climb a

small hill nearby for a better look. In the distance is the river, but it's beyond a mass of tangled alders and swamp.

What we said next is unprintable. We'd gone too far--way too far! Disgusted and weary, we shouldered our outfit and backtracked the entire two and one-half miles to camp. We set up the tents in total darkness and persistent rain. By mutual agreement we refused to discuss "the portage". It could wait until tomorrow!

We found the trail easy enough the next day. It was just a matter of careful map reading and diligent searching, unencumbered by canoes, packs, or the threat of darkness.

In the near wilderness of the BWCA and Quetico, it's common practice to carry the canoes and heavy packs over the portage first and return for the lighter packs second time around. On a wilderness river, where the trail is less sure, you'll want to reverse this procedure, or better, partially (or wholly) scout the way without a load.

If the trail looks good from the start, carry a light pack and a couple paddles across. This will give you the freedom to search out shortcuts and alternate routes around obstacles like fallen trees, washouts, and mud.

Portages are not always easy to find in remote country, though the trend (unfortunately) is to mark them with brightly colored metal signs or garrish paint. Either method is, in my opinion, an intrusion to the sanctity of the wilderness and my own sanity.

In places where there are no signs you'll find an axe blaze, jutting pole, a wide clearing...or mans' garbage. I've seen ice-cream buckets, paint cans, plastic ribbon, broken paddles and canoes, discarded boots, underwear, and once, an old parking meter used to mark portages. Humans are very creative in this respect.

The location of river portages as given in government trip guides often calls for considerable interpretation. For example, at high water, the head of a portage may be dangerously close to the rapid below, while at low water you may have to clamber hundreds of yards over a dry boulder bed to reach it. Written descriptions of the specific whereabouts of portages must be tempered by an understanding of this relationship.

Searching out portages on a complex lake requires careful map reading, good compass skills, and a bit of luck. Portages are frequently plotted incorrectly on maps so you'll want to "aim off" generously when you shoot compass bearings to them.

If you get confused on a large lake, head towards the nearest "dip" in the horizon that's in line with the suspected direction of your portage. Dips indicate channels or ravines, hence connecting links (portages) between waterways.

Being on the "correct" side of a dangerous river in your approach to the portage may be a matter of survival. Mix a quarter mile wide river with a six or eight mile an hour current (quite common on tundra rivers during the summer run-off) and the ordinarily simple task of crossing from one bank to another takes on monumental proportions. You may be in real trouble if you've put ashore just above a major falls only to discover that the route around it is on the opposite bank. An error like this may mean an hour of upstream tracking (if the shoreline permits it) and a dangerous ferry across.

If your map shows a portage just ahead but gives no clue as to which side of the river it's on, select the shore with the lowest relief (elevation) and/or least amount of vegetation. Rationale: Portages have been in use for centuries by natives and explorers which, like you, had to get around obstacles in the river. Indians and voyageurs were no better at scrambling over canyon walls than you are. They took the path of least resistance, and so should you.

More often than not, you'll find portages on the *inside* bends of rivers. Merely a matter of energy economics: The shortest way to cut off a loop is from the inside. Only if the short route is very unforgiving does man purposely select the long way around.


# PORTAGE LOGISTICS

## PACKS

Pack in *odd* units--that is, three packs or five per canoe, not two or four. This will equalize the number of trips you and your partner must make over the portage. Some canoeists can carry a pack and canoe at the same time but it's a killer and a sure recipe for a sprain.

The same applies to "double-packing"--carrying two packs, one on your back, the other over your chest. Double-packing works well enough on the groomed trails of the BWCA and Allagash but it's out of place in the rough entanglements of a river portage.

## PADDLES

Paddles should be hand carried over the portage, not hauled inside the canoe as recommended by some experts.

**Reasons include:**

**1.** Weight! At around one and one-half pounds per paddle you'll be shouldering an additional four and one-half to six pounds (three or four paddles per canoe). Doesn't sound too significant but over the long haul it is!

**2.** It's hard on canoe paddles. Everytime you jam a paddle between seat and thwarts you scrape off some varnish. Minor, perhaps, but still not the best way to treat fine equipment.

**3.** Brightly varnished or painted paddles become highly visible markers for your gear when you set it along the portage trail. "Drabness" is a major reason why things are left behind or lost on portages. There's not much color among the scrub vegetation on a northern river. Set an olive drab Duluth pack just off the trail in a maze of olive drab vegetation and you may have a real search on your hands to locate it later.* But jam a paddle upright through the pack straps and you'll have an eye-catching flag to guide the way.

Brightly colored equipment--packs, canoes, and clothing--is important in the north country. It provides an edge against loss and brightens up your photographs.

**Accountability:** Each team should take responsibility for the gear in their canoe and inventory it at the end of *every* portage. To avoid confusion as to "who has what", *don't* shift items from boat to boat after each carry. Instead, make equipment assignments on a daily basis.

**Loose items:** Except for camera bags, fishing rod cases, paddles, and gas cans,** there should be none! Shirts, raingear, etc., should all be stuffed solidly into a packsack or jammed under loops of shock cord strung through canoe thwarts. Unsecured gear is a sure recipe for loss on the portage trail...or in a capsize.

**Habits:** Develop an unyielding system of packing and portaging equipment. If you "always" carry your two paddles and camera over

---

*One manufacturer, Duluth Tent & Awning Inc., Box 6024, Duluth, MN 55806, offers any Duluth pack in their line made from bleached white canvas on special request only. These packs are every bit as tough as the unbleached versions but are easier to keep track of on land and in the "green" of the river.
**I prefer to carry stove fuel in a plastic can *outside* my pack.

the portage, and "always" set your camera behind your seat, don't vary from this procedure. Clint Waddell reports that he and Verlen Kruger left the tail section of their canoe cover along a portage in northern Canada some 3,000 miles into their 7,000 mile trip. Two thousand miles later they forgot a folding saw when they broke camp. In both cases the men violated a habit. In the first instance it was dark and they were in a hurry--Verlen "assumed" Clint had packed the cover, while Clint, who ordinarily took responsibility for it, thought the opposite. In the second case, Verlen changed his packing system slightly one morning which left no place for the saw he carried. He "assumed" Clint would get it.

Assumptions have no place on a wilderness canoe trip. Each person must communicate his intentions and stick solidly by them. Good habits are essential to prevent loss of equipment and insure you can find specific items when you need them.

# COMFORTS

You'll discover you can ease the pain of portaging if you occasionally drop one arm to your side as you carry the canoe. This transfers some of the weight of the canoe to the shoulder of the outstretched arm and gives your other shoulder a rest.

Another trick is to keep your outstretched arm straight, with the hand reversed--fingers touching the inwale, thumbs against the outwale. This position puts more muscle tissue in the "critical zone" and makes for a less painful carry.

Granted, my techniques--dropping an arm, reversing the hand, straight elbow--are aimed at the small framed person who needs every portage advantage possible. Big men with brawny shoulders may rightfully scoff at my suggestions, though even they will gain some extra comfort by occasionally practicing these procedures.

There are times when portaging is downright drudgery--all you can think about is getting over the trail quickly! But often as not, a portage is a welcome break from long hours of tedious paddling and the mental strain which accompanies running long stretches of difficult rapids. Portages are usually less numerous on the big rivers of the far north than on the small waterways of the BWCA and Quetico. In fact, it's not uncommon to canoe for days on some northern routes without making a significant carry. Then, it's good to get out and stretch on dry land even if it means carrying your outfit a substantial distance.

Even a "really bad" portage is seldom as ominous as trip guides and the testimonials of past voyageurs suggest. Canoeists have a long proud history of exaggerating the difficulties (and dangers) of rivers. Perhaps it is the passage of time which clouds our view of reality when we report "how things are". Or maybe we're just describing the river as we wish it was.

# 15

# The Joy of Soloing

It's silent, awesomely silent. And swift. With a mere touch of the paddle it turns. Instantly, precisely. It leans when you lean, slips aside willingly, goes on command. Like a dragon fly it skims across quiet water. Its bow entry, quick and sure, produces only the faintest murmur of parting water.

Confidently it twists its way down rock-strewn mountain streams, between the snags and deadheads of lazy river backwaters. Two and one-half inches of water is enough to float it, cargo, crew and all. And where the water ends and land begins it carries easily--forty or forty-five pounds light--a load handled by anyone.

It goes where no other canoe can go, does what no other canoe can do. It has grace, style, and elegance unlike any other watercraft. It is quite simply...THE SOLO CANOE.

The first two rapids indicated on the map were runnable. Just big waves, no problem. But shortly the mood of the river changed. Below us lay twelve pitches (about a mile) of substantial white water. The map indicated a gradient of 50 feet per mile!

"Let's line it on the left," suggested Paul. "No", I answered authoritatively; "Let's portage on the right." After a heated debate we parted company--Paul to line, I to portage.

The portage trail wound tortuously upward--impossible to carry even my solo canoe over. For a short time I hauled the boat behind me with its bow tracking line, like a dog on a leash. It skidded over the rocks, hung up between trees. I sweated and strained. Cussed. It began to rain. For the first time mosquitoes appeared.

Finally I had had enough. Paul was right! Enviously, I watched him 75 feet below line the first pitch successfully. I was burning with sweat, delirious for a drink of cold water. I could take no more. I then did something very stupid. I decided to run the entire rapid...blind! Anything to get off this God awful mountain. I strained my ears and

listened for the roar of a falls, the hollow drone of a ledge. There was
none. I again checked the map for signs of hidden dangers. It looked
okay. This accomplished, I slid the canoe down the bluff into a small
eddy below. I adjusted the nylon spray cover then cautiously but
determinedly, paddled into the foamy white of the river.

The first drop was the largest--an exhilerating Class III run with
big waves, unclear passages, and hundreds of rocks to avoid. I drew
hard, pulling the boat sideways to get into a clear channel ahead. But
an unseen rock caught me dead center at the port bilge. Instantly the
canoe swung sideways and grounded on the rock. Then I heard a
terrible cracking sound! But no panic. I kept the upstream gunnel high
and forcefully pushed off with my paddle. Sluggishly the canoe slid
forward to freedom. I looked down into the fiberglass walls of her
hull. There was no leakage!

I raced through the rapids, drawing, prying, ferrying to cross
currents. I discovered the trick of laying the boat on its side to pass
safely between close rocks. I quartered--ran nearly sideways--the
bigger waves to gain buoyancy. In a few minutes it was over--a mile of
white water behind me. I drifted into the quiet pool below, shared
knowing glances with Paul (who'd been waiting for me there for an
hour), and silently began to sponge the accumulated water from my
canoe.

It was a glorious run--stupid, dangerous, but nonetheless
glorious. I had come through it all without incident. My boat was
totally predictable, reliable, emminently stable in the biggest waves.

The rain subsided and the bugs disappeared. A golden sun streamed beckongly through clouds of twisted gray. There was no need for further words. Drained and gratified, we quietly drifted the last five miles to Lake Superior.


# EVOLUTION

It began in 1975, when friends Bob Brown, Darrell Foss, and I agreed to build solo canoes. Darrell responded with a wood-strip version of an old British touring kayak while Bob made a 13½ foot open canoe of his own design. Being somewhat less creative in these matters than my friends, I constructed from plans the only solo canoe available at the time--the 14 foot MCA (Minnesota Canoe Association) model.*

After months of casual paddling on quiet streams, we were ready for the test--a four day BWCA trip. Despite miserable weather, we were hooked. From then on it would take more than casual prodding to get any of us back into the bigger boats.

But our canoes were less than perfect. Though fast, the kayak was a pain on the portages and during loading and unloading operations. And Bob's canoe and mine were simply too slow for efficient touring. So back to the drawing board we went. The idea? To design a wilderness tripping canoe that with two weeks gear aboard would be fast on the flats yet turn with precision. One that was seaworthy in chop, waves, and rapids through Class III. A forgiving craft that was comfortable to paddle and portage.

Henry Rushton built boats like this a century ago, though none were big enough to suit our purposes. Nevertheless, maybe we could learn something from his designs.

After months of study and dead-filed plans we produced "our version" of Rushton's traveling canoe. Built to my specifications, it measured 15½ feet long, 11 inches deep, and a scant 30 inches at the rails (maximum beam). Weight? Just 36 pounds!**

"Too big", said Darrell, as he watched me stripping it up. "They always look big on the forms," I chortled. "Wait'll you paddle it! But Darrell had other ideas. In just 10 days he completed "his canoe--a

*Plans for this and other solo canoes are available at low cost from the Minnesota Canoe Association, P.O. Box 14207, University Station, Minneapolis, MN 55414.

**A fiberglass Kevlar facsimilie of this canoe (CJ Solo) is available from the Old Town Canoe Company. **New for 1984** is the "Lady Slipper", a sophisticated 14½ foot solo play/tripping canoe by Mad River Canoe Company, designed by Bob Brown to author's specifications.

scaled down version of my boat--a 14½ footer of profound grace and beauty.

Finally, the new canoes were ready. Several weeks of field testing on local waters suggested they were just what we wanted: Snappy, yet forgiving; equally at home in fast water and flat. Light and sweet they rode the waves, "Like a yellow leaf in autumn." We discovered the incomparable joy of paddling alone...together. Our tandem canoes gathered dust in the garage.

But deep down we wondered how our little boats would perform in the "real" wilderness. Were they strong enough to withstand the rigors of a major trip? Big enough to ride over the large waves and rapids we were sure to encounter? Fast enough? Sufficiently maneuverable to twist down a beaver stream? Would they carry the load?

## DIFFERENT STROKES

Then there was the matter of learning to paddle alone efficiently. The solo canoeist lacks the symmetry enjoyed by a tandem team. Perhaps we should consider use of the double paddle.*

In the end, only friend Paul Swanstrom liked the idea. But Paul discovered that the traditional kayak paddle was too short, so he made a special nine footer from a pair of canoe paddles. I let him use my old and slow MCA 14 foot canoe for the trip. Without the twin blades he'd never have stayed with us.

Darrell and Chic** adopted the snappy Minnesota switch (racing stroke) which they used almost exclusively. But I stubbornly stuck with the time honored "C" stroke (see Appendix A).

We argued a good deal about which stroke was best. Ultimately, we agreed that the Minnesota switch--which is basically a short fast bow stroke (you take three or four strokes on one side of the canoe; switch sides and repeat)--was most efficient. Since there's no steering component (rudder) to this stroke, the canoe describes a slightly erratic path in the water. The Minnesota switch is mindless, boring, and ugly, but it moves you along with less effort (and skill) than the classic "C".

Nonetheless, the "C" is the traditional way to paddle alone. It's a dynamic, precise stroke--the canoe barely wavers as it runs. Olympic

*At the turn of the century when soloing was in its heyday, almost everyone used double paddles. Virtually all of Henry Rushton's solo canoes were designed to be paddled with twin blades.

**Unfortunately, Bob couldn't join us for the trip. In his place went Chic Sheridan--a talented 61 year young precision welder and jack of all trades. At first Chic was apprehensive about keeping up with us "young boys", but in the end we were frequently the ones who trailed behind.

flatwater canoeists use the "C" to propel their shallow straight keeled racing hulls. Over the *short haul*, the "C" may be the fastest way to paddle a solo canoe.

I grew to love the "C" and learned to use it hour after hour without tiring. And in rapids, the stroke blended nicely into the "bow draw" and "low brace" (Appendix A). But could I maintain the pace day in and day out on a long wilderness voyage?

Granted, our little canoes were delightful to paddle--like touring the back roads of America in a vintage sports car. But could they meet the challenge of a wild northern river? Experienced canoeists we talked with were skeptical. And reference to these craft in the canoeing literature was limited to "messing around" on quiet ponds. There was no mention of using them for serious trips.

It was up to us then--a small circle of friends--to prove "it could be done". All we needed was to finalize the details of packing, portaging, and paddling...and find an isolated, awe-inspiring route that offered enough variety--large lakes, meandering beaver streams, substantial rapids, etc.--to produce a meaningful experience from which we could draw conclusions. Tough portages didn't scare us. After all, our heaviest canoe (my old 14 footer) weighed only 43 pounds!

## CARRYING THE CANOE

We wouldn't carry our solo canoes the traditional way--with a gunnel perched on one shoulder. Painful experience taught us that a true yoke, like the one recommended in Chapter 6, was essential for comfort over the long haul. But the yoke must be removeable so it wouldn't interfere with the centralized solo paddling position. The answer was to clamp* rather than bolt it to the gunnels. A length of parachute cord tethered the yoke to the forward thwart so we wouldn't lose it is an upset.

## THE ROUTE

After studying scores of maps and trip guides, we settled on the Steel River circle route. Our 1980 edition topo maps indicated it had everything we wanted: Unsurpassed beauty (bluffs to 700 feet), extreme isolation (no roads crossed the river anywhere), lots of good rapids, and a short (10 mile) auto shuttle. More important, the river was located only 500 miles from home.

Easy shuttle, fabulous scenery, challenging rapids. There must be a reason why the Steel River wasn't over-run with people.

---

*A simple hardwood bracket and wing-nut works fine. Or if you want a really slick outfit, get a pair of heavy cast aluminum and brass yoke clamps from the Old Town Canoe Company.

There was. The portages! Even the easy ones required more than casual perseverance. And the worst came at the start. For example, the government trip guided stated: "Unfortunately the canoeist will be facing the steepest and longest portage (a bit over a mile) the first day out. Portage #1 is a climb up over a steep ravine (it gains 400 feet) that will test the mettle of even the most ardent outdoor enthusiast. Packing light and being in good physical condition are prime requisites..."

# PORTAGING

We had it all carefully worked out and so weren't intimidated. We'd each carry two packs in our canoe--a number three Duluth, loaded to weigh 47 pounds, and a small day pack of 15 pounds (we used a bathroom scale to evenly distribute every ounce)!

First trip over the portages we'd carry the big Duluth, our two paddles, camera, and life jacket. Second trip we'd tote the day pack and canoe. Average weight per trip would be around 55 pounds. Pure luxury when you're used to manhandling 80 pound canoes and 65 pound Duluth packs on "traditional" canoe trips.

We set the heavy Duluth pack just forward of our feet, belly down. It made a fine foot brace and fit nicely under our fabric splash covers. The day pack--which was crammed with rain gear, wool shirt, wind jacket, and other frequently used essentials, reclined at arms length behind the seat. The trim was perfect!*

We had all the procedures down pat. All that remained was to get to our river and convert principle to practice!

Our first mistake was breakfast. We parked the van along deserted Santoy Lake road the night before our departure with the intent of having our "contact person" (owner of a local motel) shuttle it the next morning. But when we arrived at the motel the following day, our man was gone--out cutting wood. Had he forgotten about us? No matter, we'd get breakfast at a restaurant and find someone else to drive the van.

After breakfast I asked D.E. Miller, proprieter of the small cafe, if he'd shuttle our vehicle. "Sure", says D.E. "Ten bucks plus two bucks a day to store the van." That seemed reasonable enough so we agreed.

---

*The seat on most factory built solo canoes is mounted with the leading edge four inches aft of dead center. This results in perfect trim with the paddler but no weight aboard (weight of the paddler makes no difference). If, like us, you plan to carry two packs of unequal weight, and your canoe does not have a sliding seat, you'll have to re-mount the seat six inches back of center to compensate for the heavier pack.

To balance the canoe for day trips, simply set a five pound weight (a light day pack works fine) in the bow.

I opened my map and showed Miller our route. Methodically he ran his forefinger along the thin red line that represented highway 17. "Here's where you wanna start", he said, tapping his finger repeatedly on a point about five miles west of our intended Santoy Lake put-in. "That Diablo Lake portage'll kill ya."

Then he told us about this "great" trail--a two lane highway he called it--built by a youth works program a few years ago. "Hardly anyone knows about it," he said. "Not on the maps. That Diablo portage'll kill ya!"

I studied the map. It was two...maybe three miles (if the trail ran straight) to Diablo Lake--three times farther than the MNR recommended route. And the cumulative gain in elevation was close to 800 feet! "How do you know this route's better?" I asked feebly. Miller faced me squarely and with a condescending voice replied, "Hell I live here, don't I?"

I mumbled a polite reply and meekly nodded approval. Long experience in the Canadian bush had taught me to trust the locals.

A three minute drive from the restaurant brought us to the trailhead, which, snuggled in dense alders, was impossible to spot from the road.

We unloaded canoes and gear, said goodbye to Miller, and began the arduous hike skyward to Diablo Lake.

The trail was anything but a two lane highway. Barely wide enough for our solo canoes, it was a network of tangled brush, roots, and downed trees. Unyieldingly the path climbed steadily upward. It would cross two lakes, two beaver ponds, and several creeks before it terminated at Diablo Lake.

Seven hours of arduous portaging brought us to the first pond. A two minute paddle and we continued again--another mile then ten minutes of open water and another portage--this time nearly straight up through thick brush. Along the trail we met a man carrying a bright red Chestnut wood/canvas canoe. He'd begun the portage *the day before!* A smug smile flashed across my face as I passed him by. I was beginning to discover the joy of tripping in a solo canoe!

It was seven p.m. when we slid our canoes into the dark slick water of fishnet lake, a mile from our destination (Diablo Lake). Nine hours of nearly continuous portaging had brought us only two miles. Tired and drained, we made camp on a small island just off shore.

In the morning we awoke to a thick penetrating fog. I fired up the big Optimus stove and prepared bacon and pancakes. Within 90 minutes we were water borne, paddling north into the fog in search of a portage whose location we could only guess.

We found the portage easily but the scenario of the day before again repeated itself. We horsed our boats through thickets, snaked them between trees, hopped from rock to rock. Occasionally there were short stretches of water to paddle. But mostly there were portages.

We kept reminding ourselves that this was fun! But we were becoming weary and angry. We began to talk openly about finding some way to abort the trip. Half way through a swampy portage we paused to rest. Darrell spread open the map sheet, which we all stared at in disbelief. Though Diablo Lake was just ahead, we would need to carry our outfit at least another mile beyond it to reach the first "real" lake that had significant open water.

Chic reached into the side pocket of his day pack and withdrew our store of Peppermint Schnapps. We said nothing--just gloomily passed the bottle around, again, and again. We'd had it!

At three p.m. on the second day we nosed our little canoes into a quiet bay that marked the southern end of beautiful 12 mile long Cairngorm Lake. We had carried our canoes and gear for more than 16 of the first 18 hours of our trip to reach this lake. We were ecstatic--a giant load (literally) had been lifted from our shoulders. We stripped our clothes to zero and plunged headlong into Cairngorm's crystal clear waters. We swam and played, washed our shirts and socks (no soap of course). Then we lunched on a sloping lichen splashed outcrop. Kosher bagels, hard salami, cheese, salted nut rolls, and lots and lots of Wylers lemonade. Oh joy!

The discussion became strangely philosophical. Was it worth all those hours of portaging to get into this positively georgous lake? It was unanimous: absolutely not! "Thank God for little boats," we chorused. "Can you imagine carrying your 80 pound Old Town Ranger over those portages, Cliff?" asked Darrell. We passed around our carefully guarded bottle of Schnapps. Another chorus of "thank God for little boats".

## CANOE STRENGTH

Our two real fears about soloing on the Steel were wind and the questionable strength of our wood-strip canoes. Our experience on local streams suggested that the areas which receive the greatest abuse on a solo canoe are the bow stem (at the waterline) and center bottom just beneath the seat. So prior to the trip we reinforced these areas with layer after layer of fiberglass cloth.* It paid off! Not only when I solidly smacked that rock on the final descent to Lake Superior, but also in the boulders of "Darrell's mistake".

Darrell was in the lead when we heard the muffled sound of rushing water. He put ashore at the head of the rapid to check it out. I

*Be wary of ultra-light (under 40 pounds) fiberglass solo canoes. They may not be strong enough for serious use in the wilds. Most makers of fiberglass canoes will reinforce wear prone areas with additional material for a small extra charge.

**Figure 15-1**
The author runs a section of rapids along the upper Steel River in his hand-
built 15½ foot redwood strip/fiberglass solo canoe.

back ferried into an eddy to wait for his decision to run or portage.

"Hey Cliff, come take a look," he called.

"Nyah," I answered lazily"...Doesn't sound too bad, whatcha think?"

"Looks okay...straight shot..should be easy," said Darrell. "You go ahead, I'll follow."

"Sure", I muttered..."Let's put the scratches on *my* boat!"

I started down the rapid confident there would be no problem. Then I saw it--a gradually sloping five foot drop--one boulder after another, and only a few thin ribbons of water between. No way! I thought. But it was too late. I swept, drew, pryed, cross drawed, lurched, skidded, and screeched. In a second it was over and I was safely floating in the pool at the base of the drop. I was hopping mad and amazed that my "fragile" stripper had survived the beating. I gained a new respect for wood and fiberglass!

I reached for my whistle to warn the guys. Then I stopped short. "Like hell," I said to myself! "Let's see how tough their boats are!" So I just leaned back in the canoe and waited for the inevitable.

It was a commedy of errors. One wipe out after another. *Everyone* had to get out and walk, to drag their canoe over the boulders, to cuss and complain. *All except me! I loved it!*

# PADDLES

In retrospect, I'd have to attribute my good fortune in navigating these and subsequent rapids more to the extra long paddle I used rather than any superior skills. Whenever I heard the sound of rushing water I put aside my 56 inch Clint Waddell* paddle and grabbed an old but sturdy 60 inch solid ash beavertail. The unwieldy ash paddle seemed out-of-place in my modern strip canoe, but it was much more efficient in rapids. The shorter stick just didn't have enough leverage to spin the boat quickly around obstacles.

This realization came as a shock to all of us who for years had snubbed our noses at long paddles. We'd been "brain-washed" by the pro-racers into believing that "short paddles were always better" Fact is, you need plenty of length for solo slalom maneuvers. The old Red Cross canoeing manual was right on target in this respect.

Once through the rapids, however, and you'll want to return to a shaft with more reasonable length. Fifty-four to 56 inches is about right for the traditionally styled boats we paddle. Race bred hulls, like the Wenona Jensens and Sawyer DY, require less--maybe 52. And if your preference runs to the bent-shaft, lop off another inch or two.

# WIND

We came to appreciate the shallow 11 inch depth of our canoes and the low 15½ inch ends. Paddling into a headwind was hard work, but controlling the boats wasn't. We plunged ahead through the biggest waves--even the two footers we later encountered on Santoy Lake near the end of our run. As near as we could estimate, our traveling speed was about four-fifths of what we might have expected to make in larger tandem boats.

# PHYSICAL PROBLEMS

I alone suffered physical problems on the trip: My hands kept "falling asleep!" The tingling began after two very strenuous 11 hour days of rough upwind paddling in the big rollers of 30 mile long Steel Lake. The culprit was my unyielding use of the solo "C" stroke. Evidently, the constant twisting action of my wrists and iron clad grip strained the muscles in my hands until there was a physical overload. It was quite frightening at first. The solution was to "eat crow" and adopt the "Minnesota Switch" along with my friends. By trip's end my hands were back to normal and I settled into a modified style of paddling--a few moments of "C", some switching, back to the

*Clint Waddell, 8015 Sunkist Blvd., Minneapolis, MN 55444, makes wonderful straight and bent-shaft canoe paddles. And he'll mail them direct to you.

"C" again, and so on. For long distance touring--solo or tandem-- variety is essential!

# JOY

We enjoyed a freedom in soloing unmatched by the togetherness of a bigger boat. Though we traveled as a close knit group we were often separated by hundreds of yards. There were long periods of time when no one spoke, when none competed with the silent majesty of the wilds. Perhaps that's what made this trip so memorable: Good friends were near to share joys and hardships yet each of us was very much alone and in command of our own destinies. And we enjoyed a new sense of unmatched comfort as we paddled along. There was never the cramped feeling you get when paddling bow in a fine lined tandem cruiser. Even with 10 days gear aboard we had plenty of room to stretch out. And our full two piece splash covers made canoeing in wind and rain a joy.

To be sure we were somewhat slower than the big canoes on open water. But we were much faster in rapids and portages. Loading and unloading the little canoes at the base of a rocky landing was easy: There was never the awkwardness that's generally associated with manhandling longer heavier craft.

Despite the magnificence of our surroundings, our conversation invariably returned to our canoes. How could we improve their designs to make them faster without sacraficing load capacity and the critical need for quick turns? What was the optimum fiberglass lay-up for a lightweight wood strip canoe that would see use in the wilds? By trips end we had no final answers to these questions--only strong opinions. However, we agreed unanimously that solo canoes work as well in the back country as conventional tandem craft and are much more fun to paddle.

Because we pared clothing, food, and equipment to the bare minimum to save as much weight as possible, we traveled over land and water with a lightheartedness seldom experienced in "big" canoes. But most important was the joy of skillfully paddling a sweet responsive canoe. And that, plus an increased awareness of the sights and sounds of the river has kept us coming back for more.

Soloing is addictive...it rejuvenates both body and spirit.

# 16

# Commercial Carriers and the Long Drive

Travel agencies suggest that "getting there is half the fun." We know better! After long hours (or days) of elbow to elbow confinement within the padded walls of a passenger car--packs, paddles, life jackets and sundries wedged into every corner, canoes with their network of ropes strung overhead, road dust everywhere-- canoeists are more than ready for whatever freedom and tranquility the river has to offer.

About all that can be said in favor of "the long drive" is that it's *usually* the cheapest way to get everybody...and everything to the water's edge.

Our six man crew traveled in style to the Hood river (NWT) in 1982: We shared the comforts (and cost) of a small motor home! And despite the horrible gas mileage, the ride was sheer luxury and worth every penny we spent.

Even if you can find a vehicle that's large enough to carry everyone you'll still need a trailer to haul your gear. A home built model with 14-inch wheels and locking cargo box is best though a large wheeled utility trailer will work if it's strong enough. Canadian bush roads are tough on vehicles. A trailer needs plenty of ground and spring clearance. The typical commercial trailer with its 12 inch wheels is fine for trucking along smooth pavement but it won't ride through the ruts of an unimproved logging road!

Trailer accessories should include at least one extra tire, a canvas dust cover, a high lift jack (so you can change tires in the mud), and mounting brackets for one or more "Jerry" cans. It's doubtful your rig will get admirable gas mileage when loaded with canoes and packs for a long trip so carry extra gas--safely in approved Jerry cans--*outside* the vehicle. And don't forget to bring a matching gooseneck filler cap so you can pour the petrol into your tank rather than all over the highway. A plastic funnel *isn't* good enough!

It's easy to car-top two canoes, but a third one complicates matters considerably. However, it's safe enough if you set the odd boat on a pair of carpeted one by two's that bridge the paired canoes below. Tie the ends of the wood cross bars to your metal car-top carriers so they won't shift in the wind.

Each canoe should have a drum-tight belly rope fore and aft to secure it to the car racks, plus *twin* bow and stern lines run through eye bolts in the bumpers. S-hooks on the bumper edges can substitute for eye bolts but they're not nearly as secure. The "power-cinch" (Chapter 12) is the best hitch to use for locking canoes down tight.

Abrasion is a major concern on long drives. If the sides of a pair of car-topped canoes are allowed to touch, severe damage may result to one or both hulls. This is a very real problem where an aluminum canoe is paired with a non-aluminum one. The answer is to place a large boat cushion or piece of foam padding between the canoes. Tie the padding to one canoe so it won't blow away.

You'll also want to pad the car top carriers so they won't groove the gunnels of your canoe. Carpeting is the standard remedy, though rags or sections of radiator hose duct taped to the cross bars work as well. Give serious thought to the abrasion thing: You can do as much damage to a canoe in transit as on the river!

Also be careful of where and how you use steel S-hooks. An acquaintance of mine chewed up the vinyl skin of a new Old Town Ranger when he snapped an S-hook directly to the stem-mounted brass towing ring. Continuous rubbing of the hook against the Royalex hull produced quite a gouge.

Whenever I carry three canoes--or two in very high winds--I rig a towing bridle around each boat: Simply take a few coils of rope around the canoe near the bow and tie them off at the front seat. Then string a second set of lines from the bridle to the bumper. The view up front will look like "Charolette's Web" and be as secure.

Discard the fabric straps that come with most brands of car-top carriers: they're slow and awkward to use and don't snug down tight enough. And don't use rubber truck straps or shock cords...ever! They won't hold at high speeds. Knowledgeable canoeists always use quarter or three-eighths inch nylon rope. Those who scorn ropes don't know how to tie them effectively!

Nylon stretches considerably when it gets wet or is exposed to the dampness of the night. So check your ropes every time you stop for gas. If you snug ropes with a quick-release "Power Cinch" as I've recommended, it'll take only a second to re-tighten them.

Incidently, don't use your polypropylene lining ropes to tie down your canoes. Polypropylene takes a permanent set and will coil itself into impossible configurations when you remove it from the car. Lining ropes should be carefully coiled and used only for their intended purpose, nothing else.

Last thing is to apply a good coat of paste wax to the canoe bottom. This will make it easier to remove dead insects which accumulate on the drive up.

**Car-top carriers:** The best are those which hook directly to the rain gutters. Racks which have suction cups or put pressure on the roof are a waste of money, and the grooved foam gunnel blocks you buy at marinas are even worse. I know a lot of canoeists (myself included) who simply won't buy a car that doesn't have rain gutters!

By far the most popular car-top carriers among experienced canoeists are the solid cast aluminum ones manufactured by the "Quick 'N Easy" Company.* These won't rust, bend or corrode, even around salt water. Some conoeists simply buy the load brackets and bolt them to carpeted two by fours. This makes an excellent carrier, though one not easily changed from car to car.

# THOSE WONDERFUL CANADIAN RAILROADS

It was a sweltering 98 degrees the day we arrived at Moosonee on Arctic tide water. The map indicated the train station was less than a mile across town, an easy portage. But it was dreadfully hot so we casually inquired about taxi service. Almost immediately a burly red haired man drove up in an ancient one ton stake truck. "Taxi"? he asked. "You bet," I replied, and in a flash we loaded canoes and gear onto the bed of the old truck and piled aboard. A short dusty drive along pulverized gravel brought us to the well kept station which marked the end of the line for Ontario Northland's famed "Polar Bear

*Quick 'N Easy" Products Inc. P.O. Box 278, Monrovia, CA 91016

Express". A polished diesel engine with a white polar bear emblazoned boldly on its sides clanged confidently in the glaring sun while a team of 20 cars waited silently in tow.

We unloaded our outfit and inquired at the ticket counter. The fare to Cochrane was $8.75; canoes rode for slightly more.

"Eighth car back," said the agent, pointing to the hulking train. "Use that push cart over there." We nodded our thanks and shuttled our three canoes and 12 Duluth packs down the track to the appointed car. A railroad employee saw us and jumped off a flat car, eager to help. We gratefully declined the offer so he walked along side and chatted, curious about our trip.

We stacked our gear neatly into one corner of the near empty box car, fastened the necessary baggage tags, and retired to the passenger compartment. Inside the car the temperature was a scorching 110 degrees! A round faced conductor took our tickets and apologized for the breakdown in the air conditioning. "Is there a lounge?" I asked. "Yes sir," he replied..."Three cars back. Only place aboard that's cool." We bolted from our seats intent on beating the crowd. An eight hour ride in a sweltering metal box was not our idea of a good time.

The conductor was right. The lounge was cool, clean, plush...and virtually unoccupied. We settled in for the night and round after round of that famous Canadian beer.

If you've never ridden a Canadian bush train, you've got a pleasant surprise in store. The experience is almost as much fun as the canoe trip itself.

Much of Northern Canada is still dependent on "working trains" to bring goods and services to remote communities. As a result you'll rub shoulders with the heart and spirit of the north land--loggers, miners, Indians, prospectors, trappers, and wilderness travelers like yourself. The bush trains are a thrilling melting pot of personalities, occupations...and dreams.

In addition to regular service at established stations, trains will often stop at any mile marker to accomodate canoeists and their gear. But don't expect fancy porter service or dazzling pullman decor. Railway employees are friendly and helpful but they do expect you to help load and unload your own gear.

In remote areas trains frequently run in different directions on alternate days--and not all trains will stop for canoeists. So be sure to write for an up-to-date time table.

Most of the passenger train service in Canada is consolidated under VIA RAIL, which makes getting specific information about schedules, procedures, costs, etc. relatively easy. A letter addressed to VIA RAIL headquarters in Winnipeg* will bring prompt courteous

*VIA RAIL, Canada, Inc. 101-123 Main St., Winipeg, Manitoba R3C 2P8.

answers to all your questions.

Canoes accompanied by their owners are usually considered excess baggage rather than freight and travel for about the same price as a passenger, which at this writing is 12 cents a mile (one way).* This is much less expensive than driving.

Some railroads won't handle canoes longer than 18 feet in standard baggage car service. There seems to be no logical reason for this regulation as there's usually plenty of room in the box cars. And a 20 foot aluminum canoe weighs no more than an 18 foot wood/canvas one. However, they bend the rules a lot in remote areas so there's real likelihood you'll be allowed to board with whatever you're paddling. But to be safe, check the length requirements before you commit yourself to your beloved 18½ footer. The alternative might be a lonely ride home on a passenger train while your canoe travels unescorted on another freight train!

**Freight trains:** Freight trains haul freight; passenger trains carry people. There are exceptions. I know of several cases where friendly freighters have picked up canoeists by appointment...and otherwise. The bush trains are marvelous!

Virtually every Canadian railroad has a wealth of materials that are free for the asking. And when you receive them you'll understand why Canada's trains are surviving while ours aren't. The "tourist packet" I received from VIA RAIL weighed a full five pounds! Included was a wonderfully informative tour book which listed major cities, points of interest, historical information, mile markers, maps, and much more. There was also a volume of provincial and city brochures plus a surprisingly detailed guide to canoeing Manitoba rivers.

Materials supplied by Algoma Central, though less voluminous, were equally useful--it included a number of high quality canoe routes accessible by rail.

The Canadian railroads are wonderful. They work hard to get your business: The free brochures and canoe maps they supply are in itself almost worth the price of the ride.

*Algoma Central Railway rate as of October, 1983.

**Figure 16-1**
Loading a Twin Otter for the trip home. Point Lake, NWT.

# CHARTER PLANES

High noon and mist gray. An icy wind whips gentle white caps across the 40 mile lake. The wind stops, the rain (snow?) begins. I stare unbelievingly at the thin column of mercury in my pocket thermometer. Thirty degrees. Exactly! Hard to believe it's the eighteenth of August. Clad in layered woolens and bombproof rain gear, I'm warm. Barely. I shiver slightly and search longingly into the menacing sky. Nothing. Will he come? Perhaps he's forgotton us. I snug the parka around my face and nestle against a half full Duluth pack. We wait!

Minutes blend to hours. Still no sign. At last I hear the sound, muffled at first, then louder. Finally an amorphous speck of silver appears on the horizon. The speck grows larger. Pontoons, twin props--a turbo Otter! The plane cuts power and drops gracefully to the water's surface. A long glide, pause...a turn. Slowly it chugs our way.

The engines stop and the metal floats settle gently on the sloping gravel beach by our camp. The door opens and a grinning heavy-set man wearing sunglasses emerges. "Sorry I'm late, boys" says the man; "Had to pick up a load in Uranium City." But no apology is necessary. The long wait provided ample time to dream of chairs with padded back rests, tables to sit at, ice cold beer, McDonald's hamburgers...pizza. "Let's hit it guys," calls someone. It's back to reality--and to work!

Fitting three 17 foot Old Town Trippers into the belly of the Twin Otter isn't easy. We stack 'em opposite the side door, tails against the back wall. We twist, turn, grunt...the third boat fits. Luckily. The pilot makes no comment even though the stem of one canoe rests just inches from the instrument panel.

All aboard and ready to cast off. Wait...the money! Seven hundred twenty-six dollars for 220 air miles. Expensive but worth it. We peel off the fare in Canadian traveler's checks, settle into the thinly padded folding seats opposite our canoes, and fasten our seat belts. The pilot revs for take-off. There's no upholstery to deaden the sound. The noise is deafening!

I watch the "co-pilot"--a boy in his late teens. His fore-finger moves methodically across the map with anticipated precision. He looks out the window, checks the compass. His finger advances a few millimeters across the map.

Those in front are warm, but back where I sit it's downright cold. Hard to believe this is a million dollar airplane. Then the jolting begins. Rough weather, sleet ahead. I study the faces of my friends. No one looks too well. The talking stops, the queeziness begins. Ultimately we level out and the ride--and our stomachs--smooth. I'm grateful now we've got the Otter and not a pair of Cessna's. The Cessna's would be cheaper to be sure, but less safe. For me that's enough.

Minutes later we set down in a protected cove. It's over and we're homeward bound.

Almost everyone who lives and works in the vast roadless regions of the far north has access to some sort of aircraft. There are Cessnas, Beavers, Navahos, Lancers, Otters, a variety of helicopters, and more. Finding an airplane to haul you to and from the river is easy: All you have to do is match what's available with what you can afford to pay--which invariably is more difficult than it sounds.

The Provincial Bureau of Tourism can supply the names and addresses of charter aircraft companies which service the area of your interest. Write for specifics and get a firm committment before you leave home. A Cessna 185 is usually the cheapest way to fly for a party of two, though some pilots won't carry canoes longer than 16 feet on the floats of these small planes.

A single-engined Beaver or Otter is better than a Cessna if you have a lot of gear or an 18 foot canoe; and a Twin Otter is best for large parties with two or three canoes. A twin Otter is a big plane and with careful packing can easily accomodate a crew of six, a months supply of gear, and three 17 foot canoes, although you might have to explain this fact to some disbelieving Twin Otter pilots.

Costs are ordinarily computed on a per mile basis which means you pay for each mile the airplane flies from its sea base to your location and return. Prices vary slightly from one air service to another so it pays to shop around.

Some companies have an external "tie-on" charge of ten or more dollars for securing your canoe to the floats of the aircraft.* There may also be an additional per mile charge for the drag incurred on the plane from the pontoon-mounted canoe. Generally, float plane pilots are less than enthusiastic about carrying canoes outside aircraft. The canoe reduces wind speed considerably, increases gasoline consumption, and creates problems during take-offs and landings. Nevertheless, a lot of canoes are flown on the struts of airplanes...safely!

The chart at right gives the vital statistics and 1982 charter costs of some of the most popular bush planes. Prices will certainly be dated by the time you read this, but comparative relationships won't.

## CONSIDERATIONS

**Maximum load:** The amount of weight an airplane can *actually* carry depends on the distance traveled (the amount of gas required), the presence or absence of an external load (a canoe), and the length of the waterway (runway).

The "useful" load of an aircraft is reduced substantially when a canoe is carried on the pontoons. For that reason, the rule is to *double the weight of the canoe when determining load capacities, though some pilots increase it much more than that.*

A "charter weight" calculation for a new model Cessna 185 might look like this:

Basic empty weight average
(plus oil and survival gear) ............... 2247 pounds
Pilot ....................................... +175 pounds
Operational empty weight ................ 2422 pounds
Assume total fuel weight (round trip) is .... +300 pounds
                                             2722 pounds

Gross weight of the aircraft is        3320 pounds
Useful load = 3320 minus 2722 equals   598 pounds

Subtract weight of 80 pound canoe:     160 (canoe weight
                                           doubled)
                                       438 Amount of
                                           weight you
                                           can put in the
                                           cabin.

---

*All float plane pilots are not expert at tying on canoes. You'll want to oversee the procedure with a wary eye and use your own superior knot skills if the occasion demands. Canoes do sometimes fall off airplanes!

## 1982 COSTS AND CHARACTERISTICS OF SOME POPULAR BUSH PLANES

| NAME OF AIRPLANE | NUMBER OF* PASSENGERS | PAY LOAD** (pounds) | COST/PER (Canadian currency) | COMMENTS |
|---|---|---|---|---|
| Cessna 185 | 3 | 800 | $1.40 | Wheels or floats. One canoe may be carried externally. Some Cessna pilots will not carry canoes. It's generally agreed that canoes longer than 17 feet should not be carried on this aircraft. |
| Beaver | 5 | 1200 | 1.75 | Maximum canoe length on the floats is 18-18½ feet. Some pilots will carry 20 footers. |
| Single Otter | 10 | 2000 | 2.50 | One canoe up to 18 feet long is carried on the floats. A few pilots will carry 20 footers. |
| Twin Otter | 21 | 3000 | 3.30 | Wheels or floats. Will accept three 17 foot canoes or two 18-18½ footers inside. You can't carry enough gear on a normal canoe trip to overload this airplane. |
| DC-3 | 30 | 6000 | 3.30 | Wheels only--you must have a landing strip. More room than you could possibly need. |

*Number of passengers (or weight of gear) must be reduced when a canoe is carried on the pontoons.

**Includes the "rough weight" of the pilot but no gas.

Some conservative air services *halve* the "useful load" when a canoe is carried outboard, which by this calculation would leave only about 300 pounds pay load in the cabin.

Practices vary among charter companies, so get all the facts before you commit!

**Money**: In preparing this section I surveyed more than two dozen charter air services. All would accept Canadian or American cash or Canadian travelers checks. Most would also take VISA cards and American Express travelers checks, but none would honor a personal check without a guarantee (reference, past association, etc.) of some sort.

The pilot expects to be paid in full when (or before) he picks you up so plan accordingly. One solution to avoid embarrassment is to pre-pay the entire cost by mail--and *carry the receipt*. This will ensure there'll be no "extra charges" when the plane arrives.

If you lose your money on the river and can't afford to pay, the pilot will surely fly you out anyway. No self-respecting bush pilot would consider leaving anyone stranded in the bush, even if he has to foot the bill. However, there's no guarantee he won't leave your gear sit by the water's edge if he suspects you don't intend to pay!

Bush pilots are generally very considerate and understanding. They know their airplane is your link between life and death--a responsibility they accept willingly and with an air of flamboyance that commands admiration and respect.

## BY BARGE OR BOAT

If your trip terminates at a roadless settlement that receives scheduled air and boat service, you may be able to ship your canoes to a port which you can later drive to. This way you can save a bundle by flying out aboard an inexpensive commercial airliner. The disadvantage of this of course is time--it may take several weeks or months for your canoes to arrive at the port of call where you can pick them up.

Northern Transportation Company LTD* operates a tug and barge operation based in Churchill, Manitoba that services a number of remote northern communities. Some settlements, like those on the west edge of Hudson Bay (Baker lake, Chesterfield Inlet, Eskimo point, etc.) receive scheduled service during the July through October shipping season. Other places like Bay Chimo and Bathurst Inlet are serviced only when the traffic warrants.

Northern Transportation Company LTD will send you the details of their operation upon request. For comparison, the 1981 cargo rate

*Northern Transportation Co. LTD, 9945 rue 108 St., Edmonton, Alberta TSK 2G9.

from any of the Hudson Bay settlements to Churchill* was $13.17 per hundred weight, subject to a minimum weight of 400 pounds for canoes under 18 feet, and 500 pounds for those over 18 feet. Shipment from Bathurst Inlet to Hay River costs $68.19 per hundred weight. The company is licensed to carry freight only: they won't accept passengers.

Whether or not you'll save money by barging your outfit depends entirely on how much time you have, the number of canoes in your party, the weight of your gear, availability of low cost commercial aircraft, and the distance you have to drive to the port of call.

*Canoes can be sent by rail from Churchill to Winnipeg or other points South.

# 17

# Hazards and Rescue

To canoe a remote northern river without incident requires know-how, perseverance, and a lively appreciation of what it means to suffer an injury or lose a canoe when you're 100 miles from the nearest help. It requires many years under fire plus occasional "upsetting experiences" to develop the proper respect for a wild river. First, you acquire essential paddling skills, learn the basic maneuvers, and coordinate with a partner. You know your limitations and are extremely cautious. You take no chances. Yet!

In time, you get the mechanics down pat. You can do a fast forward ferry into an eddy, pivot smoothly around a mid-stream boulder in a Class III rapid,* twist confidently down a mountain stream. You can handle whatever the river throws at you, alone or with a partner. You're almost as good as you think.

Then one day, far from the nearest road, you run a tough drop your friends elect to portage. "Walk around it," they urge. "We're too far from home to take chances." But the die is cast. You'll show 'em! So down the river you go, confident of success. But you miss the clear channel; the hydraulics were more than you bargained for. The result is a cold swim to shore and a damaged canoe. It's more than "just embarrassing"--your heroics have endangered the welfare of the entire crew. You vow you'll never pull a stunt like that again in the bush.

Unfortunately, the last decade has been marred by a profound increase in canoeing fatalities across Canada--especially on the technically difficult barren land rivers. Surprisingly, the ones most likely to get hurt are neither over-cautious beginners who realize their limitations, or practiced trippers who know they "can't conquor a river." Generally, it's the paddle competent, over-confident hot-dog who becomes the statistic. And high-tech white water skills are not the equalizer. Avoiding the dangers of the river is!

In the pages that follow we'll probe some of the hazards you're likely to encounter on northern canoe routes. The anecdotes you'll

*See Appendix E for a review of the International white water rating scale.

read are real. However, I urge you not to over-react to the implied dangers. Northern rivers are very safe places for those with good skills and mature judgement. Of course there's always the unexpected, the unpredictable. And that, good or bad, is what makes wilderness canoeing such an exciting ball game. Invariably if you play by the rules you won't get hurt!

## OVER-RELIANCE ON THE MAP
### THE 100 FOOT CONTOUR INTERVAL

You're a week into the trip and so far the days have been uneventful. You've run some substantial rapids without problems, took the cautious route and portaged the questionable drops. Your maps, with their detailed profiles, have been your lifeline. You're doing a fine job as trip leader.

Now there's time to relax. Neither your map nor trip notes suggest there are imminent dangers ahead. The river is at peace; only the occasional skitter of a dragon fly across its mirror smooth green surface breaks the tranquil laziness of the moment. You want to lay back and float awhile, just take it easy.

Your friends paddle alongside, eager to go. They don't share your views of slowing down. "We'll go on ahead...get a good campsite...have coffee on when you slugs arrive," says the fast team.

You check the map again. The contours are uniform; there's no hint of danger. Surely it's okay to break the rules and separate the party for a few hours. Why not let your friends exercise their muscles? But wait! Fifty miles from the nearest road is no place to take chances. You reluctantly make the decision--"We'll pick up the pace and stay together."

Ahead the river narrows and bends sharply to the right. The current quickens and produces a barely audible gurgle. Maybe a Class I rapid, you muse. Certainly nothing stronger than that. Your friends are chomping at the bit. They pull ahead.

"Hold up," you call. "Let's check this blind corner." "Aw, it's just a swift," is the reply. But you're unsure. You decide to go ashore and have a look. You tie your canoe to a tree and struggle through thick underbrush to cut off the river bend. Ultimately, you push aside a small sapling and step into the blazing sunlight. Nothing. Just the same persistent gurgle. Then you see it--a sheer ten foot drop over glass smooth granite. And barely a sound! The falls is not a killer, but it is a canoe eater for sure. Run it and you'll have a long walk out.

Triumphantly you work your way back through the undergrowth. "Falls!" you call sharply. Let's portage!

There's no portage trail or hint of one. Getting around the falls means horsing canoes and gear through tangled vegetation. Later you walk out to the flat rock above the ledge and study the map again. You're hopping mad. How dare the cartographers miss a dangerous spot like this! Then your eyes wander to the map margin. *The contour interval is 100 feet!* Suddenly everything is quite clear: A ten foot fall is insignificant when the distance between contours is that large.

Until now I've suggested that a good map and detailed profile will keep you out of trouble. As the case in point indicates, it won't always. Maps with generous contour intervals are next to worthless for interpreting hidden dangers.

The lesson is academic: Don't assume the way is clear just because the map says so. If you can't see around a bend and feel a gnawing uncertainty in your gut, then get out and look, even if it means climbing a high hill or bull-dozing your way a quarter mile through dense alders. Certainly you should rely heavily on you map for basic information, just *don't take too literally what you don't see!*


## FALLS

It's late June on the Missinaibi River in Northern Ontario. For more than an hour the six canoeists have been intimidated by the awesome roar of Thunderhouse Falls--a canoe length slot in hard granite through which the entire volume of the Missinaibi thunders fearfully. Immediately beyond Thunderhouse falls are two more substantial falls of near equal fury. The total drop is more than 40 feet!

In the turmoil below Thunderhouse falls stands "conjuring house"-- a solitary vertical pillar of stone which was once held in awe and superstition by the local Indians. The men are excited. They are about to experience the highlight of their trip.

The Ontario trip guide indicates the one mile portage begins at the head of a small rapid on the west bank. Information received from previous parties who've run the river suggest the portage is well marked...and well used! Everyone fully understands the dangers of "getting too near the falls".

As the men approach the small rapid above the falls they spot the portage marker on the left. But the white water beyond looks easy and there's a large pool below--plenty of room to "pull out".

The trip leader starts down first. The rapid is easy, all goes as expected. He paddles the length of the pool and puts ashore a safe distance above the falls. Then he prepares to carry gear and canoe up the steep bank to the portage trail above. In a moment the second canoe snugs to shore against the first with the third boat close behind. The result is a classical canoe jam-up--everybody falling over each other and everything. Disgusted and impatient, one canoe decides to paddle out into the pool to wait, and perhaps get a better photograph of the head of the falls. The crew ferries into mid-stream and nonchalantly backpaddles to hold position. The bow man puts down his paddle and fetches his camera. He stands up in the canoe and begins · to shoot. Evidently entranced by the majesty of his surroundings and confident he's in full command, the stern man also rests his paddle. Neither one realizes the current is gently but forcefully carrying them towards the lip of the falls. Suddenly, there's an awakening! The men back paddle for dear life. Again and again. But it's too late; the silent strength of the slick tongue carries them into the rocky chasm below. One man swims to shore; the other perishes in the succeeding cascades.

Your initial reaction to the tragedy is probably, "don't mess around above waterfalls." But the error goes much deeper than that. First, the clearly marked portage began *above* the pool for a reason-- safety! Neither the trip guide nor map indicated it was okay to go beyond it. Nevertheless, it was safe enough to continue downstream into the pool if you pulled out well above the falls. The crew leader's real mistake was not that he went too far, it was allowing his less experienced crew to join him. However, he might still have saved the day had he advised everyone of the dangers and admonished them to "hang in tight", paddle upstream and "hold" to shore until each canoe was unloaded, etc. But he didn't and the result was disaster.

On a different river the scenario might have been played differently. Burr Falls on the Fond du Lac River begins in the middle of a low canyon which is preceeded by a quarter mile long pool. Above the pool is a short stretch of fast water with a small island at its head. A well marked portage begins just upstream of the island. (Note the similarity between this and Thunderhouse falls?)

Below the pool the river narrows and drops without warning. Once into the quickened flow and there's no escape--the canyon walls are sheer and at least a dozen feet high. Total drop is about 30 feet. I doubt you'd survive the fall!

Only the small rapid and quiet pool is evident from the top. When we arrived the wind was blowing strongly downstream and masked the sound of the fury below. We could hear nothing from our holding point on the island.

We put ashore on the island to study the map. We knew the falls was just below. Somehow, we'd missed the portage though we'd been searching diligently for it. The trip guide indicated the path was a few yards above our location on the east bank of the river. I searched downstream with binoculars. There was no hint of danger. All signs suggested we could proceed safely into the quiet pool. Perhaps it was the canyon wall that stopped us--and the knowledge that once committed, escape was impossible. Or maybe it was our "sixth sense" that suggested something wasn't right. But our real concern was the location of the portage--*above the island!*

We applied the rule, "If the carry starts here, there's a reason!" and backtracked accordingly. Had we violated our instincts I doubt you'd be reading these words now.

**PROCEEDING BEYOND MARKED PORTAGES ISN'T ALWAYS SAFE, EVEN IF IT APPEARS SO FROM ABOVE!**

# WIND

In case you missed a subtle point, the direction and intensity of the wind is critical in sensing--or failing to sense--a falls. A good upstream wind out of a canyon can make a three foot ledge sound like Niagara falls, and a downstream breeze can hush the most violent drop. So keep in touch with your map. *Know where the falls is!* And continually check the relative position of ground features to the river. If dead ahead the tree line abruptly drops off, there's a reason! Get ashore and check it out!

# DAMS

Dams are much more dangerous than falls. The hazard lies in the uniform drop and accompanying backroller (eddy) at their base. Float a small log over a dam and watch it tumble over and over, trapped in the turbulence below. Now picture your canoe doing the same thing. Broaching at the base of a dam may mean certain death. Your only recourse in an upset may be to abandon the craft *and your life jacket*, and swim down under the eddy to the current beneath--a frightening maneuver which calls for cool determination and a realization of what's happening.

If, heaven forbid, you find yourself being swept over a dam with no recourse but to obey the flow, then drive the canoe forward with all your strength. Your only salvation may be to get enough forward speed to breach the dangerous backroller. Running a dam--even a low one--is a life-threatening situation!

# STRAINERS

A strainer results when the river flows between the branches of a submerged tree. If you get sucked into one, there may be no escape-- especially if you're wearing loose clothing or a bulky life vest that catches in the debris.

Strainers are every bit as dangerous as dams--maybe more so because they don't look very ominous from above. As with other canoeing dangers, you're best bet is to avoid them in the first place--in this case with an evasive maneuver called the "back ferry".

## "THE BACK FERRY"

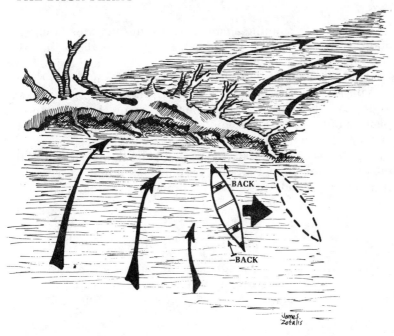

**Figure 17-1**
If you spot a strainer ahead, tuck your tail towards shore at an angle of
about 30 degrees, and **backpaddle!** Your net movement will be sideways.


If you come around a bend and spot a strainer ahead, tuck your
tail towards shore (the *inside* bend) at an angle of about 30 degrees,
and *backpaddle* for dear life. The combined vectors--forward velocity
of the river and reverse speed of the canoe, will move you sideways
towards shore (Fig. 17-1). This procedure is identical to that used by
old time ferry boat captains to cross strong currents. Only experience
can suggest the best ferry angle.

You can also spin the canoe around and cross ferry with your
nose upstream (the forward ferry). This maneuver is more powerful
than the back ferry and is the best way to cross fast currents that have
dangerous obstacles below.

Space does not permit treatment of evasive maneuvers and
paddling techniques. If you want a solid background in the basics of
canoeing white water, read and re-read Bob McNair's excellent book,
"Basic River Canoeing", published by the American Camping
Association, and "Path of the Paddle", by Bill Mason.

# CANYONS

The dangers in running a canyon are two-fold. Most obvious is the inability to "get out" if you capsize. Second, is the difficulty of determining the *real height* of waves from a vantage point on the canyon rim. Waves tend to flatten when viewed from above. And the higher you are the flatter they appear. Even a dozen feet makes a difference. A binocular (not monocular!) helps put things into proper perspective but still requires you to interpret the difference between "sheer magnification" and wave size.

There's no second guessing once you start into a canyon. Either you make it or you don't. Canyons are one place where the rule, "If in doubt, portage", should be applied religiously!

# ICE COLD WATER

Perhaps the greatest danger in canoeing northern rivers is capsizing in ice cold water. The hazard lies in the shock of initial dunking and the accompanying hypothermia which follows.

Hypothermia is a medical term which means "low temperature". Symptoms change as the temperature falls:

99-96 degrees F. -- Victim shivers intensely.
95-91 degrees F. -- Shivering worsens, slurred speech, amnesia.
90-86 degrees F. -- Shivering stops and muscles stiffen; skin becomes blue or puffy.
85-81 degrees F. -- Increased severity of the above symptoms
80-78 degrees F. -- Unconsciousness, erratic heartbeat.
Below 78 degrees F. -- Death.

Until recently it was impossible to obtain low reading thermometers capable of monitoring progressive stages of hypothermia. Now you can get two accurate models from Indiana Camp Supply, Inc. P.O. Box 344, Pittsboro, IN 46167. A hypothermia thermometer is a useful addition to any first-aid kit.

Canoe upsets invariably occur in rapids where even a good life jacket won't always keep your head above water. So you can't assume the recommended "huddle" position to conserve body heat and wait patiently in the freezing froth for a friendly watercraft to speed to your rescue. Every second is precious. You must get to shore quickly-- a feat that's next to impossible if your arms and legs are immobilized by cold.

Layered woolens covered with waterproof nylon help conserve body heat both in and out of the water, but not nearly enough. Only a neoprene wet suit cuts the cold and keeps it out. Wet suits, however, are uncomfortable, time-consuming to put on and take off, and generally impractical under typical field conditions. Far better to wear the time-proven woolens--and your life vest, and not capsize at all!

An ice water dunking requires immediate treatment, *even if the victim disagrees.* Dr. Forgey, in his excellent book, "Wilderness Medicine", (See Appendix D) recommends the following procedure:

> "Remove the victim from wind and place him in the best shelter available. Replace wet clothing with dry clothing if possible. Insulate the victim from the ground and add heat...strip the victim and place him in a sleeping bag with a stripped rescuer. A hypothermia victim alone in a well insulated sleeping bag will simply stay cold. If he is conscious, give him warm drinks* and candy or sweetened foods. If no sleeping bag or fire is available, have the party huddle together. Avoid use of alcohol..."

The one real danger in treating hypothermia is "after shock"--a condition which may result if the outside of the body is warmed too fast. The effect is to dilate the surface blood vessels and thereby shuttle cold blood from the extremeties into the already cold interior core of the body. Since the temperature of the blood in the hands and feet may be dozens of degrees below that of the inner body, the consequences of pumping it to the heart and brain are obvious--death in a matter of minutes!

A hypothermic must be re-warmed gradually and evenly. Strenuous exercise as advised by some "experts" may speed death by placing an additional load on the heart. A hot drink and the sleeping bag treatment is the most reliable procedure.

It's interesting to note that Dr. Richardson--surgeon on Sir John Franklin's ill fated journey up the Hood River (N.W.T.) in 1821,

*Here a thermos of tea or coffee is indispensable. Firing a stove and waiting for water to boil may be a luxury you can't afford.

prescribed the sandwich treatment for a Voyageur who had capsized in a bad rapid. The account reads: "...Belanger was suffering extremely, immersed to his middle in the center of a rapid, the temperature of which was very little above the freezing point, and the upper part of his body covered with wet clothes, exposed in a temperature not much above zero, to a strong breeze...By the direction of Dr. Richardson, he was instantly stripped, and being rolled up in blankets, two men undressed themselves and went to bed with him; but it was some hours before he recovered his warmth and sensations." (From "Narrative of a Journey to the shores of the Polar Sea in the years 1819, 20, 21, by Sir John Franklin. Charles E. Tuttle Co., Rutland, Vermont and Tokyo, Japan.)

The sad irony is that Arthur Moffat (see Chapter 4--LOOSE THREADS) might have survived his dunking on the Dubawnt river had his crew understood the nature of hypothermia. Evidently Moffat's friends believed his authoritative cries of "I'm okay, I'm okay", and simply placed him in a sleeping bag inside his tent. There was no "sandwich treatment" or hot drink.

## POOR COMMUNICATION/NO SUPPORT CANOE

Two inexperienced canoeists were lining their 18 foot Grumman around a rapid on the Kanaaupscow River in Quebec, when without a word each simultaneously let go his line momentarily. The canoe, now free, slipped quietly away and out of sight down the rapid. The disgruntled canoeists walked the shoreline of the river and carefully searched the rapid for signs of the canoe. Nothing! Did the craft dive for the deep currents and become wedged between rocks? The pair sat down at the edge of the pool below the drop to contemplate their misfortune when the canoe, bone dry and virtually undamaged, mysteriously floated to shore within a few feet of where they were sitting. Joyously, the men climbed aboard and smugly waited for their friends upstream to finish the half hour long arduous task of lining the rapid.

A similar case ended differently: Two young men traveling alone on a remote river in the Northwest Territories, halted their canoe near a small island to check a rapid below. Each man had a firm hold on some willow branches which jutted from the island. Cautiously, they let the canoe downstream, working their way from branch to branch. Then without a sound, each man let go his branch and leaned over to grab another. The unbalanced canoe capsized and floated away, leaving the men stranded on the island without food, shelter, or warm clothing.

The pair were rescued two weeks later only because the HBC manager in Yellowknife persuaded them to register their route with the RCMP before they left. When the two were long overdue, the mounties initiated an air search.

In each case, the near tragedy could have been averted if each man had simply told the other what he planned to do *before* he did it. In the first example there was a rescue canoe which could have chased the lost boat if necessary. In the second case there wasn't. The far north is no place for fuzzy thinkers or those who travel without a support crew. Two canoes are the *minimum* for safety; three are much better!

## CAPSIZING ON OPEN WATER

It was early July when the two inexperienced teenagers set their 17 foot canoe into the icy waters of Reindeer Lake (Saskatchewan). For several days they paddled along without incident, gaining confidence as the hours passed. When a substantial tail wind came up the boys rejoiced and adjusted their course towards open water to take advantage of it. Soon they were riding the waves, surfing along, making wonderful time. Unaware of the dangers, they let the wind push them farther and farther into the teeth of the manacing sea. When at last the pair realized their predicament, they were a half-mile from land. They panicked--tried to turn upwind, and capsized. Though both wore life jackets, one lad died in the frigid water--a victim of hypothermia. The other boy made it safely to shore where he was later rescued by fishermen.

Their mistakes included traveling without a support canoe, getting too far from land, mis-judging the weather, and inexperience in handling a canoe in rough water. Capsizing far from shore on a rolling lake is serious, especially if the water is very cold. Under these conditions even a support canoe may not be able to help: Likely they'll be too busy attending to their own problems.

The recommended procedure for running rough open water is to stick tightly together, parallel, one or two canoe lengths apart. If a canoe upsets, your first responsibility is to get your friends out of the cold water immediately. The "canoe over canoe rescue" touted by the Red Cross and Boy Scouts is generally impossible to perform in a running sea. Far better to forget about the swamped canoe and gear and put your efforts into rescuing the paddlers.

If there's only one support canoe, rescue may mean throwing some packs overboard to provide room--and essential freeboard--for the victims. If you have two support crafts, they can work as a team and share responsibility. In either case, there's real danger of swamping the upright canoes when those in the water climb aboard. And even if you are able to perform a safe rescue, it's doubtful you'll ever recover the gear you tossed into the lake.

The worst canoeing disaster of the decade occurred on June 12,

1978, when four replica North canoes (20-24 foot freight canoes of 18th Century vintage) carrying a total of 31 people, capsized in four to six foot waves at the headwaters of the Ottawa river. Twenty-seven teenagers and their four adult leaders had just embarked on a 16 day canoe trip into the wilds of Quebec when it happened. Far from shore, one canoe capsized in the big waves, spilling its occupants into the icy water. A second canoe tried to help but it too upset. The remaining two canoes put ashore to dump packs then set out to rescue those still in the water. But the victims panicked and capsized the canoes as they climbed into them. Thirteen people died!

In retrospect: All wore life jackets and were good swimmers. The boys were reasonably skilled in the art of paddling and self-rescue.

There are no patent procedures guaranteed to save you in a rough water upset. Staying ashore and calmly waiting for "the weather to pass" is your best insurance.

## FAILURE TO HEED THE ADVICE OF LOCALS

Grand Rapids on the Mattagami River (northern Ontario) is more than a mile long and one fourth as wide. When the water is high the rapid is quite lively and produces a hollow drone which can be heard for several miles upstream. Nevertheless, the rapid is relatively easy if you choose the correct side of the river and stay alert.

When the two young lads on their way to James Bay came to the rapid, the bowman stood up, cast a long glance downstream, and puposely selected a route *opposite* that advised by local residents of Smoky Falls, some 30 miles upstream. Their aluminum canoe went over a ledge, swamped, and wrapped around a rock. Unable to salvage their canoe or gear, the boys abandoned their trip and walked the shoreline back to town, which took them nearly three days.

The antithesis is taking the advice of local residents too literally. Our two day portage on the Steel River (Chapter 15--THE JOY OF SOLOING) bears testimony to what can happen when you seek advice from a non-canoeist. Nevertheless, you can get reliable information from non-paddlers if you compare the input from several sources. For example, Santoy Falls was a major obstacle on our 1981 descent of the Steel River. We'd heard the falls was a killer and that the portage around it began dangerously close to the drop. Naturally we were intimidated by this information so we asked some fishermen on the lake about its location. Seven of the eight people we surveyed authoritatively reported that the carry began just west of the falls in a small bay. It did, and there were no problems.

## POOR PLANNING/INEXPERIENCE

It was 1968 and the man was a high school teacher with a free summer. His friend was a business man who had precisely 14 days vacation. The idea was to paddle about 200 miles of Manitoba's South Seal River. To save time, they'd drive to the Pas* then fly commercial air to Lyn Lake. There, they would charter a float plane to the "put in". The canoe would be sent by rail from their home in Minneapolis to Lyn Lake ahead of time. Fast and neat; the canoe would be waiting for them when they arrived. Or so they thought!

First stop, Lyn Lake train station. "What, no canoe?" Checking revealed that customs authorities had impounded the craft for payment of duty. "The canoe was being shipped to a Canadian, *wasn't it?*" No matter, the misunderstanding could be cleared up in a few days. *A few days* indeed! Precious time was ticking by. The business man didn't have "a few days".

So the men went shopping for a canoe. A thorough search turned up the only canoe in town--an old but relatively sound 17 foot wood/canvas Chestnut. The craft weighed at least 100 pounds, had a deep fin keel, and a square stern. But it *was* a canoe, and it cost only 80 dollars!

The teacher was hopping mad. Everything was going wrong. He looked at the bright yellow fabric cover he had made for his Alumacraft. It wouldn't fit the Chestnut, but it might come in handy for *something!*

Problems compounded from the very outset. Instead of averaging 25 miles per day as they had anticipated, they were making only 10. They had the wrong footwear, the wrong raingear, the wrong canoe...and the wrong attitude. Only the teacher's insistence that they bring a small Optimus stove saved the day. Without it they'd have been miserable in the incessant rain.

What worried them most was that they were falling drastically behind schedule. So to compensate they took to paddling well into the evening. They grew impatient and careless. On the ninth day around nine p.m. they encountered *the* rapid. It looked easy enough from the top so they decided to run it blind. The moment of reckoning came quickly: man-sized rollers at the bottom swamped the canoe and the boulder field took out the keel and one gunnel. The old Chestnut was wrecked beyond repair. The trip was over!

The men salvaged the gear and struggled to shore. An inventory of their food revealed there was a seven days supply. The river was too fast and narrow to land a float plane on, so the next day they carried their outfit about six miles overland to a small lake that had a sand

*"The Pas" is located on Canada highway 10, about 150 miles south of Flin Flon.

beach. There they devised elaborate signals--made a huge SOS on the beach and cut flags from their yellow canoe cover. And each afternoon the men flashed their signal mirror hopefully across the empty skies.

Twenty-one days later they were picked up by a search and rescue plane. It was the flash of light and yellow flags that caught the pilot's eye. "Good thing you boys registered with the mounties...otherwise we'd never have found you," the pilot told them.

Total cost of the rescue came to nearly 3200 dollars (a fortune in 1968), which the men paid sheepishly but gladly.

The errors speak for themselves: inexperience in running white water, impatience, poor planning, and lack of a support crew. The one thing the men did right was to register their trip with the authorities. Wilderness rivers bear no malice towards the unprepared, but neither do they grant immunity from error!

## FOREST FIRES

As a forester in Oregon many years ago, I fought several good sized fires. But I've never been canoeing when the woods were ablaze all around me. If you're caught in the canoe country with a raging fire in progress, here's the recommended "survival procedure" according to Walt Tomascak, Fire Management Officer for Minnesota's Superior National Forest:

"If you smell smoke or see a convection column rising in the distance, remain calm and evaluate the safety of your position. Generally, fires move in a predictable direction so you may be able to outflank it by moving perpendicular to its path, that is so long as you can stay on or near water. If the fire has reached the lake you're on, move to the opposite shore and stay near the water's edge. If the shoreline is burning all around, get out in the center of the lake and stay there. Wet down your clothes, hat, and life jacket. Remove *all* nylon clothing! Flaming nylon produces the most severe burns--instantly!

If sparks are flying badly, overturn your canoe in the middle of the lake and get under it for protection. The canoe will retain a large air bubble inside in which you can breathe and talk normally.

An intense crown fire often generates its own winds. In extreme cases these winds may reach speeds in excess of 100 miles an hour! If that happens you may be in trouble whatever you do. Generally though, you should be able to survive even very large fires if you're at least 100 yards from a burning shoreline.

I would not recommend leaving your canoe under any conditions since it offers a means of eventual escape as well as protection from radiant heat. Its best use as I've suggested, is as a heat and ember shield when overturned in the water.

Under some conditions, forest fires may jump one-half mile or more--another reason why you should stay put near a large body of water. If you must travel through an area that is burning, wait until the fire activity is lowest, which is generally late evening through mid-morning."

**Figure 17-2**
Bob O'Hara pushes through ice on Aberdeen Lake (N.W.T.) on July 17, 1969.

## ICE

You can portage or line around difficult rapids or wait out a running sea, but the only thing you can do about an ice-choked lake is stay put and pray for a good wind to break things free. Sometimes the wind comes, sometimes it doesn't. If it doesn't, you wait, gripe, and exhaust your food supply for no gainful purpose.

In 1969, Bob O'Hara* and crew flew into the junction of the Thelon and Hanbury rivers with the intent of paddling the Thelon to the community of Baker lake. On July 17, they nosed their canoes into Aberdeen Lake...and broken ice, four feet thick! Aberdeen was jammed shut. It would take a strong north wind to blow it free.

*See Bob's testimonial in Chapter five.

For two days the men made what time they could by skirting the shore, sliding, dragging, and pushing their canoes over the ice. Tempers flared, muscles ached; everyone became physically and emotionally exhausted. Their weary bodies needed huge quantities of precious food to maintain the pace. They were making no time at all and were consuming food at an alarming rate. Bob stopped the work and put everyone on half rations.

The men waited. And waited. Entertainment was provided by the short wave radio they carried. "I remember sitting on a big rock staring into the sky while the radio blasted out the incredible news we'd landed two men on the moon. And here we were landlocked by a mini-glacier," said Bob.

Ten days passed and still no wind. Then the crew crossed paths with a wildlife biologist and eskimo who were also iced in. The worry now was food. Would there be enough to last the trip?

Fortunately, the crew had a rifle which the eskimo used to kill a caribou. The six men consumed the entire animal in less than two days!

Finally, on the twelfth day, wind broke the ice free and the men continued on to Baker Lake. "We hit an ice fog on Shultz Lake," recalls Bob. "Visibility was zero so we ran compass and dodged floes the whole way. It was pretty tricky...and dangerous weaving between those heaving ice masses."

O'Hara followed the ice out of Shultz Lake--an exhilerating experience. He said "It was a helluva ride! We clicked off 60 miles in four hours--took us two days to do that on the Dubawnt (river). The run was so fast we damn near passed Baker Lake right by."

No one can give you advice on how to handle an ice-locked lake. It's something you look at, think on, then act...or sit as the case may be. There are hazards: Most serious is getting behind schedule and perhaps running out of food down the pike. On a very long trip, your concern may be finishing up before you're pelted by the snows of winter.

Traveling in broken ice is a perilous procedure. Leads open and close quickly as wind blows the ice around. If you get caught between floes--a real possibility if the wind is up--there may be no escape. And the effects of capsizing in frigid water are obvious. For all these reasons, you'll plan your trip to ensure ice-free water. And if your plans are thwarted by a quirk of nature, just be sure to carry enough food (10 days supply is recommended) to weather the inconvenience. Bring along an extra measure of patience too, plus a flexible schedule so you can complete the run without rushing mindlessly through it and thereby endangering your safety.

**Figure 17-3**
A 20 Foot Grumman canoe stranded on the tidal flats of Wager Bay. Tides
to 14 feet inundate this area every 12 hours.

# TIDES

The Kellet River begins about 20 miles north of Wager Bay at the
edge of the Arctic Circle. It's a remote challenging river that to date
has not been canoed. The problem is ice. Lots of it. Bob O'Hara and a
friend attempted the river in their 20 foot Grumman canoe in 1980, but
were unsuccessful.* The path to the Kellet remained ice-choked the
entire season.

Bob also experienced unusual tides in the area. "I didn't have an
up-to-date tide table, so we used what we had," he commented. "One
afternoon we stopped for lunch on a rocky outcrop in Wager Bay, tied
the canoe to a boulder then went off to explore. When we returned a
few hours later the tide had gone out. I mean *really* out! There was a
half-mile of huge boulders between the canoe and open water. So we
just sat and waited for the water to return."

O'Hara learned that tides to 14 feet inundate Wager Bay every 12
hours. After their first "tide-bound" experience, the two men made it a
practice to always stop (and camp) on a high hill that had a near
vertical drop to the sea. "That way we could lower the canoe to the
water if necessary--like dropping into a swimming pool", said Bob.

O'Hara also discovered that tide water sometimes moves rapidly
and forcefully. "Once on a side trip down river we lined around a good
sized ledge. Later, when we followed the tide back upstream, we rode
a full blown rapid, hell bent for leather. The ledge was completely
washed out!"

If Bob O'Hara had been new to the arctic, this episode might have
ended tragically. Bob's best advice? Get a current tide table and learn
to use it. And bring an accurate watch!

---

*Bob originally planned to canoe the river with a crew of six in two 20 foot canoes, but
he lost four men during the final planning stages. His partner for the trip was an
experienced canoeist and an M.D.

# LINING

The object of lining is to work the canoe downstream around a bad rapid--one which you don't want to paddle or portage. One person controls the bow line, the other the stern. Together you walk along the shore and snake the canoe *slowly and carefully* around obstacles (rocks and ledges) in the water. Steering is accomplished by pulling in or playing out the appropriate rope. A tug on the bow line while releasing the stern sets the canoe at an angle to the current and allows the side wash to push it into mid-stream. Doing the opposite snubs the boat to shore.*

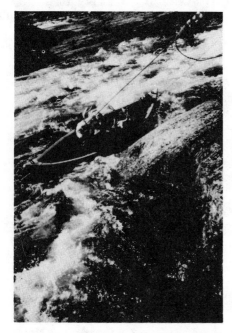

**Figure 17-4**
Lining a canoe around a ledge on the Hood River (N.W.T.) "Things aren't always as easy as you'd like."

An aluminum canoe with a deep fin keel will usually scoot right out into the river when you set it at the proper "ferry angle". But a Royalex or fiberglass boat with no keel and rockered ends has little surface area to give the current good purchase (a plus when running rapids) and so often stays put. Then, generous shoves, kicks, and an occasional cuss word are necessary to coax the canoe into the mainstream.

---

*Keep your rope loosely coiled so you can toss it to your partner with a minimum of fuss when the occasion demands. And don't put monkey fists or knots on the end of your ropes; they'll catch between rocks and snag.

Canoeing texts make lining sound like a lark. It isn't! More canoes are probably damaged (or lost!) on northern rivers due to errors in lining than to any other cause. The problem stems from letting the tail of the craft get too far out in the current as you work the canoe downstream. Once the canoe turns broadside to the river, you're done!

Successful lining requires team coordination and a shoreline which is relatively free of vegetation. If you've got to pick your way between over-hanging trees you might as well portage. Lining down a major rapid--one which will eat up your canoe if you goof, takes practice and patience. It's not a skill you can learn from a text book!

**Figure 17-5**
Tracking is the opposite of lining.

## TRACKING

"Tracking" is the opposite of lining. Here, the idea is to haul the canoe *upstream*. The rules are the same as for lining except the ends of the boats are reversed and an "upstream ferry angle" (stern tucked to shore) is maintained.

# SALVAGE

"It had been only four days since our four man canoe team arrived by helicopter at the headwaters of the South Nahanni River. Gordon Lightfoot and I were lining his new Old Town Voyageur canoe through some very turbulent water down a drop between two boulders when without warning, the canoe spun broadside to the current and swamped. We pulled the packs from the canoe just as it submerged and watched, horrified, as the canoe bent backwards and wrapped tightly around the boulder. All that was visible was one gunnel and side of the hull. This demoralizing scene brought to mind Gordon's hit song "The Wreck of The Edmund Fitzgerald", but in this situation it was our own wreck and a hopeless predicament.

We spent the balance of the day trying to salvage the boat but it was no use. The combined strength of four men, a strong rope, pry bar (log) and sophisticated application of all the physics we knew, was of no avail. After hours of frustrating failure, we gloomily retreated to the head of the rapid to set up camp and develop our strategy for the immediate future. We were now four men with one canoe. Things couldn't have looked worse!

It was then that we met a party of five canoes led by Dr. Brian Gnauck of Marquette, Michigan. Now there was new hope. Could the combined strength of 14 men pull the canoe free? I remained skeptical. Fourteen or forty--what difference could it make?

But Fred Nelson, one of the new arrivals, produced a block and tackle which we hoped could provide the edge. We combined forces and attached the block and tackle to our bow line which we had wrapped around the hull. The idea was to pull the canoe away from the boulder against the full force of the current--a near impossible task without the aid of pulleys. Perhaps if we also pryed with a large log as we worked the winch line...But I was pessimistic. Even if we succeeded in retrieving the canoe it would be irrepairable. Or so I thought.

Together we pulled, pryed, pulled some more. In an instant it was over and the canoe popped free, like a cookie from a mold. We pulled the canoe quickly up the rocky shore then watched in amazement as its grossly distorted

**Figure 17-6a**
Paul Pepperall (L) prys while Ted Anderson (center) and Gordon Lightfoot (R) use a large stick as a tournaquet to shorten the rope.

Photo: Fred Gaskin

Photo: Fred Gaskin

**Figure 17-6b**
Ted Anderson (L) and Gordon Lightfoot (center) attempt to lift the canoe while Paul Pepperall prys from the upstream side.

**Figure 17-6c**
Canoe has been recovered and has returned to its original shape. Only a slight wrinkle in the side gives any indication the canoe was abused.

Photo: Mark Schieder

**The South Nahanni River Recovery
(1980)**

shape, now free from the pressure of the pounding water, slowly returned to its original form. Only a small wrinkle on each side of the hull gave any indication the canoe had been 'abused'.

Truely, ABS Royalex is a miracle material."

Fred Gaskin
South Nahanni river (1980)

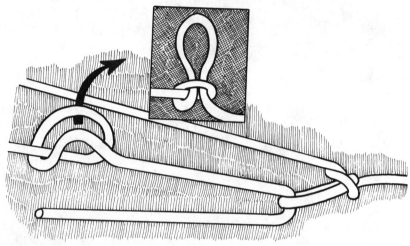

1.   Make "second loop" in "free end" of rope as shown.

2.   Pass free end through this loop.

3.   Pull free end of rope to winch out canoe. Additional loops may be added if necessary to gain a greater mechanical advantage.

**Figure 17-7**
The multiple power-cinch makes a powerful winch for retrieving a pinned canoe. See chapter 12 for instructions for making the basic knot.

If you pin a canoe on a boulder on a remote river, you've just got to find a way to free it. If weight and space is a minimal concern, your best bet is to carry some bona-fide retrieval gear--block and tackle, one or two hundred feet of braided three-eighths inch rope, etc. The water pressure on a pinned canoe is at least a ton, which means you'll need a pulley with a mechanical advantage of three to one or better to budge it. If you don't have pulleys you should rig a *multiple power cinch* like the one shown in figure 17-5. This hitch makes a powerful winch despite the great amount of friction in the system.

Salvage ropes should always be attached *around the hull* of the canoe--never to seats, thwarts, or lining rings which may break loose. Position ropes on the canoe to take advantage of the force of the current. Often, you can free a pinned canoe by jockying it around only a few inches.

Nearly every north country canoeist has at least one horror story to tell about a rapid that was "almost lineable". The Gaskin/South Nahanni near disaster is not unique. My files are filled with similar cases.

Wilderness canoeists know they're "tempting the patience of the river" when they line a difficult drop, so they proceed with caution and give the river the respect it demands.

# 18

# Barren Land Travel

If you've never been to the barrens you may wonder why anyone would choose to canoe there. After all, what could be attractive about a place that's frozen solid four-fifths of the year and covered with perma-frost the rest? A stark forbidding land of lichen-covered hills, devoid of trees, save for the enduring scrub willow and tag alder; where ice, polar gales, pounding rapids, and near freezing water are expected hazards; where isolation is absolute, and danger, physical hardship and uncertainty are daily companions. A silent awesome scape of endless tundra where skill, common sense, resourcefulness...and even luck, are essential ingredients for making a safe "adventure-free" canoe trip.

Just why would anyone want to paddle an arctic river?

Reasons are diverse and often impossible to relate. There is the great thrill of seeing and photographing some of the largest and most interesting animals in North America. The barrens are home to the solitary tundra grizzly--which, though often portrayed as forboding and aggressive, is usually quite timid in the presence of man; the dazzling white arctic fox and wolf, the shaggy muskox--remnant from a prehistoric age, and the plentiful caribou.

Along the Arctic Ocean there is an abundance of unusual marine life too. From mid-July to the end of August--heart of the canoeing season--you may encounter herds of playful whales, seals, and even a walrus or polar bear.

The bird life is equally fascinating. There are bald and golden eagles, peregrine falcons, whose diving speed has been clocked at over 100 miles an hour! Gyrfalcons, snowy owls, jaegers, fulmars, terns, ptarmigan, kittwakes, ivory gulls, loons, and many more. In all, nearly 300 species of avions call the barrens home, making this area one of the richest havens anywhere for bird fanciers.

Fishing is inevitably a prime attraction. Even a rank amateur with rod and reel can, within an hour, catch his daily limit of grayling, char, or giant lake trout.

Everywhere in this vast roadless region there are bountiful fish, birds, and animals. The tundra is a mecca for the biologist, birder, angler, and for everyone who feels an affinity for the unspoiled wild.

As inseparable from the land as its fish and wildlife, is the "Inuit" or Eskimo. Though now confined to outpost settlements, these once nomadic people still depend heavily on fish and wildlife resources for their livelihood. They routinely hunt caribou, seal, and bear, and build their ingenius igloos during their winter travels.

Arctic explorers have described the Inuit as "unspoiled man". Carefree, proud, and unquestionably honest, these kindly people willingly share their homes and sustenance with complete strangers in need. Traveling with an Inuit family for a few hours or a few days provides an eye-opening glimpse into a world forgotton by the hustle and greed of modern man.

Some tundra rivers abound in eskimo sign--decades old tent rings (circles of water-smoothed rock once used to hold caribou skin tents in place), "inukshuks" (human likenesses made by piling rocks designed to scare caribou towards awaiting hunters), food cache's, and artifacts. The thrill of camping at a traditional Inuit site or of finding relics is profound and everlasting. Genuine artifacts are of course protected from theft and vandalism by Canadian regulations, but no self-respecting canoeist would think of stealing or obliterating them.

You cannot canoe an artic river without developing a deep concern and respect for the land and its inhabitants.

Not to be overlooked is the challenge of canoeing a brawny, demanding waterway. Though many arctic routes are technically no more difficult than ones deep within the timberline, they are generally free from the traffic of other humans. To canoe the barrens is to be utterly alone and dependent upon your own resources and knowledge. And it is this feeling of self-sufficiency, of individual challenge, that to many is the greatest lure. The rivers of the high arctic are to the wilderness canoeist as are the Himalayas to the obsessive mountaineer. To experience the solitude, the dangers, the raw untamed beauty...and to live in harmony with the land without incident is for many the supreme accomplishment.

## SKILLS

There are few "second chances" in the barrens: A serious map reading error may send you scurrying down the wrong waterway into subsequent disaster. Overturning in a rapid or swamping far from shore in the rollers of an icy wind-tossed lake, could cost you your canoe, your equipment, and possibly your life! A polar gale may keep you pinned down for days, at best playing havoc with your schedule, at worst shredding your tents into a mass of useless nylon. In the arctic there is no turning back once the float plane drops you off. The only way "out" us usually down river!

**Figure 18-1**
The Barrens promises the grace of beauty and the virtue of solitude. A
remote campsite on the Hood River, N.W.T.

For these reasons only the best canoeists with the best skills and
equipment should canoe the northern reaches of the Northwest
Territories, Alaska, and Labrador. To suggest otherwise is to
minimize the hazards and invite disaster.

If you want to paddle above the timberline and are uncertain of
your skills, make your first trip with an experienced guide. Scores of
routes are advertised in the classified pages of outdoor magazines,
notably CANOE. Most of the trips are led by highly experienced
arctic travelers who understand the need for caution. If you have a
good basic canoeing background, can turn the other cheek to bad
weather and persistent bugs, have a high tolerance for the pain of
portaging long distances and paddling many hours without sleep,
you'll get along fine under a competent tutor. But select your guide
with care. Get testimonials from others who have canoed with him or
her. And shun large parties! Any group larger than eight is unwieldly
on a dangerous river. The logistics of getting everyone through the
rapids safely, of maintaining effective control between canoes in
heavy seas, of locating enough level tent sites, etc., becomes
increasingly more difficult as the group size enlarges. As I've

suggested in Chapter Three ("Picking A Crew), four or six people is about right, with six being the logical choice for safety.

Some specific canoe skills you should master include:

## THE FORWARD AND BACK FERRY

These tactics are essential when negotiating rapids and "muscle" sections of arctic rivers. When the river races violently, you'll need to stay on the inside of all bends (the place of slowest flow and usually, lowest waves), to avoid being swept into the violent outer currents. If the river is very wide, staying inside curves may mean making frequent cross-stream ferry's in accellerated water. Ferrying across a quarter mile wide fast moving river while a substantial rapid looms ahead, requires good judgement and precise control of your canoe. A foul up and subsequent broadside in icy mid-stream can be disastrous.

Practice ferry maneuvers *with your partner* before the wheels roll north!

## EDDY TURNS

Eddy's are a safety valve: They provide a place to "take out" above a falls or rapid, a spot to rest before you proceed into dangerous waters below. Be well practiced in both bow upstream and bow downstream eddy-in, eddy-out procedures (See *Basic River Canoeing*, by Bob McNair or *Path of the Paddle*, by Bill Mason).

You need a good coordinated canoe team to paddle an arctic river. A skilled bow partner is a necessity, not a luxury. You can't horse a heavily loaded canoe around boulders by sweeping or prying from the stern. Both canoe partners should be darn good!

## EQUIPMENT

Arctic rivers seldom give second chances so there is no room for equipment failure. Canoes, tents, clothing, and footwear which is suitable for use "down home" may not be the best choice for the demanding conditions of the barrens. Take canoes, for example: The testimonials you read in Chapter five all honestly suggest that above all you need a very strong high volume canoe. Considerations regarding speed, light weight, and aesthetics, are all secondary to the basic premise that *your canoe is your lifeline!* It must get you safely through mile after mile of punishing rock fans, across heavily running seas and through difficult rapids. The water temperature on Point Lake at the start of our 1982 Hood River (Northwest Territories) trip was a scant 39 degrees Farenheit. It never warmed beyond 47 degrees on the Hood river. An "upsetting experience" cannot be taken lightly when you're working with such low water temperatures. This is why a high volume intensely seaworthy canoe (and by this I mean a boat that keeps the water out!) is the logical choice.

Some canoe writers suggest using a fine-lined skinny canoe with full fabric cover for negotiating arctic waterways. Certainly such a boat may be used to advantage if your route contains few rapids or rapids which are wide open and uncomplicated. More than likely, however, you'll encounter nicely runnable drops which simply require intensive maneuvering--something that may be difficult if you have a canoe that "doesn't turn". Canoe stems--especially square ones--may take a terrific beating in the rocky arctic shallows, another consideration when selecting your canoe.

The ice cold water of a tundra river dictates that you use extreme caution when running rapids. Even if your fabric canoe cover keeps the water out, the bow person is apt to get drenched in the bigger waves, a major reason why the vote goes to canoes with enough forward volume to keep the partner up front reasonably dry.

**Figure 18-2**
The Cannondale Aroostook

# TENTS

As I suggested in Chapter 10, your tents should be large enough for prolonged comfort and to insure that there will be sufficient shelter to sleep the crew if one tent is destroyed in a gale or lost in an upset. This means three or four person (six feet by seven feet or larger) tents should be used to sleep each pair. Most important is a reliable high altitude design that will withstand persistent gale force winds.

Once, on our Hood River trip, we were tent bound for 62 hours-- pinned down by icy rain driven by an unrelenting wind which raged at 50 miles an hour. Fortunately, our Cannondale Aroostook tents never failed us.

Some of the best woodland tents just aren't windproof enough for use on the barrens. You might get away with a low-to-the-ground two person version of a good forest tent, but I don't recommend it. At the risk of snobbery I'll suggest that if you can't afford a good high altitude tent you probably can't afford to canoe in the barrens. The arctic is no place to second guess the weather and what it may do to your equipment.

## COOKWARE AND STOVES

Double up on cookware and stoves. Carry an extra back up set of both in another canoe, "just in case". And don't put all your stove fuel in the same boat. Allow *at least* one gallon of gasoline per week for a crew of four. If this sounds extravigant, remember that arctic waters are much colder than those in the South, and hence require more heat energy to boil.

## MEDICAL KIT

On the tundra, more than anywhere else, you should have a complete medical kit which includes a variety of wide spectrum perscription antibiotics. Shortly after the start of our Hood River trip I developed a throat so sore I could barely swallow my food. Fortunately, we carried a half dozen different antibiotics. The right drug seemed to be Erythromyacin which I took on a regular schedule for nearly a week. In a few days I was fine.

Stress to your family doctor that you will be *totally* isolated and you'll probably get the prescriptions you need. And be sure to carry enough tablets of each drug so that the affected person can rely on them for at least seven to ten days.

Equally important, make sure at least one member of the crew is skilled in the use of everything in the medical kit. On a long trip it's essential to have someone along who has much more than a casual acquaintance with intricate first-aid procedures.

With the exception of bandaids and moleskin, and the one instance mentioned above, I've never had to resort to the sophisticated underpinnings of a complete medical kit. Nonetheless, it's only common sense to be prepared! For kit examples and ideas see "Appendix D".

## CLOTHING

The suggestions I've given in Chapter 8 (Gearing Up), though quite complete, may be enhanced by these few considerations:

**Hats:** Bring an extra stocking cap--at least one or two extras for the crew. Warm headgear is essential in the artic and loss of a knit wool hat can be serious.

**Wool:** is the key word for everything, except long underwear which may be polypropylene or synthetic (but never cotton).

A windbreaker of some sort is absolutely essential in the arctic. A light zippered nylon shell with hood is all you need.

**Severe outerwear:** It's surprising how cold it can feel on the windblown tundra when the thermometer registers relative warmth. For example, I remember waiting out a fierce north wind on Takijaq Lake in the Northwest Territories while wearing the following: Thin wool long johns *and* Damart long underwear, wool shirt and trousers, down ski jacket and nylon wind shell, wool gloves and heavy stocking cap. Though the thermometer hovered at a balmy 43 degrees, I was only "comfortably" warm.

Perhaps it is the sustained exposure to chilling weather, or the physical let down which accompanies the end of a tough day. Whatever the reason, you need plenty of warm clothes for arctic canoe travel.

# MAP INTERPRETATION

The northern regions of the arctic generally receive less than a foot of annual rainfall, so except in spring when the ice goes out, water levels in the small rivers are apt to be too low for canoeing. Almost without exception, wherever a waterway narrows to a single line on a 1:250,000 scale map, you're in for a long walk. If your route includes many of these "single lines" be sure you have sturdy hiking boots. You'll need them!

# PORTAGING

If you're accustomed to portaging along well marked trails within the timberline, carrying your outfit overland on the tundra will be a unique and generally pleasant experience. Since there are no trees on the barrens, portage trails don't exist. You merely strike off cross country in the appropriate direction.

Where you must portage into a lake some distance away, your best bet is to follow a marked drainage (you better know how to interpret contour lines) or plot a compass bearing to the objective. As I've pointed out in Chapter 13, compasses are very reliable in the arctic as long as you apply the declination correctly.

When the direction of travel has been determined, the crew strikes off *together*, completing each leg of the carry in approximately half mile increments. At each rest stop the gear is placed in a tight pile, paddles strung through packstraps, blades skyward for good visibility (it really helps to have brightly painted blades). Then the crew returns for another load. The portage is continued in this manner--the crew moving in a continuous phalanx--until it is completed.

There are several important benefits to portaging as a group.

1) It prevents loss of gear in the drab heather of the tundra.

2) By maintaining an advancing set of markers you insure a direct bee line to your destination.

3) Overland travel is perhaps the only place where you might encounter a grizzly bear. Grizzly's as I've indicated, are usually quite timid and will ordinarily run from humans at the first whiff. But if you're upwind and the bear fails to sense your presence until the distance between you and him is a matter of feet, there can be dangerous consequences. By traveling together you keep the noise level--and "nose level" high. I might add that "bear bells", so popular in western mountains, can be used to advantage in the tundra if you're worried about a bear encounter.

In reviewing this chapter, my first impression was that I had been too dogmatic in my suggestions. For in most ways, canoeing an arctic river is no different than paddling any challenging waterway within the timberline. But as my thoughts began to meld I realized that the one thing which makes the barrens much different than most Canadian and U.S. routes, is remoteness. *Absolute awesome isolation!* This fact, coupled with the ice cold water temperatures and polar winds, demands that canoeists exercise extreme care.

Adopt a humble rather than "hotdog" approach to the water and weather; do your homework well; equip yourself with the best equipment you can afford; plan a route of resonable length, and you'll make an enjoyable "adventure-free" canoe trip. But watch out, arctic fever runs high. Tundra rivers are addictive: They'll capture your heart.

**Figure 18-3(a)**
Perhaps the most remarkable aspect of
the barren lands is the incredible wildlife encounters.

Photo: Bob Dannert

**Figure 18-3(b)**
The powerful surge of a northern
caribou thrashing across our path
on the Hood River.

Photo: Bob Dannert

**Figure 18-3(c)**
Fishing in the Northwest Territories is inevitably a prime attraction. Here, Bob Dannert holds
a 23 pound lake trout caught along the Hood
River.

# 19

# Some Interesting and Significant Canoe Trips of the Last Decade

In this chapter we'll follow three adventurers as they descend a major river in the Northwest Territories. Each story is written in the author's own hand and has a different emphasis and rationale.

In AH WILDERNESS, by John Turner, you'll experience the unspoiled beauty of the river and awaken to the harsh realities of its dangers.

Fred Gaskin's expedition from Lake Athabasca to Hudson Bay is less "free-swinging" and more historical: it parallels the 1893 route of J.B. Tyrrell and gives a valuable insight into the lives of the modern Eskimos which still inhabit the land.

Finally, there is Christie Buetow's dashing descent of the South Nahanni river--one of the most dangerous and spectacular in the far north. You'll view the awesome power of this great river through the eyes of an all women's team who had been told "it was for men only".

Read carefully between the lines and you'll discover again and again, the application (and occasional mis-application) of the skills and procedures I've suggested thoughout this book. You'll also come to realize that these modern day voyageurs have a deep love for the river and its human and animal inhabitants. They are sincere in their desire to protect wild places from the encroachment of civilization and mans' pollution. They subscribe dogmatically to the ethic "Leave only footprints"!

## ABOUT THE AUTHOR

John Turner holds advanced degrees in jurisprudence and civil law. He has served as Registrar General of Canada, Minister of Consumer and Corporate Affairs, Minister of Justice and Attorney General of Canada, and Minister of Finance. He resigned from Parliament in 1976 to join the law firm of McMillan, Binch in Toronto as a partner.

John Turner was a Canadian track and field champion, winning the 100-yard dash and 220-yard dash in 1948. In 1950-51 he was a member of the English Track and Field Team.

Despite his very active public life, John finds time to pursue his great love--canoeing the remote rivers of Northern Canada. Most unusual and commendable is that he commonly travels with his family--his wife Geills and four children, three of whom were with him on the Burnside--and who in 1980, when this trip was taken, ranged in age from 11 to 15.

That the Turners were the first family in history to descend the remote Burnside River from Kathawachaga Lake to Bathurst Inlet, alone makes this story significant. But more important than "being first" is this family's deep concern for the future of the river and others like it. Strands of "I care" are richly woven throughout this personal story of joy, hardship, and togetherness. (C.J.)*

## AH WILDERNESS

### by
### John Turner

We stood that August afternoon on the shores of Kathawachaga Lake, 60 kilometers south of the Arctic circle, watching the Cessna 206 take off. We were alone. And in the Great Barrens, one of the last really large areas of uninhabited virgin wilderness on the planet, the word "alone" has a meaning southerners can't know. The nearest trace of civilization--and of help, if it were needed--was Yellowknife, 480 kilometers to the southwest. Ahead of us lay our frontier canoe

*AH WILDERNESS, by John Turner, first appeared in the August issue of TORONTO LIFE Magazine. It has been slightly condensed here.

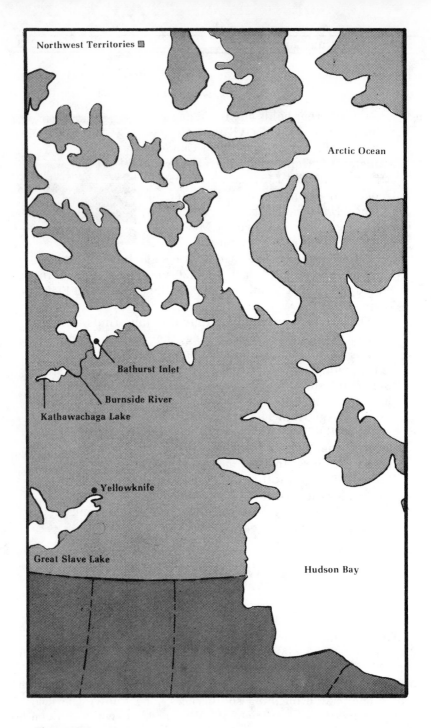

**Figure 19-1**
The remote waters of John Turner's expedition from Katawachaga Lake to
the Bathhurst Inlet via the Burnside River.

trip northward down the white water of the Burnside River, across the Arctic Circle, dropping 1,300 feet over 210 kilometers into Bathurst Inlet on the Arctic Ocean.

Only four parties of canoeists had ever done the river before. We were the first family to try it, just as we had been the year before on the Hanbury into the Thelon, and before that on the lower Lockhart, both demanding northern trips. Experience is vital. Maps are not always accurate and topography can change without warning. For us, this trip was the culmination of a lifetime of canoeing. I had canoed the rivers of Ontario and Quebec since I was seven. My wife, Geills had been taken as a girl down the waters of Manitoba and northwestern Ontario by her father and uncle. The three of our children who were with us, Elizabeth, then 15, Michael, 13, and David, 11, had been with us on many a trip. The other three in our party of eight were all experienced. Bob Engle, a frontier pilot and now president of Northwest Territorial Airways of Yellowknife, had canoed all over western North America since he was a boy. Two 17 year-old students from Winnipeg, Donald Konantz and Fraser Norrie, grew up on the summer waters of the Winnipeg River and the Kenora Rainy River district. Without this kind of collective experience, canoeing in the north can be hazardous. The terrain is magnificent, but unforgiving. Even in summer, there can be abrupt and dramatic temperature changes, including freezing. Fatigue and cold, causing hypothermia, can affect morale and judgement. Polar winds can be violent, and there are no trees for wood or shelter. The water temperature ranges from close to freezing in the larger lakes and rivers to about 13°C. An upset canoe too far from shore can mean death within five minutes, no matter how good the swimmer. Ravaging mosquitoes and black flies can drive people mad. The Barrens are also home to the grizzly. Bears are very rarely encountered, but there is no escape if a bear decides to charge. It can out run a horse. The Barrens, too, are still utterly isolated. Help is not available. Mistakes can quickly be fatal.

The eight of us would share each other's company for the next 10 days, until we reached the wildlife sanctuary on Bathurst Inlet where Glenn and Trish Warner ran their lodge for bird watchers and fishermen. We would see no one else. Our company would be the sky, the river, the birds, the caribou. The terrain was rugged; hills dotted with boulders, large areas of massive rocks and muskeg. There were stands of dwarf birch and scrub willow but no real trees. Everywhere there were Arctic flowers of extraordinary brilliance and delicacy.

As the noise of the Cessna faded away, we turned to setting up camp and preparing dinner. Wood was, of course, scarce, but we managed a fire and dined on steak, potatoes, onions, corn and applesauce. There was a steady northwest wind and the weather was cool at about 4°C which meant no bugs! We hit the tents at 9:30 p.m. It was still light.

The next morning, after a leisurely breakfast, we made our way down the lake to the mouth of the Burnside River. We were soon in swift water. As the speed picked up, we ran some white water and then a series of rapids. By late afternoon, still making very good time, we were approaching Bellanca Rapids. This was to be our first real test. We'd run several rapids during the day and our confidence was high. But the Bellanca proved too rough and we had to line the canoes. At one point we lined when we should have portaged. A better scouting job would have saved us some grief; one canoe swamped and we nearly lost some gear.

Below Bellanca we found a fine campsite at an esker, a glacial moraine of stratified gravel and sand. Eskers allow burrow areas for ground squirrels, the arctic white wolf and the occasional grizzly. Ground squirrels in turn attract bald and golden eagles, peregrine falcons and gyrfalcons. We dried our wet gear and swam in the bracing 10°C water. We had covered 32 kilometers on our first day down the Burnside.

The next day was beautiful, cloudless and warm at 13 to 18°C.. The river was fast, and we reached the mouth of the Cracroft River in about an hour. We were now in good-sized water. But the river was moving faster and dropping 10 feet a kilometer (about 16 feet per mile)--a very steep gradient. For the rest of the day we had to run white water and line our canoes. We were surrounded by high, treeless hills. The going became tricky when the river narrowed. We had to watch our own over-exuberance--risk-taking would be severely punished. We did not know what was ahead. Our map did not have much detail. Experience reminded us that failure to stop and walk along the river bank in places where the water got rough or the river bent out of sight, to inspect for impassable rapids, or even a waterfall, might prove fatal.

At some points the river was dropping so quickly that we could actually look downhill. The river banks sped by and we were gripped by the exhilaration of knowing we were committed and couldn't escape its rush. We were hitting standing waves three to four feet high at the end of every set of rapids caused by the fast water colliding with the slower water at the bottom. These waves were coming over the side of our canoes. We were taking in a lot of water.

When we camped that second night our gear was wet again from swamping, and we decided we would have to improve our packing. We had covered 40 kilometers.

We hadn't seen any game--only ducks, loons and geese. Later we were to see several small clusters of caribou, stragglers left behind from the huge late summer migration of the 150,000 head Burnside herd which had already passed on its way south.

The weather was blessed. Sunny, for the most part, and warm. For the next few days we ran a good deal of white water and slower pools. We did some fishing, caught a land-locked Arctic char, stopped for a ceremonial photo at the point below the junction of the Mara River where our best guess located the Arctic Circle. We enjoyed some magnificent scenery of massive, barren hills; from one campsite we climbed a hill and reached a promontory where we could see 16 kilometers downriver.

On the sixth day some of the realities of the north reasserted themselves. The Burnside was wide and slow with only occasional fast water. But as the afternoon came on, the river started to narrow and pick up speed, and we were forced to line more often. We had to bail out all three canoes. In a narrow passage, Fraser's canoe swamped and was carried onto a rock; we had a tough rescue from the rock to the bank of the river by line rope. Luckily, the weather was warm, otherwise we would have risked hypothermia. We lost our general reserve bag and all our cooking utensils.

Our trip was suddenly no longer a luxury paddle but a survival course. We were moving down difficult water. We were having to line the canoes more often, and we were becoming tired. My canoe, with Geills and David, nearly swamped once, but we got ashore. Too many encounters with standing waves as we came out of a series of connecting rapids had left us no chance to bail out the water. The river was becoming rougher and the banks higher. There was no landing in sight. Time was running out and the need to search for a campsite was becoming urgent. By the time we finally found one, up a steep 100-foot slope on an esker, we were all exhausted.

The weather had been good, but during the night it rained hard. We were being followed be a strong south wind; in the morning there was the smell of smoke from forest fires hundreds of kilometers to the south. It had turned cold, down to about 5°C, and we made a slow start. From the one pot that had survived, we had a double portion of oatmeal. We converted our reflector baking oven into a frying pan and cooked bacon, eggs, and some fish that Bob had caught the day before.

Our progress continued slow in breaking camp, and we didn't get started until afternoon. We had only 16 kilometers to go, but they were brutal. We ran our first set of rapids without trouble, but the river remained narrow, with many bends. We were forced to line our canoe repeatedly, and to portage once around high rocks.

We were losing our touch. We began to hit rocks. We were bailing constantly. Fatigue was lowering our performance. Our map and intuition told us we were coming close to the final gorge. We had to resist the urge, stemming from impatience, to run every set of rapids

**Figure 19-2**
John Turner and party line their canoes around a bad rapid on the lower
Burnside River N.W.T. Bow to Stern: John Turner, Robert E. Engle, Frazer
Norrie, Donald Konantz. Photo Credit: Geills Turner.

in sight. After one final long run, we reached the last safe spot before
the river narrowed and dropped 300 feet through a seven kilometer
gorge over a series of three waterfalls--including Burnside Falls--and
into the ocean.

At nine p.m. we set up camp on a rise above the river gorge and
dried our clothes, which were wet from swamping. The next day, a
long, six-kilometer portage would carry us past the falls and to the
Arctic Ocean itself.

The first kilometer or so of that portage proved very tough--
straight uphill. We reached the top of an esker and saw the valley
between Burnside Falls and the third falls. We left the river valley on
our right and began the long trek down to the ocean. From the final
headland we could see 50 kilometers out into Bathurst Inlet.

The next morning was our final day. Don and Fraser travelled
back over the portage for the third canoe. The rest of us breakfasted,
broke camp, and then walked back to the Burnside Falls following the
river gorge. On our way we saw a nest of rare peregrine falcons. The
channel was carved out of feldspar, a reddish rock. The canyon was
over 100 feet deep. The falls dropped 60 feet over a lip 100 feet wide.

At one p.m. we paddled off into the estuary and followed swift
water into the bay. After a two hour paddle we arrived at Bathurst
Inlet Lodge, thoroughly wet. Trish and Glenn Warner came out to
meet us, with almost the entire Inuit population--25 people, including
children.

Once again we had shared another unique family experience.
Together we had escaped into our northern frontier--and we had

survived. Before us had been a big unspoiled, majestic country of treeless land and water, game, and birds in their undisturbed habitat. Wildlife bloomed everywhere. Many times on our trip I wondered how long this river would remain untouched and unspoiled. How much longer would this solitude last? What a privilege to have run these waters so much alone. We had travelled one of the last frontiers of the world. Because we love the country, we are careful to leave it as we found it, with no signs of our passing. And like my family, I have never felt more Canadian than when alone with my thoughts in the remote northern vastness.

## RETRACING TYRRELL'S TRIP INTO THE BARREN LANDS

**by**
**Fred Gaskin***

## ABOUT THE AUTHOR

Fred Gaskin's story is condensed from the January, 1977 issue of the prestigeous Canadian Geographical Journal, and is noteworthy not only because of its 1060 mile length, dangerous rapids and extreme isolation, but also because Joseph Burr Tyrrell, who died in 1957 at the age of 99, was Canada's greatest land explorer of his day.

"Retracing Tyrrell's Trip Into the Barren Lands" is more than just an epic canoe adventure; it is a step backward into a time when men lived simply by their own keen instincts and resourcefulness.

(C.J.)

Seven years before the turn of the century, Joseph Burr Tyrrell, a geologist-engineer with the Geological Survey of Canada, began an exploratory survey of "terra incognita" in the Barren Lands of the Northwest Territories, a subarctic land of mystery, devoid of trees, and home of the semi-nomadic Eskimo.

*As mentioned in Chaper five, Fred Gaskin has canoed most of the major historical canoe routes in the Northwest Territories.

It was in 1893 that Tyrrell, armed with some slight information and sketch maps procured from Saskatchewan Chipewyan Indians, headed north by canoe in search of the great "Telzoa" River. It was believed to flow northward through the unexplored Barrens of the former Hudson Bay Company territory which Canada had purchased only 24 years earlier.

In 1974, Tyrrell's journey served as an inspiration for my own canoeing adventure; the contrast in style and composition of the two journeys was remarkable. The original expedition was outfitted with one 19-foot basswood canoe and two 18 foot cedar canoes, each weighing 120 pounds. Our equipment consisted of supposedly indestructable 18-foot canoes weighing only 80 pounds with dazzling colour and water-repelling deck covers.

Tyrrell assembled an eight-man team comprising himself, his brother James (who served as topographer and Eskimo interpreter), and six canoemen who were chosen for their strength, endurance, and skill in boiling rapids.

Our team included significant Arctic canoeing expertise and some international glamour, plus proof that, although it was a man's world in 1893, such was no longer the case. Along with my good friend Jack Purchase, came his wife Susie, who had paddled the Kazan with us the previous summer.

Staffan Svedberg, who had led a Swedish team on a 1000 mile Arctic canoe trip in 1972, journeyed from Kiruna, Sweden to join us. And teamed with him was Gretchen Schneider of Kitchener, Ontario. Paddling with me was Katie Hayhurst, a North York-Toronto alderman and veteran canoeist.

Carrying maps and a copy of Tyrrell's report to the Geological Survey of Canada, we launched our canoes on June 30 at Uranium City, Saskatchewan and headed east along the north shore of Lake Athabasca to the Indian villages of Fond-du-lac and Stony Rapids. From here we continued east to Black Lake then north into what James W. Tyrrell described in his book "Across the Sub-Arctic of Canada", as the "great untravelled wilderness." We were aware that we had left civilization behind as we began the two-mile Wolverine portage, knowing that there was no one between us and Baker Lake, and Eskimo hamlet 870 miles to the northeast. For Tyrrell's men, the sensation must have been awesome, with no maps and no assurance that they would reach Chesterfield Inlet.

We took four days of comparatively easy upstream paddling to reach the Height of Land portage between Selwyn and Flett Lakes. Once over the Height of Land our pace quickened as we crossed Flett and Wholdaia Lakes and began the descent of a river known to Tyrrell as the Telzoa, meaning "broad shallow river," and now identified on our maps as the Dubawnt. We were to travel this river system with its

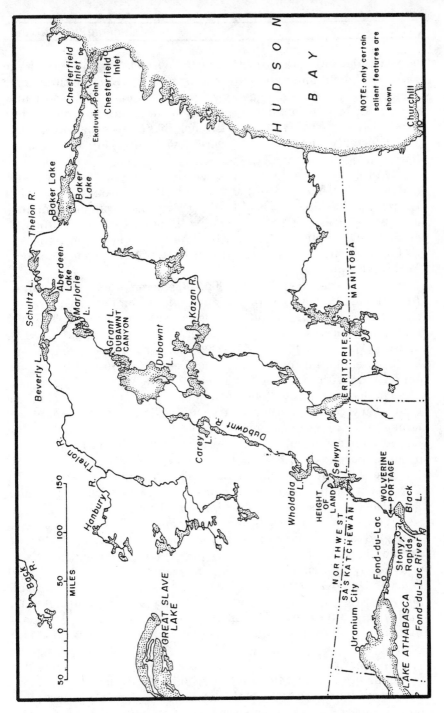

**Figure 19-3**
Map of Tyrrell's 1893 and Gaskin's 1977 route to Hudson Bay from Lake Athabasca via the Dubawnt & Thelon Rivers. Map courtesy Canadian Geographic Magazine.

large windswept lakes for the next few weeks. The forest began to shrink in height and to become less dense; the world appeared to be rapidly going bald. Pike gave way to lake trout. Bitter head winds were frequently encountered, pinning us down for as long as three days. And, when the wind abated, black flies and mosquitoes become uncomfortably numerous. We were now well on our way into the Barren Lands.

On July 22, we arrived at Carey Lake. About half our provisions had been flown here and dropped on Cairn Point the day before we left Uranium City. Four drums of food and supplies awaited our arrival, and July 22 was Susie's birthday. Nothing was spared for the gala occasion. We celebrated both the birthday and completion of the first half of our journey with extra rations of Drambuie, canned food, and fresh lake trout.

The next day we reinacted Tyrrell's ceremony at this point on August 1, 1893. It was here on an enormous boulder of red granite, situated on the highest point that the explorers built a cairn. They left a map and message stating the progress to date and, as stated by James Tyrrell, "the flag that for 1,000 years has braved the battle and the breeze floating overhead." The Geological Survey of Canada supplied us with Canada's Royal flag, the Union Jack and a message.

The location of our food cache at Cairn Point was symbolic in light of Tyrrell's experience 81 years earlier. Tyrrell encountered large herds of caribou, impossible to estimate in number, but measured in acres and square miles. His party killed 20 animals and dried the meat over a fire.

The greatest obstacle on the Dubawnt River encountered by Tyrrell and later explorers had been ice on Dubawnt Lake. Seventy-five miles long, it is the largest lake in the Barrens. The last trees were left behind us as our flotilla, heavily laden with cut logs, struggled against the wind in the approach to Lake Dubawnt. Fortunately, the lake was clear of ice, and the weather abated sufficiently to permit our crossing in five days.

The Dubawnt River exits from the north end of Dubawnt Lake and enters a two mile canyon immediately above Grant Lake. We made camp at the canyon and spent three days relaxing and enjoying its majesty. Tyrrell saw musk-oxen here, though we observed only caribou, Arctic ground squirrels ("sic-sics") and rough legged hawks.

On the first evening while portaging we met a cloud of black flies of plague proportion. My light brown shirt and trousers appeared to be covered by a deep layer of thick black fur, and at that moment my most treasured possessions were a head net and bottle of "Off".

The distance from Dubawnt Canyon to Baker Lake, by our route, was less than 300 miles, but the ever-increasing head winds made it seem like 3,000. Being windbound 50 percent of the time, we had

**Figure 19-4**
The magnificent two mile Dubawnt Canyon, where the Dubawnt
River leaves Dubawnt Lake. Jack Purchase stands on the right
shore. Photo credit: Staffan Svedberg.

ample opportunity to experiment with new menus featuring local
produce and fish. Although we were one week behind schedule, there
were plenty of fish, berries, and mushrooms to supplement our
dwindling larder.

Taking advantage of good weather when it came, and carefully
scouting all the remaining rapids, we finally reached Beverly Lake
and the Thelon River. At Beverly Lake, Tyrrell noted large quantities
of driftwood, the first wood seen since crossing the timber line. We
lost no time in stocking large quantities of wood for the crossing of
Aberdeen Lake.

In Tyrrell's time, there were no Eskimo communities as we know
them today. The Eskimo population lives "on the land" migrating
from place to place in search of good hunting areas. Although the
Tyrrell brothers recorded many encounters with small bands of
Eskimos camped along the river, we found only abandoned
campsites, numerous graves, and rings of stone used to secure tents.

We saw "inukshuks" or stone men, built of rocks by the Eskimos
as land-marks and to scare caribou toward waiting hunters. All of
these reminded us of a people who, only a generation ago, were losing
a thousand year struggle for survival in one of the world's most
inhospitable environments. Caribou, upon which the inland Eskimo
depended for survival, were estimated at two million at the turn of the
century, but 50 years later their numbers were reduced to
approximately 200,000.

**Figure 19-5**
An Eskimo Inukshuk stands sentry along the Thelon River where it enters Schultz Lake. Photo Credit Staffan Svedberg.

Our crossing of Aberdeen and Schultz lakes provided ample evidence of the old culture and the stone inukshuks seemed to be indicating our way. While paddling across Schultz Lake on one of the rare windless days, and lost in my thoughts about the old Eskimo ways, I was startled to hear the roar of an outboard motor. We were soon over-taken by a family of Eskimos in a large freighter canoe, returning to their summer camp after a successful caribou hunt. An invitation to share their camp was readily accepted, and that evening we dined on a feast of steaming caribou meat.

**Figure 19-6**
A group of Eskimos camped along the shore of the Dubawnt River, **September 2, 1893.** Photo Credit: Staffan Svedberg.

With the older children acting as interpreters, we learned that the family had come from Baker Lake by dog team the previous May to live and hunt on the land, and would return to Baker Lake in November. Although living in tents, it would only be another month or so before they could start to build the traditional snowhouses or igloos.

**Figure 19-7**
Joseph Burr Tyrrell stands beside the ruins of an ancient Eskimo
stone house by the mouth of Chesterfield Inlet at the Coast of
Hudson Bay, **September 12, 1893.**

Three days later we arrived at Baker Lake, eight days behind
schedule. Gale-force winds ruled out plans of paddling our canoes on
the Chesterfield Inlet, and with our timetable already in disarray, it
was necessary for everyone but Katie Hayhurst and I to return south.

With two Eskimos, William Aupuluktuk and his son Thomas
Kudloo, and their freighter canoe, it was possible, when the wind
moderated, for us to continue on Tyrrell's route to Hudson Bay.

Our two companions planned to visit William's dying father in
Chesterfield Inlet and to hunt caribou along the way. Often kept to
shore by severe winds, there was ample opportunity to hunt, and on
the third day, Tom bagged three caribou--two with one bullet!

It was 4:30 p.m. and snowing as we witnessed a centures-old
scene. First the skins were removed, revealing lean dark red meat, and
then the carcass was butchered into sections and stored in a casually
constructed cache to await the return journey to Baker Lake. Tom
estimated the weight of each carcass at approximately 150 pounds,
and  so, at supermarket prices, we were piling rocks over a small
fortune! At 8:30 p.m. William served a tasty dinner of caribou steaks
and liver--a delightful improvement over more mundane provisions
obtained from the Hudson Bay store in Baker Lake.

We were now on salt water and subject to the Hudson Bay tides,
tides which William, who spoke little English referred to with a giggle
as "that crazy Chesterfield water." To complete the remaining 75
miles of our journey, it was necessary to wait two days for calm
weather to permit crossing of the inlet to the south shore at Ekatuvik
Point. Those two days were spent with a few Eskimos camped on the

shore of the inlet where they planned to hunt and fish until their return to Baker Lake in November. Supper that night featured large chunks of caribou meat boiled in a cut down oil drum over a fire fueled with dead moss. There were about 10 of us huddled together in the tent that night, eating our caribou and raw arctic char, and drinking tea--an almost nonstop social custom. And although only the young children could speak English, I understood the universal language of smiles and laughter. Later, as I participated in their games of matchsticks and pebbles and watched the shadows on the faces of my companions in the candlelight, I could see that we had been welcomed as their own.

The following day, after a slow and careful five mile crossing to the south shore, we came upon Eskimos from Chesterfield Inlet tending their seal nets; the winds vanished as we approached the broad blue expanse of Hudson Bay.

On September 1, we stepped ashore at the hamlet of Chesterfield Inlet, successfully concluding a canoe journey of some 1,060 miles and 64 days, retracing Tyrrell's route from Lake Athabasca.

For myself, our arrival provided a feeling of celebration and satisfaction, remembering the anxiety of the early explorers who, having arrived at the same place on September 12, 1883, were then faced with a 400 mile voyage along the coast of the bay and into the jaws of winter.

**Figure 19-8**
Fred Gaskin's "Crew to the Hudson" Left to right is: Susie Purchase, Jack Purchase, Gretchen Schneider, Staffan Svedberg, Fred Gaskin, Katie Hayhurst, at the "Height of Land" headwaters of the Dubawnt River. Photo Credit: Staffan Svedberg.

# THE SOUTH NAHANNI RIVER EXPEDITION
**by**
**Christie Buetow**

## ABOUT THE AUTHOR

Christie Buetow is a complete outdoorswoman, as much at home on skies, snowshoes, or behind a team of sled dogs, as on an arctic river. She lives near Grand Marais, Minnesota in a log cabin that has no electricity or running water. Her one luxury is a telephone

Christie began canoeing with her family at the age of five and carries on this important tradition with her husband and young son. When not canoeing, hiking, or otherwise enjoying the wild beauty of nature, Christie works as a family planner. To Christie, the wilderness is home, breath, life. She is an itegral part of nature.

Her story, the South Nahanni River Expedition is re-printed from the Minneapolis Tribune Picture Magazine (Sunday, November 13, 1977.)

[C.J.]

After a 50-minute plane flight from Ross River, Yukon Territory, over the continental divide and the Christie Pass, we were in the Northwest Territories at the headwaters of the South Nahanni River. Our emotions, as we stood all alone and watched the plane take off and circle around Mt. Wilson, were very mixed.

There was a feeling of excitement, aloneness, apprehension, with some fear, wondering, finality. There were no more decisions to be made. We were there and we had to go. With common sense, good judgment, skill and a bit of prayer, we would make it out a month later, August 2, 1976.

The South Nahanni River Expedition began a year before the trip with Katie Knopke, 30, Ely, Minnesota, and Lisa Holzaphel, 25, formerly of Rochester, Minnesota, now of Eugene, Oregon. Four months later, the rest of us--Kay Lee, 28, also of Eugene; Sherry Renton, 29, Columbia Falls, Montana; Jeannie Bourquin, 25, St. Paul,

**Figure 19-9**
Route of Christie Buetow and crew's expedition down the Nahanni River.

and myself, Christie Buetow, 30, Grand Marais, Minnesota--had made our commitment, too.

We had a massive amount of wilderness experience among us. Katie and I had often talked of traveling in the Norhtwest Territories during our years of counseling and guiding at the St. Paul YMCA's Camp Widjiwagen in Ely. Since then, she had been an instructor with Minnesota Outward Bound School, and I had, among other projects, done a wilderness program with the Twin Cities Institute for Talented Youth.

We'd met the others at other camps, in other wilderness education settings. Jeanne, Sherry, Kay and Lisa had all worked for Outward Bound Schools too, and Sherry had additional experience from the National Outdoor Leadership School in Lander, Wyoming.

Planning this trip was difficult as the six of us were scattered across the country. Katie became the trip organizer and clearing house as we gathered information about the river and its natural and human history, sent for maps, planned meals and decided on equipment, transportation, first-aid and food.

Finally, after a year of planning and five days of non-stop driving from Minnesota, four of us met Lisa and Kay (who had driven from Oregon) at Dawson Creek, B.C., the beginning of the Alcan Highway. Two days later, after a 240-mile truck ride and our plane flight, we were on the South Nahanni with our gear; three Old Town canoes, on loan from the company, wood and fiberglass paddles, seven (full) Duluth packs, two Kelty frames with waterproof packs, six life jackets and two tents.

The upper Nahanni was by far the most challenging as the river drops 33 feet a mile, and you can literally watch it run downhill. It began so narrow that you could hardly turn a bend without coming to a stop, but the current was there from the beginning.

We practiced in the early riffles--ferrying, making eddy turns--to sharpen our skills and get used to our partners. We decided to paddle with the same people for the entire trip, which worked well as the white water often demanded instinctive communication.

We were soon into continuous white water, which meant stopping at every bend to read the water and decide whether to shoot the rapids, line them, or portage, which was extremely difficult in the dense spruce forest and boulder-strewn shores. Our self-confidence increased with practice. But it was still slow going. A good day would mean three to five miles of stopping at every bend. It took us nine days to go 40 miles.

The scenery was spectacular. We were in alpine tundra with mountains rising out of the river. The melting snow from the peaks sent streams rushing into the Nahanni. The flowers, mosses and trees, unique to the far North, intrigued us. Stopping to read a set of rapids often turned into a hands-and-knees picture-taking session of the flowers--artic cotton, dwarf lupine, mountain avons and many more.

The river was cold, and we were too. We had to make fires at lunch to warm up feet. Half the group had some wet suit gear which worked very well. Those of us who didn't--suffered. Our appetites were outrageous because of the energy drain. And it rained. By the end of the trip, we had logged 20 days when it rained at least once. We even had snow in the early part of the trip.

Entries from my Nahanni journal:

## (DAY 5)

There are so many rapids, one around every corner, I can't even count how many we've shot. This is the part that everyone warned us about not doing. Once again, it feels good to be in the unknown and unpredictable and to be surviving--comfortably, skillfully and ecologically.

**Figure 19-10**
Christie Buetow and Katie Knopke punch through a big roller on the
South Nahanni River. Canoe is an Old Town Tripper with full
splash cover.

## (DAY 6)

It's impossible to distinguish the rapids. They come one after the other with virtually no regular paddling between them. There was a biggie today...really high standing waves and two major rocks to avoid in the chute. Lisa and Kay went first, then Sherry and Jeanne, and then us. It was like the baptism! I've never paddled bow in rapids--I've always avoided it--but WOW! When the bow got buried in the waves and plowed through, straight on, I was amazed, exhilarated, scared, a bit hysterical--it was really a rush.

By this time we were settling into the experience. It began to feel easy, natural. We had nowhere else to go, nothing else to do, but keep on going down the Nahanni. It was feeling good--good because we were swinging up and down, angry and happy, at each other, at the river, as into the present moment as we could be.

The meals were good and filling. We ate mostly freeze-dried dinners (always with extra peas!) plus soup and a dessert; breakfasts swung from hot cereals to granola to mashed potatoes and gravy; lunches were combinations of sardines, voyageur bread, jersey cremes, honey, nuts, gorp, cheese, peanut butter, jelly, dried fruit, home-make jerky and--for a treat once in a while--smashed-up Oreo cookies. In addition, we had daily breaks of hard candies and caramels. The food was organized by Lisa and Kay and based on caloric needs for cold weather and hard work. I found that the first nine days I couldn't get enough to eat, but after we quit lining through the rapids, I was fine.

All of a sudden on the ninth day we passed an unnamed stream on the left, and--as predicted--the river changed like magic. It widened dramatically, and we were on our way to Rabbit Kettle Hotsprings and Virginia Falls. We went from paddling less than five miles a day to 15 miles on our ninth day and close to 30 miles on the tenth day. And then it rained and blew and snowed on us, and we had a layover day.

The next day was cloudless and cold, with new snow on all the mountains. We paddled by several ranges including the Backbone Range and the Mackenzie Range. They were high mountains with glaciers and ice fields and snowy peaks. It warmed up, and we could finally paddle without all our clothes on.

The Rabbit Kettle Hotsprings were definitely a scenic wonder, difficult to get to (we ended up swimming a cold mountain stream to get there) but worth it. Amazing formations of calcium carbonate rising 70 to 90 feet above the Rabbit Kettle River. They are terraced in odd half-moon circles all the way up and on top. We had heard that seeing the pool empty meant that your life was about to end, so we were glad to see it full.

After two 40-mile days, we made it to Virginia Falls. We could hear the low roar and see the spray from our campsite, a mile upstream. In the next two days each person went on her own to meet this fabulous cascade. It drops over 300 feet between canyon walls that tower above the falls and has more volume than Niagara.

After completing the mile-long portage around Virginia Falls, we prepared ourselves for Five Mile Canyon--a stretch of the Nahanni with no way out or off. You have to make it on the river. This was where I found out what standing waves really are. They ran four, five and six feet high--or deep, depending on which way you happened to be looking. There's nothing like heading on through and maintaining balance. Sometimes I was looking at water as we went down and the waves came up. This was pure current and depth.

The canyon walls were fascinating and very distracting, so

concentrating on the water was difficult. We had been told that the area from Virginia Falls to the Splits had not been touched in the last glaciation. Up until Virginia Falls the mountains ran parallel to the river. From the falls to the Splits they ran perpendicular. The canyoned mountains rose out of the river on either side to heights of 3,000 to 4,000 feet.

From Five Mile Canyon, we made it next to Figure 8 Rapids, also called Hell's Gate. It's where the river makes a right-angle turn, crashes into a rock wall and forms two huge whirlpools, one upstream and one down. We decided to portage the gear and two canoes. Katie and Jeanne decided to shoot it despite the unpredictable boils that were surfacing. They had no difficulty making it, but the place can be very treacherous.

The sound of the river changed all the way. After Hell's Gate it was light, musical in comparison to the previous day's roar. It changes at each bend, and the country adapts, the people adapt. We thought often of the admonition in Herman Hesse's *Siddartha,* "Love this river, stay by it, learn from it."

The canyon country came next, slicing through eons-old sandstone, shale, limestone and dolomite. The colors and patterns on the slopes caused us to stare for hours. The river was easy at this point, and we found we could float 20 miles a day, easily, with no paddling, which allowed us to study the canyon walls, huge caves, and left-over oxbows high up in the rock.

The first break in the canyons was Deadmen Valley, so named for a pair of brothers who were mysteriously found headless one spring. They had been prospecting for gold about 1907 or so, and their mysterious deaths still make people suspect that somewhere near here there is a lost gold mine.

This valley is a broad, wide, open area, very unlike the canyons. We spent several days here at a cabin provided by the Nahanni National Park. All travelers here have left their names. We were no exception.

From here, you can hike up Dry Canyon Creek or up Prairie Creek in search of Dall sheep and goats and see them if you're lucky (we weren't). The fishing was wonderful in the little pools just off the Nahanni. We caught enough fish for three days--mainly Dolly Vardens and arctic grayling.

There was only one canyon left, First Canyon, and at the end of that was Kraus Hotsprings. These were truly hot with a sulphury, rotten-egg smell, but they felt good. To get to the main pool you walked through garden-like fields of wild dill and flowers.

**Figure 19-11**
And meet the crew of the ambitious South Nahanni River. Left to
Right: Sherry Renton, Lisa Holzaphel, Kay Lee, Jeanne Bourquin.
Christie Buetow, Katie Knopke.

The next day took us through the Splits, about 30 miles of
meandering channels, where it was very difficult to find the current.
It is also treacherous because of submerged logs and trees. At the end
of the Splits is the end of the Nahanni, the town of Nahanni Butte.

The mountains and canyons were gone, and we were down into
the broad reaches of the Mackenzie River Valley. At the Butte was the
Nahanni National Park Headquarters, where we spent the night
fighting the worst mosquitoes of the entire trip.

This was the end of the joint canoeing effort. Katie, Kay, Lisa and
Sherry decided to take a barge another 120 miles down the Liard River
to Fort Simpson. But Jeanne and I didn't consider the trip finished
without paddling every stroke of the way and so departed at 10 one
night for Fort Simpson.

We paddled through most of that night with the sky full of
Northern Lights. The next day we pulled over for a few hours rest at
Poplar River and watched the barge with our comrades go by. The
highlight of this section was the roller-coaster ride through the
Beaver Dam Rapids, a 10-mile stretch where two Americans had
drowned a week before. We had no trouble, however, and camped on a
gravel bar just below it for our last night.

The next day we floated on down, watching as the Laird lost itself
in the mighty Mackenzie when we came to Fort Simpson. It was
August 2, and we'd made it out.

# 20

# Bush Roads

### by
### Don Mitchell and Bill Simpson

**Don Mitchell** is a freelance technical writer currently under contract by the 3-M Company in St. Paul, Minnesota. He's a former psychology teacher and leader of a blue grass musical group called "Northwest Passage". In his spare time, Don leads groups of all ages on canoe trips into the Canadian bush.

**Bill Simpson** teaches special education in a Minnesota high school. He's co-founder of the "Wilderness Inquiry Association"--a non-profit organization committed to providing wilderness experiences for educationally, emotionally, and physically handicapped persons.

Together, the men carry the banner for ethical management of the American and Canadian backcountry. Don and Bill are active environmentalists who practice what they preach!

Portions of this chapter first appeared in the Spring, 1982 issue of "Park News", a publication of the National and Provincial Parks Association of Canada.

You follow through a curve and another climb, now through deep forest cover. It is a relief to get out of the sun. A hundred yards more, then another curve, another little ascent. Suddenly, the woman ahead of you stops cold in her tracks, and you see the legs of more members of the group, bunched ahead of her. They are standing in a flood of sunlight. Packs and canoes are down, the people wait in confusion.

You wedge the bow of your boat between two convenient trees, lower the stern, then walk out from under your canoe. You walk past three or four members of the group, then out into the glaring openness. Everyone is strangely silent. You have a sickness in your stomach;

you know in advance what has happened. Your eyes can only confirm the disaster.

## You have come upon a bush road!

The road itself is not yet in view--only a waste land of trees, clear cut. The valued trunks have been dragged out, and the brush, the unwanted boles of unworthy species, left to rot. Carnage is strewn all over the slopes, down to the spot where you stand. Beneath your feet is the last dusty remnant of the portage trail, choking off abruptly beneath impassable ragged heaps of slash.

The others watch as you pick your way gingerly over and around the debris, up toward the embankment that you now recognize as the outside of a curve. Your mind races ahead:

Supposed to be a mile-and-a half portage. Maybe a third of that done. The footing--unthinkable with canoes or packs; one slip and we'd have a medical disaster. Maybe with teamwork and infinite caution we could get through to the road...But then what lies beyond it? More clear cut? Will we be able to find the trail again? Map showed a ridge. They probably followed that. Ran about east/west...well, better check that.

*You get out your map and compass.*

Kind of bisects the trail here. Unless maybe it curves sharply (decent chance of that) and would go somewhere near the lake. We might be able to crash down, unless there's more of this slash. Okay, assume it would go down, one way or the other. But which way to start walking?

You shudder at the idea, praying silently that you'll be able to pick up the trail at the far side of the cut...

Stepping from trunk to trunk you approach a large boulder, and clamber up its side. From here you can look down at the road. Your heart sinks as you absorb the sweep of the clear cut on the far side--a quarter mile at least, just as rugged as the terrain you have just covered. You scan the forest edge desperately for a blaze, a tattered plastic ribbon--*anything* that might have been left to mark the portage. There are broad, bright scars on the trees from the passing of the bulldozers, but nothing that looks like a blaze.

The road itself is a boulderfield, shoulderless with threatening washouts at every low spot. It has not really been built at all, but dumped out over the landscape from the gravel and sand excavations that yawn at you over to the west. Beneath the washouts are smooth floodplains of sand, from which the rust-colored limbs of hacked pines strain disjointedly. The destruction is so complete that not even the miles of wilderness, the abundance and vigor of the world's most beautiful boreal forests, survive untainted in your mind.

*Why didn't they tell us at the Ministry?*

It's a legitimate question, but no good thinking about it now. Reluctantly, you organize a couple of teams to search along the far edge of the clear cut, in hopes that the trail did not parallel beneath the road for any distance. Your partner glances at the declining sun, and reminds you that you could still be looking two hours later. Shouldn't somebody walk the road a ways?

*Yes, they should. Both directions.*

Which means, of course, a couple hours minimum--even if someone lucks onto the lake or the trail--to reassemble the scattered group. And while everyone else is busy searching for the lake or the trail, you'd better rethink your whole route. An extra half-day here, maybe a whole day, with the possibility of crossing it again somewhere up ahead, depending on where the damn thing is going...

There is no consolation in this setting--unless you are one of those miserables who love company. You have plenty of company, because the same story is recurring, every day of the canoeing season, all over the Canadian Shield. We know, from bitter experience, that the insidious network of these roads has stretched out from Fort Frances, from Ignace, from Dryden, Kenora, Minaki, Thunder Bay, Atikokan. We have heard that it stretches from Ear Falls, Red Lake, Sioux Lookout...In how many hundreds of instances, perhaps thousands, is it the work of an afternoon for a man on a D-9 to obliterate a pathway that has served quiet passerby for millenia? Does the man on the Caterpillar even realize that the trail was there?

The men on the machines are not at fault. In fact, many of them have come upon us in these settings and have assisted us in any way they could. Have they ever been told to mark portage paths when they cross them? Have they ever been told that a clear trail must be maintained?

In the United States our roadless areas have dwindled to a tiny percentage of our land mass, and even the few havens left to us are under constant attack by development interests. We may win a few of the battles that remain, but the outcome of the war is not in doubt.

We only hope that our Canadian friends can learn the disastrous consequences of our course and get a grip on the mechanism whereby these seemingly irrepressible roads are pushing outward from every town in the northwest.

Oh yes, regarding that question about why the Ministry didn't say anything about the road, when they were so helpful and informative about everyting else...Seems they didn't know where the road was going either!

The preceding account indicates the obvious emotion a canoeist feels whenever he or she encounters an "access road" in the Canadian wilderness. Having said this much, is there anything that can be done in a more constructive vein to defend wildreness from exploitation?

The answer, fortunately, is yes. Even without political franchise in Canada, out-of-province and even American visitors can legitimately become involved by providing input to the Ministry of Natural Resources on land use issues. Government policies are open to public scrutiny, and are dependent on informed opinions from all land users. An American canoeist's input should weigh no less, at least in theory, than an American corporation's.

It is a sad irony that so few canoeists, of any nationality, are willing to lift a finger in support of conservation efforts. Even men and women whose livelihoods depend completely on the availability of wilderness, will not speak out publicly, though they freely share their private concern.

Activism means different things to different people. You don't have to travel long distances to participate in hearings, though some dedicated people do. You don't even have to write letters--though such letters can have great importance if the timing is right. Maybe the first step should be to join a Canadian conservation group--we have yet to find such an orginazation that excludes foreign members.

More importantly, do your conservation "homework" when you are out of the woods. Get serious about political issues like acid deposition, that directly threaten both northern wilderness areas and Canadian/American relations. *Inform your groups about these issues.* The truth of the matter probably is that what we do in our homes and businesses, hundreds of miles away, may have more ultimate impact on the canoeing wilderness than our immediate behavior on the water or at the campsite.

**Figure 21-1   OUCH!**

# Mending The Tears

## A Primer on the Art of Modern Canoe Repair!

I recently talked with a guy who'd smashed a RAM-X (polyethylene) Coleman canoe against a mid-stream boulder on Wisconsin's Brule River. The damage included a jagged tear near the keel, a broken seat, and a lot of bent aluminum. "I can straighten the metal", said the voice on the phone. "But how do I fix the rip?" Without thinking I sarcastically replied, "you don't!! Polyethylene's not repairable, but chewing gum and duct tape might work for a while." Later, I began to wonder about the validity of my advice, so I wrote Coleman in Wichita. To my chagrin, I learned that RAM-X could indeed be repaired, though admittedly, not by ham-fisted clutzes like myself. That knowledge sparked my interest in learning more about the science of modern canoe repair.

I began my research by contacting several ghurus of the boating industry. From Grumman came detailed instructions and photos for fixing tempered aluminum; from Eugene Jensen,* tips for repairing fiberglass covered wood-strip canoes; from Coleman and Hollowform, procedures for mending polyethylene hulls; and from Blue Hole and Old Town, suggestions for patching Royalex craft. The art of canoe repair, I learned has come a long way since furnace tape and fiberglass.

Included in this chapter then, are tips for making field and permanent repairs to all the new synthetics in addition to the venerable old aluminum and fiberglass canoes. The Red Cross canoeing manual contains enough information about wood/canvas craft to permit deleting it here.

Frankly, I hope you'll never have to use any of the techniques contained herein on a canoe--at least not on your canoe! But in the event your good judgement fails in a bad rapid, here are the recommended repair procedures:

*Eugene Jensen is one of North America's best long distance canoe racers. He is a master canoe designer and builder. Jensen designed canoes are manufactured by at least a half dozen performance-minded companies.

# ALUMINUM

### Holes and breaks in the skin.

Emergency repairs to aluminum are usually accomplished in the field by simply covering the affected area with silver furnace (duct) tape. If you want a stronger and more permanent repair, apply aluminum proven epoxy* putty to the break before you tape it.

Some canoeists report good luck with chewing gum. Just apply a bead of well-chewed gum to the break; heat the gum with a match or candle, and work the gum through the tear. Then tape over the gum (optional).

Inside View                                    Outside View

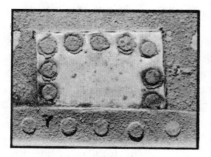  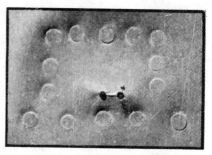

**Figure 21-2(a) & (b)**
Repair a break in the skin of an aluminum canoe by affixing a riveted patch.

### For a more permanent repair, apply a riveted patch as follows:

1. Secure the proper size, alloy, and thickness of aluminum patch from the manufacturer of your boat. Get the correct rivets and waterproof caulking compound.

2. Pound out the damaged area to its original contour (use a rubber or wood mallet) and drill one-eighth inch diameter or smaller holes at each end of the tear so it won't "run".

3. Center the patch over the damaged area, form it to the curve of the hull, and draw a pencil line around it.

4. Remove the patch and drill a rivet-size hole in each corner of it.

---

*Does not necessarily mean that the epoxy works only on aluminum.

5. Place the patch against the boat again and drill through the hole (and hull) at one corner.

6. Secure the drilled corner to the canoe with a small bolt, then drill and fasten each corner of the patch as above.

7. Lay out a hole pattern on approximate one inch centers staying well in from the edges of the patch.

8. Drill all the holes and remove the patch.

9. Remove burrs and shavings from the patch and boat skin, and apply a thin layer of waterproof caulking compound (or contact cement a patch-size piece of neoprene rubber) to the patch face.

10. Re-fasten the patch to the canoe with the bolts.

11. Rivet the holes progressively around the exterior. (See "To install a rivet" for the proper riveting procedure.)

12. Remove the corner bolts and rivet the holes.*

## DENTS

There are two schools of thoughts regarding dents. Some say don't remove them as "working" aluminum weakens it. Others advise removing all dents, claiming that the amount of strength lost by hammering the metal is insignificant. Nevertheless, even gentle working of aluminum with the proper materials stretches and thins it, with the result that a drum-like oil-can ping develops whenever the re-formed dent strikes an obsticle. For this reason, and the loss of strength factor, I prefer to remove only dents that are large enough to affect the performance of the craft. I treat small dents as battle scars and leave them alone.

Removing dents along a river bank requires determination and resourcefulness, especially if you don't have a hammer or hand-axe. However, you can make an effective mallet by wedging a rock in your boot or sneaker. It's also acceptable practice to place the canoe in shallow water, sand, or grass, and jump inside it to remove dents.

## STRAIGHTENING KEELS AND GUNNELS

It's almost impossible to straighten perfectly a bent keel or gunnel in the field. I think the best procedure here is to place the canoe on level ground and stomp the hull into a shape that will paddle efficiently enough to finish the trip. If you try for perfection along a river bank with primitive tools, you may just complicate the precision job later at home. Equipment needed to precision straighten keels and gunnels includes a two foot long section of two by four, a light sledge

*A special thanks to the Grumman Co. for these detailed instructions for applying a riveted patch.

hammer, a small hydraulic auto jack, a heavy vice grip pliers, ingenuity, and a friend.

## LOOSE RIVETS

To determine if a rivet is leaking, look for a ring of black aluminum oxide--which indicates rivet movement--around the rivet head. Tighten the loose rivet(s) by holding a bar of steel or the backside of an axe against the rivet head while striking the bucktail with another metal hammer.

## BROKEN RIVETS

If a rivet breaks in the field in a structurally non-critical place, simply tape over the damaged rivet head (or hole) and continue the trip. If the rivet shears in an important area (such as a seat brace) you may have to effect a more rigid repair. One method is to carefully punch out (use a drift pin) the broken rivet and install a bolt in its place (use a washer on each side of the bolt).

Personally, I don't like to mess with rivets in the field. It's too easy to damage a rivet hole which makes later installation of a new properly sized rivet difficult. I've had to resort to the bolt procedure only once--when a canoe (not mine!) went over a falls and tore loose one end of its keel. I straightened the keel as best I could, punched out a few of the broken rivets, and installed bolts in their place. The job was completed with several feet of duct tape and the party paddled the remaining miles of the trip with much embarrassment but little real discomfort.

To minimize damage to rivet holes when removing rivets, follow this procedure:

1. Center punch the rivet head lightly on center.

2. Drill to the depth of the rivet head using the proper size drill (see chart below).

3. Break off the drilled head of the rivet with a punch and light hammer taps parallel to the hull. (Stubborn flush rivets can be removed by lightly drilling the rivet heads with the next size larger drill.)

4. Hold a bucking bar against the aluminum skin adjacent to the bucktail and drive out the rivet shaft with a punch and hammer. (Use a round shank drift punch the next size under the rivet size.)

## DRILL COMBINATIONS

1/8 inch rivet--use #30 drill
5/32 inch rivet--use #21 drill
3/16 inch rivet--use #11 drill

1/4 inch rivet--use #F drill
5/16 inch rivet--use #P drill
3/8 inch rivet--use #W drill

**To install a rivet:**
1. Select the proper rivet for the job and insert it into the rivet hole (consult the manufacturer of your canoe for the correct rivet size).*
2. Place a steel bucking bar against the rivet head and hammer (use a ballpeen hammer) the inside bucktail until the rivet seats tightly.

If you use a rivet gun, place the bucking bar against the bucktail side of the rivet and hold it firmly during the riveting operation. (Take care not to push the rivet back through the hull.) Pressure on the bar should be much less than that applied to the gun.

## BROKEN WELDS

Lots of luck! Breaks in spot-welded canoe parts are almost impossible to repair on the trail and not a lot easier to fix at home. About the only thing you can do is to plug any holes with epoxy or gum, tape the area, and hope you don't hit something there again. At home take the boat to a *good* aluminum welder. Better yet, return it to the manufacturer for repairs. Or, if you want a stronger repair, drill out the spot welds in the affected area and replace them with rivets-something the manufacturer probably should have done in the first place!

## PULLED DECK PLATES

If a deck plate pulls loose on a canoe trip, punch out the broken rivets, hammer the plate back into position, and secure it to the canoe with small sheet metal screws. Later at home, replace the steel screws with aluminum pop rivets.

**Note:** Non-aluminum metals will corrode aluminum if placed into prolonged contact with it. For this reason, permanent patches and fittings should be made of aluminum (preferably the same alloy) or a non-metal. If you must use a steel, copper, or brass part, on an aluminum hull (example, a steel washer over an aluminum rivet), protect the aluminum by placing a thin plastic or rubber gasket between it and the foreign metal. It's okay to use non-aluminum parts for temporary repairs, however.

---

*If the rivet hole was enlarged when the canoe was damaged or drilled, you'll have to use the next larger size rivet.

## PAINTING

If your canoe has been factory painted, touch up scratches with the special matching paint provided by the craft's manufacturer. If you want to tackle a complete painting job on an unpainted hull, proceed as follows:

Wash off any anti-oxident varnish on the surface of the metal with a commercial pre-wash primer or household vinegar. If you use vinegar, allow it to remain on the metal over night (it will etch the aluminum slightly) then wash if off with clean water. Dry the hull completely with a clean soft cloth and allow the boat to air dry thoroughly (preferably in the sun). Apply a *thin* coat of zinc-chromate primer and paint. Though high quality alkyd, silicone-alkyd, and polyurethane paints are generally recommended for use on aluminum alloys, many canoeists report good luck with brush applied enamels.

If you don't feel up to tackling a major paint job, take the canoe to an auto body shop that is experienced in painting aluminum. They'll do an excellent job.*

Suggested materials for the field repair of aluminum canoes:

†roll of silver duct tape.
†hand axe or hammer.
flat mill file and rat-tail file (for removing burrs).
†coil of fine copper wire (for securing torn fittings and seats).
†assortment of small bolts, washers, and sheet metal screws.
†small vice grip pliers.
aluminum epoxy.
chewing gum.
†drift pin.

*Additional detailed information about repairing aluminum canoes may be found in "Repairing Aluminum Boats" by Vin T. Sparano (Outdoor Life Magazine, February, 1976). Re-prints of the article are available from the Grumman Co., Marathon, New York 13803.

†These materials are considered most essential.

# FIBERGLASS

Most paddlers rely exclusively on duct tape to repair fiberglass canoes in the field. With enough duct tape and ingenuity you can usually repair anything--even boats which border on the "unrepairable". Furnace tape on a canoe is a paddlers' gray badge of courage"!

Generally, it's best to stick with tape for field repairs and save the application of fiberglass patches for the controlled conditions at home. Fiberglassing along a river bank without the proper tools (like a long-bladed sharp scissors, sabre saw, "moto-tool" type rotary grinder, and sandpaper) will likely produce an unsightly--though adequately strong--patch, and in fact may make a proper repair job later at home more difficult.

Nevertheless, where extensive hull damage has occurred, you may have no choice but to fiberglass in the field. Fortunately, patching with glass is easy--though it often takes some skill to effect a repair that is completely unnoticeable.

Although I've had considerable experience patching fiberglass canoes and have built several glass-covered redwood "strippers", I am not an expert in fiberglass repair. Lengthy books have been written about "how to fiberglass", and for good reason: numerous resin formulations, fabrics, and techniques, are used for building and repairing boats, and each material and method has its advantages and disadvantages.

To learn the intricacies of fiberglass repair, I consulted several books and canoe manufacturers. To my chagrin, I learned that every expert has specific ideas on exactly how repairs should be done. So after much confusion about "the right way to do things", I called a friend, Bob Brown, building chairman of the largest state canoe club in America--the Minnesota Canoe Association. Ther result of my conversations with Bob, and my research and experience, has produced the methods suggested below. Possibly you may know an easier, faster, and better way to fix fiberglass boats. If so, I hope you'll share your knowledge by writing me care of the publisher. In the meantime, I offer the following time-proven easy-to-use techniques.

First some terms:

**FIBERGLASS CLOTH:** "Cloth" is composed of twisted strands of fiberglass which are woven at right angles to one another. You can get cloth in a variety of weights per square yard, though for canoe repair, the seven and one-half ounce and ten ounce weights are most popular.

Fiberglass cloth has the highest glass to resin ratio (about 1:1) of all the fiberglass fabrics and therefore has the greatest tensile strength. For this reason, most canoeists make repairs exclusively with this material.

**FIBERGLASS MATT:** Matt is composed of chopped, crosslinked glass fibers which are held together with a dried resin binder. Matt has a glass to resin ratio of about 1:3, which means it's only about one-third as strong as woven cloth. However, matt is easier to work into tight corners than cloth, so despite its lack of strength, it is very useful for some applications.

**ROVING:** Roving is a much coarser weave than cloth. Its glass to resin ratio is slightly less than that of cloth but its impact resistance is greater. Despite this advantage, roving doesn't conform well to sharp bends, and so it is seldom used for canoe repair.

**GEL COAT:** an abrasion resistant waterproof resin used on the outside of a fiberglass canoe. Liquid gel coat is mixed with a coloring agent and activator prior to application. If you want a cosmetically perfect patch, you'll need to apply color matched gel coat over the outside layer of fiberglass cloth. Gel coat is hard to apply smoothly and it's hard to sand. For this reason, most canoeists don't use it.

**MEKP (methyl-ethyl-ketone-peroxide):** the hardening agent used for polyester resin. Comes in small plastic tubes and smells terrible.

## MATERIALS

You'll need the following materials to repair fiberglass in the field: Fiberglass cloth (seven and one-half ounce weight or heavier), polyester resin or quick-curing epoxy, a one inch wide paint brush, MEKP (for polyester resin), 50 grit sandpaper, mixing container for the resin and hardener, and duct tape (to provide support for the glass cloth in the event you need to span large holes).

You can repair a polyester boat with either polyester or epoxy resin, but only epoxy will work on an epoxy boat. Epoxy is considerably stronger than polyester but it's more difficult to sand and is more sensitive to temperature and humidity. If you apply epoxy on a cold damp day, it might take days for it to cure, whereas polyester will set up in minutes with an overdose of MEKP.

Use polyester for field repairs unless you have an epoxy boat, in which case, get some fast curing epoxy for your repair kit.

For more aesthetic home repairs, you'll also need: A long-bladed sharp scissors, small rotary grinder, matching gel coat, cardboard, aluminum foil or Saran wrap, masking tape, wet-dry sandpaper, buffing compound, and electric drill with buffing wheel.

## PROCEDURES FOR PATCHING WITH FIBERGLASS

You'll be able to handle almost every fiberglass canoe repair problem if you can apply:

1. An "emergency field patch" to a damaged area that's accessible from both sides of the hull.
2. An "emergency field patch" to a damaged area accessible from one side.
3. A "cosmetic patch" to an area accessible from two sides.
4. A "cosmetic patch" to an area accessible from one side.

Before we examine the specific procedures for patching, there are some general considerations you should be aware of. First, is the matter of strength. Canoes flex much more than other watercraft and they occasionally hit rocks! Consequently, a repair that's strong enough for a fishing boat may not be durable enough for a canoe. Second, is aesthetics. Many paddlers are very conscious of "how pretty" their boat looks. With care you can make a patch that is both strong and beautiful. However, "invisible patches" which result when you lay up layers of fiberglass cloth over gel coat from the inside of the hull (no locking outer cover patch) may not be strong enough for a canoe and are therefore not recommended (by the Minnesota Canoe Association building chairman).

## EMERGENCY PATCH TO AN AREA THAT'S ACCESSIBLE FROM BOTH SIDES OF THE HULL:

1. Trim away the broken pieces of fiberglass with a sharp knife. This will leave a jagged hole, through one with structurally sound edges.
2. Sand off the gel coat about two inches back from the edges of the hole.
3. Sand the area around the inside edges of the hole.
4. Mix the polyester or quick-curing epoxy according to directions and lay two or three layers of patches across the inside hole. Add an outside patch or two. For greater strength, fill the area between the inside and outside patches with smaller "hole size" pieces of fiberglass cloth.
5. Paddle the boat home, cut out the patch, and do it right (see instructions for applying a "cosmetic patch" below).

If the hole is very large (several inches across), you'll have to provide support for the fiberglass until the resin sets up. The easiest way to do this is to place thin strips of duct tape across the hole on the inside of the hull. Lay two or three fiberglass patches over the duct tape and fill the break with "hole size" patches. Cover the "hole size"

Figure 21-3

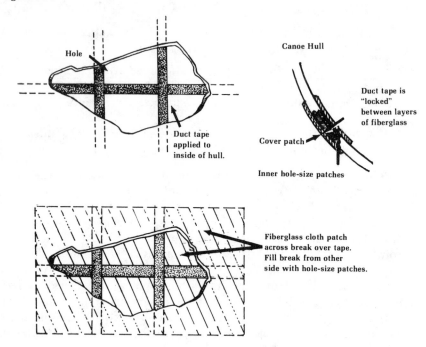

patches with a large piece of fiberglass cloth to "lock" them in place. (Note: the tape will remain imprisoned between the layers of fiberglass.) This patch is ugly, but it will keep out water and stay put until you get home.

## AN EMERGENCY PATCH TO A DAMAGED AREA ACCESSIBLE FROM ONE SIDE ONLY

About the only place you could have a problem like this is where a break occurs adjacent to a flotation element at the bow or stern (another reason why canoe makers should use suspended flotation in canoes).

If you're in paper birch country you can make a form of birch bark and patch the hull according to the directions given for making a "cosmetic patch to an area accessible from one side". If you don't have a form, you'll have to wall in the hole from the inside a strip at a time as follows:

1. Wet out two fiberglass strips (strips should be two to four inches wide) and poke them through the hole with your fingers.*

---

*You may have to cut out some flotation foam to provide a working area behind the hole.

**Figure 21-4**

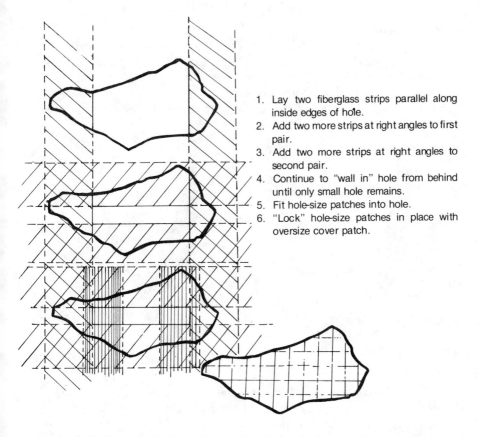

1. Lay two fiberglass strips parallel along inside edges of hole.
2. Add two more strips at right angles to first pair.
3. Add two more strips at right angles to second pair.
4. Continue to "wall in" hole from behind until only small hole remains.
5. Fit hole-size patches into hole.
6. "Lock" hole-size patches in place with oversize cover patch.

Work each strip flat along the edges of the hole (as always, first cut out badly damaged glass and sand the inside edges of the hole) so that about half the width of each strip is supported by sound fiberglass.

2. Overlap another pair of fiberglass strips at right angles to the first set. Keep this up until only a small hole is left in the center of the damaged area (Figure 21-4).

3. You may have to allow these layers of glass to set up before you can proceed to the next step.

4. Carefully fit several fiberglass patches *into* the damaged areas. The patches should seal the small hole left from overlapping the strips and extend to the edges of the damaged area.

5. "Lock" the fitted patches in place with a large oversize patch. (Be sure to sand off all gel coat in the affected area or the outside cover patch won't stick.)

6. Sand the edges of the patch to blend.

## COSMETIC PATCH TO AN AREA ACCESSIBLE
## FROM BOTH SIDES

(home repair):

  1. Cut out the splintered glass with a fine-toothed sabre saw.

  2. Feather the inside edges of the hole with a small rotary grinder.

  3. Place Saran wrap, wax paper, or aluminum foil over a flexible piece of cardboard (be sure there are no wrinkles in the wrap) and tape the cardboard--wrap side against the hull--to the canoe (Figure 21-5(a)).

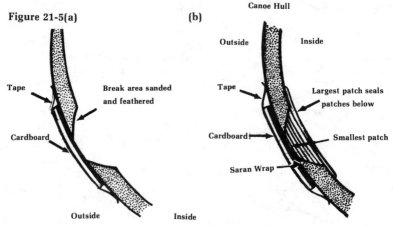

Figure 21-5(a)          (b)

  4. Use a sharp scissors to cut several fiberglass cloth patches to fit into the hole from the inside of the hull. Cut each patch slightly larger than the previous one to accomodate the increased taper (feather) of the hole (Figure 21-5(b)).

  5. Wet out the patches on a board and place them into the hole- smallest one first, then next largest, etc., until you've reached the level of the inside hull.

  6. Cut a large patch to seal the smaller patches. This patch should extend beyond the last patch at least an inch all around. (Be sure the area around the hole has been sanded thoroughly.)

  7. When the patch is dry, remove the cardboard form and sand off the gel coat about two inches back, all around the repaired area.

  8. Apply an oversize fiberglass cloth patch to the outside of the hull.

  9. When dry, sand and feather the inner and outer cover patches until they blend in with the contours of the hull.

  10. Mask around the outside patch and apply color-matched gel coat. Sand and feather the gel coat to the contour of the canoe (use progressive grits of abrasive).

Because gel coat is difficult to "work", many canoeists prefer to simply paint the area with color-matched epoxy paint. Gel coat, however, produces a nicer looking patch.

If you want a really pretty patch, leave off the outside "locking" patch and apply gel coat from the *inside* of the hull directly to the Saran wrap (foil or whatever) before you lay up the patches (the gel coat must be hard before you begin patching).* Don't think you've erred if the color of your hardened gel coat doesn't match perfectly the factory color of your boat. No one has yet found a way to get a precise color match.

## A COSMETIC PATCH TO AN AREA ACCESSIBLE FROM ONE SIDE ONLY:

1. Cut out the bad glass and feather one edge of the hole.

2. Cut a piece of cardboard to the approximate shape of the hole, only slightly larger and more oval in shape.

3. Cut a couple fiberglass cloth patches the size of the cardboard, place them on the cardboard, and wet them out with resin.

**Figure 21-6**

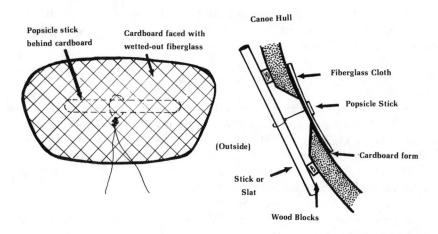

4. Run a small copper wire through the center of the cloth and cardboard, around a popsicle stick, and back through the glass covered cardboard (Figure 21-6).

*Inner and outer "locking" patches are recommended for strength. These large patches will have a minimal effect on the appearance of the boat.

5. Force the wet glass/cardboard form into the hole (you'll have to bend the cardboard slightly) and align it so the cloth butts against and overlaps the inside hole edges.

6. Pull on the wire to tighten the form firmly against the inside of the hull; wrap the wire around a wood stick or slat and block the stick at the ends to provide pressure for the patch until it dries.

7. When the patch is dry, snip off the wire and complete the repair from the outside hull as in a "cosmetic patch accessible from both sides". Note: the cardboard form and popsicle stick will remain inside the boat.

### Gouges:

Gouges which go through the gel coat can be repaired by brushing in color-matched liquid gel coat.

### Chunks:

Where a chunk of fiberglass has been knocked out, as along a stem, the best procedure is to build up the damaged area to its original contour with matt, chopped cloth stirred into resin, or miniature "logs" rolled from fiberglass cloth. Fortunately, fiberglass sands easily, so if you goof, you can easily destroy your mess and begin anew.

bias cut

Fiberglass patch

### Tip:

If you cut fiberglass strips on the *bias* (diagonal cut) they'll lay easily into tightly curved areas. Where possible, use bias strips in place of mat or chopped cloth, as it is much stronger.

## SUGGESTED FIBERGLASS FIELD REPAIR KIT

- One pint of polyester resin (for epoxy boats, choose fast curing epoxy). Resin is best stored in a tin can with a friction cap.
- One tube of MEKP (for polyester)
- One, one-inch wide paint brush. Saw off the handle so the brush is the same length as the can.
- One yard of 7½ ounce fiberglass cloth.
- Two sheets of 50 grit sandpaper.
- One 18 inch square of aluminum foil. (With this and duct tape you can span large holes.)
- Roll of silver duct tape.
- Two paper "Dixie" cups for mixing the resin. (Mash the cups flat.)

Tape the materials to the resin can and place the kit inside two plastic Zip-lock bags set into a nylon or canvas sack.

# KEVLAR

Kevlar boats are repaired just like fiberglass ones only an "invisible" patch is harder to make. This is because Kevlar doesn't sand well. In fact, it doesn't sand at all--it just fuzzes up and makes a mess. This means you can't "feather" the edges of a Kevlar patch to blend in to the contours of the hull. For this reason, most canoeists prefer to patch Kevlar canoes with fiberglass instead of Kevlar. It's less hassle, and the loss of strength is insignificant.

# WOOD-STRIP CANOES

You can patch a wood strip canoe just like a fiberglass one, but if you want an unnoticeable repair, you won't! A stripper is the prettiest watercraft afloat: the last thing you want is to destroy its beauty with an ugly fiberglass patch.

Damage to strip boats tends either to be superficial (just through the outer layer of glass cloth) or catastrophic (major structural damage). Superficial injuries are simply repaired by sanding and applying polyester or epoxy resin to the affected area. A final sanding and rub down with extra fine steel wool and pumice will restore the hull to a semblance of new. Deep scratches may be partially removed by progressive sanding and buffing.

Catastrophic damage calls for resourcefulness since it's almost impossible to re-structure large areas of broken out hull with matching wood strips. Your best bet is to cut out the damaged area and install a wood inlay.

Obtain a contrasting piece of three-eighths inch thick wood (most strip boats are laid up with quarter inch thick strips) slightly larger than the damaged area. Trace an attractive pattern on the wood (perhaps a fish or diamond), and cut out the pattern with a sabre saw. Sand and smooth the inlay and trace it onto the hull around the hole. Carefully saw out the tracing (this will remove all the damaged wood) and glue in the inlay with epoxy. Sand the inlay to the level of the hull on both sides and "lock" it into place with a fiberglass cloth patch on each side.

Sand and buff the glass patch and apply several costs of paste wax. This repair will be very attractive.

If the hull has been damaged along a severe curve, such as a section of extreme tumble home, the repair process will be more complicated. Because of the curvature at the break, a solid inlay won't work (unless of course you use a very thick board and sand away great amounts of material). The solution here is to use the curve of the hull as a temporary form for laying up a strip inlay that will fit into

**Figure 21-7**

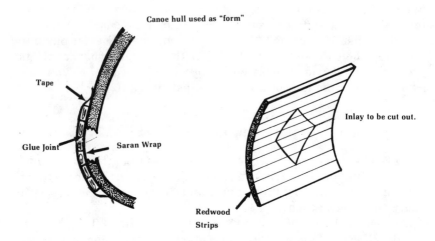

Canoe hull used as "form"

Tape

Glue Joint          Saran Wrap

Inlay to be cut out.

Redwood
Strips

the damaged area (Figure 21-7). Edge glue the strips with Elmer's glue as shown in the diagram and secure the strips to the form (canoe hull) with tape.* The "form" should be heavily waxed or covered with Saran wrap so the edge glued strips won't stick to it.

When the strips have dried, remove them, saw out the inlay, and glue it into the damaged area. Finally, cover each side of the inlay with fiberglass cloth.

If this method sounds like too much work, simply saw out the damaged strips and replace them with new strips of approximate matching colors.

## THERMO-FORMED PLASTIC BOATS
### (ABS, Royalex ABS, and Polyethylene)

Though some kinds of thermo-formed plastic boats have been around for more than a decade (ABS and Royalex ABS), only a handful of people have had much experience repairing them. This is because molded plastics are very strong; they seldom break, even when severely impacted against a rock. And that's fortunate, for tears in these plastics are not at all easy to repair.

---

*All glue joints will be covered with fiberglass so there's no danger of the Elmer's glue dissolving in water.

# ROYALEX

Royalex is a laminate of cross-linked vinyl, ABS plastic, and ABS closed cell form. The stuff is very strong but it dents. Shallow dents which are visible only on the outside of a Roylex hull will usually disappear in time. You can help "time" along simply be exposing the dented area to warm sunlight for several hours. The heat from the sun will cause the dent to level itself somewhat.

Deep dents which are visible on the inside of the hull are repaired (with some effort) by applying *moderate* heat to the dented area. An electric iron adjusted to a "rayon" setting, a 75 watt light bulb, hair drier, or commercial heat gun, will work fine. Where extensive reshaping is required, a bank of two to four heat lamps and a friend is recommended.

Apply heat slowly to the dented areas. Don't let the vinyl outer layer get too hot. Royalex is an excellent insulator, so if you apply too much heat too fast, you'll broil one side of the material without even warming the other side.

When the dent is soft enough to be moved, gently push it back into shape and hold it there until it cools.

## Mending holes and tears

**Holes:** The standard procedure for mending holes in Royalex is to fill them with epoxy putty or epoxy resin and shredded fiberglass. If you undercut the ABS foam around the hole, the epoxy will bond more strongly. Wipe off excess resin (putty) from the vinyl surface with a wet rag. When the epoxy is dry, paint it with polyurethane or acrylic base enamel, or use fuel-proof model airplane dope (excellent!).

**Note:** There are dozens of epoxy formulations. Some types of epoxy bond tightly to ABS while others don't bond to it at all. The general purpose epoxies sold at marinas are fine for emergency repairs, but they may not be the best for use where high strength and long term durability is required. Royalex canoe makers will sell you the proper repair materials in kit form,or they'll suggest specific adhesives which you can buy locally. Some ABS proven epoxies are indicated below:

| SUGGESTED EPOXY | AVAILABLE FROM |
|---|---|
| Uniroyal #OC 2490 | Adhesive Dept., Uniroyal, Inc., Mishawaka, IN 46544. |
| Ren 1250 | Ren Plastics, 5424 S. Cedar Rd., Lansing, MI 48910. |
| Thermoset 110 | Thermoset Plastics, 5101 E. 55th St., Indianapolis, IN 46226. |

Epoxical 606                     U.S. Gypsum, 101 S. Wacker Dr.,
                                 Chicago, IL 60606.


Bob Lantz of the Blue Hole Canoe Co, recommends the following procedure for **mending a tear in Royalex** with epoxy:

1. Cut out the ragged edges of the tear with a knife and undercut the ABS foam to provide "purchase" for the epoxy.

2. Apply "Epoxybond" epoxy putty (available at most hardware stores) to both edges of the tear and press the edges together.

3. Apply two layers of fiberglass cloth to each side of the hull over the tear. (Sand the vinyl lightly and clean it with rubbing alcohol before you apply the fiberglass cloth).

4. When the repair has dried, sand the patch to blend into the contours of the hull and paint it.

A fiberglass patch correctly applied with the proper epoxy probably exceeds the tensile strength of the surrounding undamaged hull material. However, it's doubtful that this or any other patch will restore the damaged area to its original flexibility. In all likelihood, only re-molding the break (virtually impossible) can do that.

Dick Roberts of "White Water West" suggests bonding the ABS material with a glue made by dissolving ABS plastic in methyl-ethyl-ketone (not the MEKP used for activating polyester resin). Dick mixes chips ground from discarded ABS canoe paddle blades with MEK to make a *very thick* paste. He then applies the paste to the break in *very thin* layers to prevent the solvent from dissolving too much of the undamaged hull.

MEK/ABS glue is toxic and touchy to use. It also tends to harden with age. For this reason I recommend that you use epoxy and fiberglass instead.

It's interesting to note that the best epoxies for bonding ABS may stick poorly (or not at all) to the outer skin of a Royalex boat, and vice versa. So if you want a first class repair job you should probably either grind off the vinyl surfaces of the hull and use ABS proven adhesives throughout, or use two different adhesives--one for bonding the ABS, and the other for glueing the fiberglass cloth to the vinyl*.

---

*Bob Lantz reports good luck in bonding fiberglass to vinyl with commonly available hardware store epoxies.

# RIBBED ABS CANOES

Ribbed ABS canoes have about gone the way of the passenger pigeon, and for good reason. They were badly designed, difficult to repair, and not really inexpensive. Nevertheless, a few of these old hulks are still around (and intact) so a word about their repair is in order.

For field repair use duct tape. Solvent bonding with MEK/ABS glue or ABS specific epoxy and fiberglass cloth is the best way to make permanent repairs.

# POLYETHYLENE CANOES*

Polyethylene canoes are touted by their makers as being the toughest watercraft afloat. They better be, because it is impossible to repair them in the field and only slightly easier at home.

About all you can do about a break in the skin (rare in polyethylene hulls) is to cover it with duct tape and pray it doesn't get worse. Holes--which might result from hitting sharp granite or a spike in a bridge piling--are more likely. One manufacturer (Hollowform) suggests you fix a small hole by installing a steel bolt through the hole (a water-tight washer should be placed on each side of the bolt)!

Coleman, however, advises use of their special repair kit which consists of three flat pieces of "RAM-X" for patching, a two part adhesive, and instructions which must be followed *exactly!* Things get interesting when you realize that the plastic must be "flame-treated" with the *oxidizing* (not *reducing*) flame of a propane or butane (not gasoline) torch before the adhesive is applied.

Since Coleman was kind enough to send me a repair kit, I gave the procedure a try. I can report that the technique requires some skill but is not difficult. Patching a curved surface with this outfit, however, borders on the impossible.

Fortunately for RAM-X owners, Coleman has found that tears along curves and hard-to-reach areas can be mended by welding polyethylene into the break with a nitrogen torch. To accomodate owners of broken canoes, Coleman has set up a number of nitrogen welding stations around the country. Contact Coleman for information about the welding station nearest you if you have a RAM-X canoe that requires this type of repair.

Another way to repair polyethylene is offered by Dick Steinke, Senior Chemist for the H.B. Fuller Co., in St. Paul, Minnesota. Dick suggests melting parent polyethylene into the hole or break with a

*Some trade names for polyethylene canoes are: Coleman (RAM-X), Hollowform (Xylar), Keewadin (K-Tek), and Perception (Marlex).

medium-hot flat iron. This method takes some skill to effect a neat repair, but it welds the break and thus restores the area to its original strength.

A final tip: Be careful how you handle any plastic boat in ultra cold weather. An acquaintance of mine recently witnessed the demise of an ABS (not Royalex ABS)hull that was accidently dropped from the top of a van in the minus 28 degree Fahrenheit northern Minnesota cold. The canoe shattered into an undetermined number of pieces!

In case you're wondering why anyone in his right mind would be messing with a canoe at these temperatures, I can report that the boat was purchased as a Christmas present for a 14 year old boy. The canoe was being taken home for the holiday!

# A Plea For Conscience

Every river has places which are "special". These may be awesome mist-filled chasms, musty beaver ponds, high lake-locked bluffs, or just your own perception of something very ordinary. What and where these places are is not important. That they exist in your own mind is what counts.

When you find your "special place", you'll know. Then all the weeks of planning, the exhausting drive up, the black flies of the day before, will all be eclipsed by the beauty of what you see. And even if you're not a reverent person you may find yourself softly whispering..."Thanks God for letting me be here."

The magic of your special place is everywhere--in the lush green of the forest, the champagne-clear sparkle of the water, the crisp persistent breeze. You experience deep satisfaction--privilege--in being here alone, if perhaps only for a few fleeting moments.

Your eyes casually wander to a small open area and the charred remains of a fire. You know others have camped here before. But no matter. Does the revelation make this place any less beautiful for you than them?

Then you see it, the thoughtless refuse of voyageurs who preceeded you--rusty cans, a broken whiskey bottle, lengths of parachute cord, scraps of paper, the rotting viscera of fish. Suddenly this place is no longer special. It is an abomination, a trash heap, an insult to man and God. You stare in disbelief at the mess scattered about and feel a deep gnawing pain growing upwards from the pit of your stomach. The pain surfaces as rage, and you swear loudly, determinedly, again and again!

What kind of people have done this? You ask. Surely, they must be big city folk--from Chicago, Detroit, or New York, where wallowing in filth and selfishness is the order of the day. Hardly! Slobs (and selfish people ) come from all walks of life, from cities large and small, from suburbs, exclusive country homes, and from the depths of the wilderness itself. Regardless of background, they share a common attribute--ignorance of the simplest ecological relationships; their lack of knowledge about the fragility of the land, its water, fish and wildlife is absolute. Most are amiable people with warm hearts and a good sense of humor. Their failing is that they've never been taught the *proper way* to do things outdoors.

That, friends is our job!

Many years ago I sat on an island campsite along the Minnesota/Ontario border and watched with growing anger, a man on a nearby peninsula scrape and wash his dishes in the lake. His actions created a small but determined raft of suds which a gentle breeze pushed my way. The longer I watched, the madder I got. I was about ready to jump into my Sawyer Cruiser, paddle in hand , both barrels blazing, cuss words flying, when I remembered the old cliche, "You can catch more bears with honey than guns." So I clamed down, forced a smile, and in a stately fashion canoed to the peninsula.

When the man saw me he waved, smiled, and mumbled something about coffee. Then he stepped candidly into the water and helped me embark from my canoe. "Don't wanna scratch that pretty blue boat", he said cheerfully.

My hostility melted to confusion. This was a "really nice guy"!

For an hour I shared the man's fire and hospitality. I told him tactfully how organic wastes increased bacterial levels in the water; why soaps--biodegradable or not--kill essential microorganisms; how improperly disposed of human feces leech into the water and pollute it; how fires can creep hundreds of yards underground and spring to life when conditions are favorable; how it may take dozens of years to replace a tiny patch of lichens which a thoughtless camper picked because "they looked pretty"; that forest service and park personnel have neither the time nor budget to pick up the garbage of campers.

We had quite a talk, he and I.

The man freely admitted his ignorance of ecological relationships. "I'm willing to learn," he said honestly. "But *where* do you learn this stuff? Why didn't the Forest Service or my outfitter tell me these things?"

"Yes," I agreed. "Why didn't they!"

Over the years I've run into scores of polluters, many of which, like the man I met along the border, were unaware of the impact of their actions. I've cussed out a few to their faces, reported some to authorities, and once, even pretended I was a Conservation Officer and threatened to write a citation. But mostly, I've used the "honey rather than guns" approach.

You'd think that over-crowding of canoe routes, and the accompanying scars it leaves upon the land, would be limited to local streams and popular places like the BWCA, Quetico, and Allagash. Not so. Virtually all the great northern rivers--from Ontario to the Northwest Territories--are now paddled regularly...and trashed regularly by canoeists who should know better.

The day may come when all who use the backcountry will have to be licensed and show competency in ethical land and water use practices. I view that day with mixed emotions. On the one hand I yearn to be free to enjoy my wilderness pursuits unencumbered by bureaucratic regulations which are designed to protect the environment.

But I am weary of being my brother's keeper. So I plead for conscience and an army of knowledgeable outdoorspeople who care about the future of our wild places. The answer lies in education--by schools, government, commercial outfitters, guides, youth camps...you--not in the impersonality of blind regulation.

There are still hundreds of free-flowing unspoiled rivers in North America which have not yet felt the darkening influence of man. Whether these rivers will continue to exist in their unpolluted form in the next century depends on all of us--our attitudes, our beliefs, our willingness to "get involved". Fortunately, we are born of a well educated concerned generation--one committed to chartering a new course towards environmental responsibility and action.

# A REVIEW OF
# TANDEM STOKES

These are the basic strokes. Space precludes the inclusion of all the variations and sophisticated maneuvers. For a complete course on white water paddling, see the book "Basic River Canoeing" by Bob McNair (published by the American Camping Association) or the new "Red Cross Canoeing Manual" which incorporates material from that book, or Bill Mason's wonderful text--"Path of the Paddle".

## KEY TO PADDLE DIAGRAMS

**BACK-SIDE OF PADDLE BLADE**

**NORMAL POWER FACE OF PADDLE**

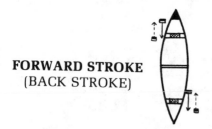

## FORWARD STROKE
(BACK STROKE)

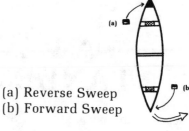

(a) Reverse Sweep
(b) Forward Sweep

Paddle is brought straight back *parallel* to keel line. Paddle should not be carried beyond your hip.

Useful turning strokes for flat water. Not enough power for white water.

**DRAW**

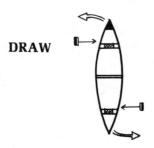

### CROSS-DRAW

Paddle shaft is held at 45 degree angle to water.

Your most powerful turning stroke. Paddle blade is submerged completely and pulled rapidly towards the canoe. Use an aerial recovery.

Used in the *bow only*. Very powerful stroke for turning canoe away from bow person's paddling side. An excellent stroke for use in shallow water.

## J-SROKE

**Essential stroke in stern of canoe.**
Keeps canoe tracking straight. A
reverse form of this (the reverse
J) is used by the bow paddler to
keep a straight course when
backpaddling.

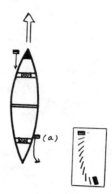

## DIAGONAL DRAW

By varying the angle of the
"Draw" from the perpendicular, a
variety of moves are possible.

**Note:** Paired diagonal draws on
the same side would unbalance
and possibly upset the canoe.
Except when paddling in a cross
wind, it's never a good idea to
paddle on the same side as your
partner.

## SCULL

Useful in bow, stern, or in the
center of a solo canoe. Turns
canoe in the direction of the scull.
Excellent shallow water stroke
and has good bracing action in
whitewater. Maintain same
power face throughout scull. A
"reverse" scull can be performed
by using the opposite power face.

**Paddle remains in water
throughout stroke.**

## BOW PRY

Paddle is pried forcefully around bilge and over the gunnel. Greatest power--and least control--results when both hands are above the gunnel. This stroke has a stabilizing effect in heavy water but the paddle can catch on rocks and upset the canoe in shallows.

In shallows, the preferred bow stroke for turning "off-side" is the cross-draw. Use an *underwater* recovery for the pry; an *aerial* recovery for draw and cross-draw.

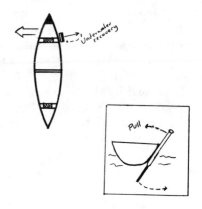

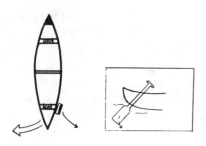

## STERN PRY

A powerful stroke for turning to the "off-side". Paddle is pried smartly over the gunnel and an underwater recovery is used. Unlike the "bow-pry", the paddle is angled to the waterline as indicated.

## LOW BRACE

Used in both bow and stern to stabilize (brace) the canoe and keep it from capsizing in heavy water. Flat of blade is nearly parallel to the water. Stroke requires a powerful downward thrust.

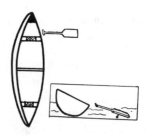

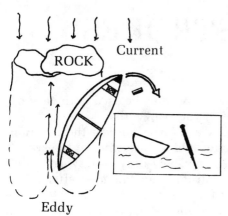

Current

ROCK

Eddy

## HIGH BRACE

A combination brace and draw. Paddle is held stationary, its face against current or at a strong climbing angle to it. The success of this stroke depends on speed (either paddling or current) and a strong lean. Useful for making eddy turns and as a pure bracing stroke when paddling solo.

# SOLO STROKES

All the typical tandem strokes above may be used with varying success in the solo canoe as long as you realize that:

1) The net movement of the boat is in a true line with the direction of the stroke since the paddler is located at the center of the craft.

2) Many strokes like the cross-draw, bow-draw, and sweeps (and of course, the braces) require a strong lean for good effect. For example, it's very difficult to turn a fine-lined straight-keeled solo canoe without leaning it considerably and using the rocker in the side wall. Some small solo canoes will lift their stems clean out of the water and pivot sharply when "layed down" in this fashion.

The accomplished solo canoeist blends a variety of hard-to-define (and diagram) strokes and techniques into a free-flowing show of grace and beauty. Paddling an open solo canoe in traditional fashion is an art form--one that requires years of practice to master.

The modern solo paddler who scorns tradition--and the customary "C-stroke"--will use a short bent shaft paddle and take three or four strokes on each side of the canoe. This switching procedure (called the "Minnesota Switch" or "HUT" stroke) is remarkably efficient in keeping the canoe on a straight course. Though ugly to watch, it is the only practical way to paddle alone for long distances, especially up-wind.

The *complete* canoeist should know and appreciate both methods!

*Some* of the paddle strokes unique to the solo canoe are shown below:

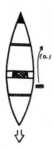

### BACK-STROKE

A powerful stroke for going backwards. Often completed with a pry off the gunnel at (a).

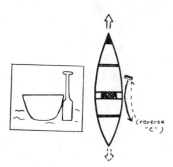

## C-STROKE

The soloist "J-stroke"-- used to keep the canoe tracking straight when paddling on one side. Paddle is nearly vertical to the water, blade brought under the hull. Some paddlers finish the stroke with a pry off the gunnel. The arc described by the paddle is actually less severe than shown.

## "ACUTE" DRAW (BOW DRAW)

This one takes practice because of the awkward hand position (wrist of top hand is turned so the thumb is down). Throw your shoulders into the stroke. This is your most powerful stroke for turning the canoe towards your paddle side.

## CROSS-DRAW

Identical to the tandem cross-draw. Mentioned here because it is your most powerful stroke for turning to the off-side.

## CROSS BACK-STROKE

When you need a powerful back-
stroke and turn at the same time.
Rotate your shoulders and flip
the paddle across the canoe, as
for a cross-draw, only more
severe. Canoe may be backed
straight by angling the paddle
outward at the start of the stroke.

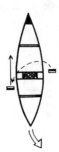

## COMPOUND BACK-STOKE

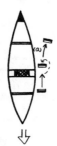

Requires twisting your upper
body more than 90 degrees at the
start of the stroke. The power
face of the paddle is reversed part
way through the stroke. The procedure is thought by some to be
more powerful than the standard
back-stroke. Some paddlers finish the stroke with a pry off the
gunnel at (a).

## OUTSIDE PIVOT

Part cross-draw, part sweep.
Looks impressive but is actually
less efficient than two cross-
draws which can be done in
about the same time. Useful for
picking your way between
obstacles in quiet water.

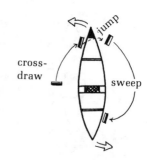

## PRY

Useful in heavy water for moving
the canoe sideways away from
your paddle side. Indentical to
the "stern pry" except the paddle
shaft is more vertical to the
water. Power should be applied
at or just behind the center of the
canoe.

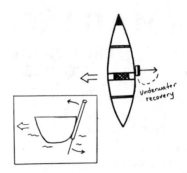

## INSIDE PIVOT

A combination reverse sweep
and bow draw. Used to turn the
canoe sharply towards your
paddle side. Actually, no more
effective than two bow draws
which can be done in about the
same time. The advantage is that
the "reverse sweep" component
can be blended with a back (low)
brace for stability when turning
in heavy water.

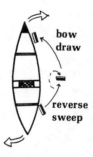

# APPENDIX "B"

# MAILING ADDRESSES
## PROVINCIAL AND TERRITORIAL
## TOURIST INFORMATION*

For free travel information write to:

**Alberta**
Travel Alberta
Box 2500
Edmonton, Alberta
Canada T5J 2Z4

**British Columbia**
Tourism British Columbia
1117 Wharf Street
Victoria, British Columbia
Canada V8W 2Z2

**Manitoba**
Travel Manitoba
Department 2020
Legislative Building
Winnipeg, Manitoba
Canada R3C 0V8
(204) 944-3777 (collect)

**New Brunswick**
Tourism New Brunswick
P.O. Box 12345
Fredericton
New Brunswick
Canada E3B 5C3

**Newfoundland**
Tourism Branch
Department of
   Development
Box 2016, St. John's
Newfoundland
Canada A1C 5R8

**Northwest Territories**
TravelArctic
Yellowknife
Northwest Territories
Canada X1A 2L9

**Nova Scotia**
Department of Tourism
P.O. Box 130
Halifax, Nova Scotia
Canada B3J 2M7

Nova Scotia Tourist
Information Office
129 Commercial Street
Portland, Maine 04101
1-800-341-6096
(from the United States,
except Hawaii, Alaska,
Maine) 1-800-492-0643
(from Maine)

**Ontario**
Ontario Travel
900 Bay Street
Queen's Park
Toronto, Ontario
Canada M7A 2E5
1-800-828-8585
(from continental
United States)
1-800-462-8404
(from New York State)

**Price Edward Island**
Visitor Services
   Division
P.O. Box 940
Charlottetown
Price Edward Island
Canada C1A 7M5

*This information courtesy of the Canadian Government Office of Tourism, 235 Queen St., Ottawa, Ontario, Canada K1A OH6. From *Canada Travel Information*, 1982-83.

**Quebec**
Tourisme Quebec
C.P. 20 000
Quebec, Quebec
Canada G1K 7X2
(514) 873-2015
1-800-361-5405
(from Quebec)

**Saskatchewan**
Sask Travel
3211 Albert Street
Regina, Saskatchewan
Canada S4S 5W6

**Yukon**
Tourism Yukon (CG)
P.O. Box 2703
Whitehorse, Yukon
Canada Y1A 2C6

**National Parks**
Parks Canada
Ottawa, Ontario
Canada K1A 1G2
(for information about
Canada's national parks,
historic parks and sites
and heritage canals)

# FOR INFORMATION ABOUT PARKS AND RESERVES, HUNTING AND FISHING REGULATIONS AND LICENSES, WRITE:*

**Alberta**
Fish and Wildlife Division
Alberta Energy and
    Natural Resources
8th Floor, South Tower
Petroleum Plaza
9915, 108 Street
Edmonton, Alberta
Canada T5K 2C9

†**British Columbia**
Fish and Wildlife Branch
Ministry of Environment
780 Blanshard Street
Victoria
British Columbia
Canada V8V 1X5

†**Manitoba**
Travel Manitoba
Department 2020
Legislative Building
Winnipeg, Manitoba
Canada R3C OV8

**New Brunswick**
Department of Natural
    Resources
Fish and Wildlife Branch
349 King Street
Fredericton
New Brunswick
Canada E3B 5H1

†**Newfoundland**
Tourism Branch
Department of
    Development
P.O. Box 2016
St. John's
Newfoundland
Canada A1C 5R8

†**Northwest Territories**
Wildlife Service
Government of the
    Northwest Territories
Yellowknife
Northwest Territories
Canada X1A 2L9

**Nova Scotia**
Department of Lands
    and Forests
P.O. Box 698
Halifax, Nova Scotia
Canada B3J 2T9

**Ontario**
Ministry of Natural
    Resources
Wildlife Branch
Queen's Park
Toronto, Ontario
Canada M7A 1W3

*Re-printed with permission from *Canada Travel Information*, 1982-83. Courtesy of Canadian Government Office of Tourism.

†Fishing license may be purchased by mail.

**Price Edward Island**
Fish and Wildlife Division
Department of
   Community Affairs
P.O. Box 2000
Charlottetown
Price Edward Island
Canada C1A 7N8

**Quebec**
Ministere du Loisir
   de la Chasse et
   de la Peche
Direction generale des
   parcs et du plein air
150, boul. Saint-Cyrille est
Quebec, Quebec
Canada G1R 4Y1

**Saskatchewan**
Sask Travel
3211 Albert Street
Regina, Saskatchewan
Canada S4S 5W6

**Yukon**
Tourism Yukon (CG)
P.O. Box 2703
Whitehorse, Yukon
Canada Y1A 2C6

**National Parks**
Parks Canada
Ottawa, Ontario
Canada K1A 1G2

# ALASKA INFORMATION

**For general tourist information, write:**

Alaska Division of Tourism
Pouch E
Juneau, Alaska 99811

**For Alaskan hydrographic charts, write:**

Chart Sales & Control Data Office
National Ocean Survey
632 Sixth Avenue
Anchorage, Alaska 99501

**For hunting and fishing regulations and licenses:**

†Alaska Department of Fish and Game
230 South Franklin St.
Juneau, Alaska 99801

**For the Alaska Catalog:**

"The Alaska Catalog"
Box 4-907
Anchorage, Alaska 99509

†Fishing license available by mail.

**Agencies which can supply additional information regarding recreational opportunities:**

Bureau of Land Management
701 C Box 13
Anchorage, Alaska 99513

National Park Service
Alaska Area Office
540 West 5th
Anchorage, Alaska 99501

U.S. Forest Service
Box 1628
Juneau, Alaska 99802

Bureau of Sport Fisheries & Wildlife
1011 E. Tudor Road
Anchorage, Alaska 99503

**If you're planning to drive the Alaska Highway, write:**

Alaska Department of Transportation and Public Facilities
Pouch Z
Juneau, Alaska 99811

**For information regarding state park facilities:**

Department of Natural Resources
Division of Parks
619 Warehouse Ave.
Anchorage, Alaska 99501

**ALASKA FERRY SYSTEM**

Alaska Department of Transportation and Public Facilities
Division of Marine Highways
Pouch R
Juneau, Alaska 99811

**CANADIAN SECTION**

Canadian Government Travel
Bureau
235 Queen St.
Ottawa, Ontario K1A OH6

# GENERAL INFORMATION ADDRESSES

**Canadian Addresses**

Canada Map Office
615 Booth St.
Ottawa, Ontario K1A OE9

(Source of topographic maps and aerial photos)

Hydrographic Chart Distribution
Office
Dept. of Fisheries and Oceans
1675 Russel Rd., P.O. Box 8080
Ottawa, Ontario K1G 3H6

(Source of Canadian charts and tide tables)

Canadian Wildlife Service
Room 1000, 9942-108 St.
Edmonton, Alberta T5K 2J5

(Information about fish and wildlife, sancturaries, firearms regulations, etc.)

Johnson Diversified Canada, Inc.
Yorkbury Square
3345 N. Service Road
Burlington, Ontario L7N3G2

(Source of Johnson Repellent Jackets, Silva compasses, and Eureka tents)

Hudson Bay Company
National Stores Dept.
77 Main St.
Winnipeg, Manitoba
R3C 2R1
Phone: Area Code 204: 943-0881

(U-paddle canoe rental, general merchandise, credit vouchers.)

Department of Information
P.O. Box 1320
Government of the Northwest
　Territories
Yellowknife, N.W.T. X1A 2L9

(Free catalog listing over 200
　publications, including some
　useful canoeing pamphlets.)

Northern Transportation Co.,
　LTD
9945 rue 108 St.
Edmonton, Alberta T5K 2G9

(Tug and barge service based in
　Churchill, Manitoba. Services
　remote communities.)

VIA RAIL Canada, Inc.
101-123 Main St.
Winnipeg, Manitoba R3C 2P8

(Largest railroad system in
　Canada)

Communications Canada
200-386 Broadway Ave.
Winnipeg, Manitoba R3C 3Y9

(Write here to register your CB
　for use in Canada)

## American Addresses

U.S. Geological Survey
Denver Distribution Branch
Federal Center
Denver, Colorado 80225

(Source of Alaska Maps and states west
　of the Mississippi River.)

U.S. Geological Survey
1200 South Eads St.
Arlington, Virginia 22202

(Source of maps of areas east of the Mississippi River.)

Johnson Camping, Inc.
One Marine Midland Plaza,
P.O. Box 966, Binghamton, NY 13902

(Source of Silva compasses and Eureka
　tents)

Recreational Equipment, Inc.
1525 11th Ave., P.O. Box C-88125
Seattle, WA 98188

(Headquarters store: wide assortment of
　outdoor gear.)

Voyageur Enterprises
P.O. Box 512
Shawnee Mission, Kansas 66201

(Waterproof plastic bags with sliding
　tube closures.)

Phoenix Products, Inc.
U.S. State Road 421
Tyner, KY 40486

(Waterproof camera and gear bags.)

Duluth Tent & Awning, Inc.
1610 West Superior St., Box 6024,
Duluth, MN 55806

(Your most complete source of canvas
　Duluth packs.)

Recreational Equipment, Inc.
710 West 98th St.
Bloomington, MN 55420

(Source of six-mil thick plastic Duluth
　pack liners, plus other outdoor gear.)

Hoigaards, Inc.
3550 South Highway 100
Minneapolis, MN 55416

(Source of six-mil thick plastic Duluth
pack liners, plus other outdoor gear.)

Martensen Co., Inc.
P.O. Box 261
Williamsburg, VA 23185

(Liquid waterproofing material for
maps.)

U.S. National Ocean Survey
Lake Survey Center
Dept. of Commerce
630 Federal Bldg. and U.S. Courthouse
Detroit, Michigan 48226

(Source of U.S. Hydrographic charts.)

Forestry Suppliers, Inc.
205 West Rankin St.
Jackson, Mississippi 39204

(Your most complete source of forestry
and surveying equipment--map aids,
clear plastic for covering maps, compasses, stereoscopes, etc.)

Eastern Mountain Sports, Inc.
Vose Farm Road
Peterborough, NH 03458

(Outdoor gear of every type including a
wide selection of canoes and accessories)

Indiana Camp Supply, Inc.
P.O. Box 344
Pittsboro, Indiana 46167

(Best source of medical gear and freeze-
dried foods. Extensive book list and
outdoor gear accessories including 6-
mil thick pack liners. Mail order source

L.L. Bean, Inc.
Freeport, Maine 04033

(Source of the famous "Maine Hunting
Shoe" and other fine camping equipment.)

Dragonfly Designs
California Rivers, Inc.
P.O. Box 468
Geyserville, CA 95441

(A lot of unique canoeing software,
including the ingenius "Otter bag" mentioned in chapter 6.)

Chicago Sponge Company
512 North State St.
Chicago, IL 60610

(Source of fine natural sponges for
bailing the canoe.)

Perception, Inc.
Box 686
Liberty, South Carolina 29657

(Manufacturers of high performance
canoes and kayaks and the stainless
steel paddle tip kit mentioned in
chapter six.)

Cannondale Corp.
9 Brookside Place
Georgetown, CT 06829

(Manufacturers of Cannondale Tents and
other outdoor equipment.)

Bendonn Co.
4920 Thomas Ave. South
Minneapolis, MN 55410

(Makers of the unique Bendonn Tote
oven.)

Precise, Inc.
3 Chestnut St.
Suffern, NY 10901

(Distributors of high quality imported
knives, Suunto compasses, and
"Phoenix" trail stoves.)

AirZone Mfg. Co.
303 Sharpe Road
Anacortes, WA 98221

(This company makes a unique three-
fingered neoprene/nylon mitten which
is ideal for paddling in bone-chilling
weather.)

Northwest River Supplies
P.O. Box 9186, 430 W. 3rd.
Moscow, Idaho 83843

(Specialized gear for canoeists, kayakers,
    and rafters.)

Sierra West
6 East Yanonali St.
Santa Barbara, CA 93101

(A variety of outdoor gear including
    "EVA" (ethyl-vinyl-acetate) foam--
    ideal for making glue-in knee pads.)

Quick 'N Easy Products Inc.
P.O. Box 278
Monrovia, CA 91016

(The most popular...and in my opinion,
    best car-top carriers made.)

FAST BUCKSAW CO.
110 East 5th St.
Hastings, MN 55033

(Source of what is, in my opinion, the best
    folding saw made.)

Seda, Inc.
P.O. Box 997
Chula Vista, CA 92102

(A large assortment of outstanding gear
    for the white water canoeist, including
    the excellent SEDA life jacket.)

Early Winters, LTD
110 Prefontaine Place South
Seattle, WA 98104

(A wide assortment of exotic outdoor
    gear, including the unusual "Moonlight
    flashlight.)

Great World
250 Farms Village
W. Simsbury, CT 06902

(Lots of specialized canoe tripping gear
    plus an extensive book list.)

Moor & Mountain
63 Park St.
Andover, MA 01910

(Speciality items for the canoeist in the
    old world New England tradition.)

Damart, Inc.
1811 Woodbury Ave.
Portsmouth, NH 03805

(Long underwear made of Acryllic and
    Vinyon. Very warm and not scratchy.)

HACH Chemical Co.
P.O. Box 389
Loveland, Colorado 80537

(Makers of some of the best water testing
    equipment around--and source of the
    nicest waterproof field notebook )jour-
    nal) I've seen.)

Cole Outdoor Products of America
6801 P. St.
Lincoln, Nebraska 68508

(Source of the "Shoo Bug" repellent
    jacket. Repels all types of biting
    insects).

Clint Waddell Paddles
8015 Sunkist Blvd.
Minneapolis, MN 55444

(Custom built paddles at reasonable
    prices. Bent and straight shaft models
    available in all lengths. Clint makes a
    fine straight paddle of my design for
    solo slalom.)

# EQUIPMENT LIST*

## COMMUNITY GEAR

\_\_\_\_\_Canoe, rigged with yoke, shock-cords, and tracking lines.

\_\_\_\_\_Three piece canoe cover.

\_\_\_\_\_Seat pads for canoe (optional).

\_\_\_\_\_"Otter bags" for canoe (optional).

\_\_\_\_\_"Running compass" (seat or thwart mounted) for canoe.

\_\_\_\_\_Large sponge for bailing.

\_\_\_\_\_Two quart plastic pitcher with cover (for bailing and mixing powdered drinks).

\_\_\_\_\_Tent and ground cloth.

\_\_\_\_\_Nylon rain tarp.

\_\_\_\_\_100 or more feet of parachute cord.

\_\_\_\_\_50 feet of three-eighths inch diameter nylon rope per canoe.

\_\_\_\_\_Cook-kit* and oven.

\_\_\_\_\_Biodegradable soap/cleaning gear for cook kit.

\_\_\_\_\_One or two stoves (Expeditions above timberline should carry *two* stoves.)

\_\_\_\_\_Stove fuel (allow at least one-half gallon per week for a party of four).

\_\_\_\_\_Hand axe and sturdy sheath.

\_\_\_\_\_Folding saw.

\_\_\_\_\_Rubber ropes and nylon cords for securing packs in the canoe.

\_\_\_\_\_Duluth packs: waterproof liners and abrasion liners for packs.

\_\_\_\_\_Pack basket.

\_\_\_\_\_Medical kit (see Appendix D for contents).

\_\_\_\_\_Compact first-aid kit (pack separate from medical kit and carry in another canoe).

\_\_\_\_\_Canoe repair kit (see Chapter 21 for suggested items).*

\_\_\_\_\_Equipment repair kit (sewing materials, pliers, sharpening tools, etc.)*

\_\_\_\_\_Candles, fire-starters.

\_\_\_\_\_Aluminum tube shovel.

*For expeditions into remote areas where help is unavailable, *double* these items.

_____Plastic or nylon folding water jug.
_____Binoculars.
_____Weather forcasting instruments: thermometer, barometer,
          tables
          (optional).

# EQUIPMENT LIST

## PERSONAL EQUIPMENT

_____Life jacket (one extra life vest *per crew* is recommended for very
          remote trips).
_____Two paddles
_____Two wool shirts.
_____Two pairs wool or polypropylene long underwear.
_____Heavy wool sweater or jac-shirt.
_____Two pairs wool or cotton/canvas trousers.
_____Two pairs gloves (neoprene, wool, buckskin)
_____Two or three hats (rain, sun, cold).
_____Extra glasses if you wear them. Security strap for glasses.
_____Polaroid glasses--helps you navigate rapids better.
_____Waterproof boots.
_____Boots for camp use and general hiking.
_____Small nylon pack for day hiking (optional).
_____Flashlight and/or candle lantern (one per tent).
_____Pocket knife on lanyard.
_____Matches, butane lighters (2).
_____Whistle.
_____Wind parka.
_____Rain suit.
_____Paddling shirt (optional).
_____Wool socks (4-5 pairs for a three week trip).
_____Camera and waterproof bag.
_____Wrist-watch.
_____One cotton T-shirt for warm weather.
_____Hand cream/lip balm/sun-screen.
_____Towel, toiletries.
_____Map set in waterproof case.
_____Insect repellent, Johnson bug jacket, 2 headnets.
_____Two colored bandannas.

_____Journal and pencil.
_____Compass.
_____Thermos bottle.
_____Sleeping bag and foam pad.
_____Fishing gear, fillet knife.

## EMERGENCY ITEMS

_____Compact signal kit (red smoke, flares, mirror) (optional).
_____Carabiners and nylon pulleys (for canoe salvage).
_____Firearms and ammunition, case, (optional).
_____Cleaning equipment for gun.

# ———— APPENDIX "D" ————

## THE MEDICAL KIT

This *non-perscription* medical kit is the one suggested by Dr. Bill Forgey in his state-of-the-art book, "Wilderness Medicine". Dr. Forgey emphasizes that these drugs should be administered only to healthy young adults who are not suffering from hypertension, diabetes, glaucoma, kidney, liver, or thyroid disease, or women who are pregnant or nursing.

For lengthy expeditions into remote areas where help is flatly unavailable, a more sophisticated *perscription* medical kit should be assembled. The particulars of this kit--and its use--along with other essential medical information is detailed in "Wilderness Medicine"*

### THE BASIC KIT
*(Adequate for 2-10 persons)*

| | |
|---|---|
| Percogesic | 24 to 48 tablets |
| Pseudoephedrine .30 mg | 50 tablets |
| Chlorpheniramine 4 mg | 25 tablets |
| Yellow Oxide of Mercury opthalmic 1%, ⅛ oz. tube | 1 tube |
| Schein Otic Drops (or equal), 1 ounce bottle | 1 bottle |
| Triple Antibiotic Ointment, 1½ ounce packets | 10 packets |
| Dibucaine Ointment 1%, 15 gram tube | 1 tube |
| Meclizine 25 mg tablets | 10 tablets |
| Bacid Capsules | 20 to 30 capsules |
| Bisacodyl tablets .5 mg | 10 tablets |
| Camalox tablets | 20 to 40 tablets |
| Povidone-iodine Prep Pads | 10 pads |
| Bandages, 1″ × 3″ (plastic strips) | 20 each |
| Gauze pads, 12 ply, 3″ × 3″, sterile | 20 each |
| Gauze roll, 3″ × 10 yards, sterile | 1 each |
| Elastic Bandage, 4″ × 10 yards, top quality | 10 each |
| Butterfly bandages, medium | 10 each |
| Tape, 1″ × 10 yards | 1 roll |
| Spenco Skin Guard Padding 2 × 10 strip | 1 each |

*Available from Indiana Camp Supply, P.O. Box 344, Pittsboro, IN 46167. Indiana Camp Supply is your most complete source of medical equipment and non-perscription drugs. Write for their catalog.

## SUGGESTED MATERIALS TO AUGMENT THE BASIC KIT

| | |
|---|---|
| Vaseline Gauze, sterile, 3″ × 9″ | 3 each |
| Hibiclens Surgical Scrub | ½ to 4 ounces |
| Needle Holder, Mayo-Hegar | 1 each |
| Bandage Scissors, Lister-or Operating Scissors | 1 only |
| Scalpel, disposable, #10 or # 11, sterile | 1 only |
| Splinter forceps | 1 each |
| Ethilon Suture 3-0 | 3 packs |
| Ethilon Suture 5-0 | 3 packs |
| Plain Gut Suture, 3-0 | 1 pack |
| Cutter Snake Bite Kit (not essential for northern rivers) | 1 kit |
| Tinactin Ointment 1%, 15 gram tube | 1 tube |
| Tooth Ache Gel, ⅛th ounce | 1 tube |

# INTERNATIONAL SCALE FOR RATING RAPIDS

Ratings of rapids as given in guide books and trip guides usually reflect the river's *normal* flow. Be aware that flood conditions can turn a bubbly class II rapid into a formiddable run that even experts wouldn't attempt. Conversely, a prolonged dry spell may tame the most violent drop. Water levels *are* important!

It's common practice to increase the difficulty rating substantially (about half a grade) for rapids which are extremely remote and/or whose water temperatures are below 45 degrees Fahrenheit.

### GRADE I: Easy

Waves are small (a foot or so) and the route is recognizeable from above without scouting. Some artifical difficulties like piers  and bridge pilings.

### GRADE II: Medium

Fairly frequent but unobstructed rapids with waves up to three feet. Course generally easy to recognize, passages clear. River speeds may exceed hard back-paddling speed. Occasional low ledges.

### GRADE III: Difficult

High, irregular, numerous waves. Course may be difficult to recognize; rapid requires careful advance scouting. Frequently requires complex maneuvering. This is about the limit for an open canoe. Loaded wilderness canoes should stay out of Class III water unless they are manned by competent paddlers and have full splash covers.

### GRADE IV: Very Difficult

Long, powerful rapids and boiling eddies. Requires powerful and precise maneuvering. This is no place for a wilderness canoe, regardless of cover or expertise.

## GRADE V: Extraordinarily Difficult

Long, violent rapids with big drops, souse holes and boiling eddies. Class V rapids should be attempted only by *expert* paddlers in slalom canoes and kayaks.

## GRADE VI: Limit of Navigability

Extremely powerful and dangerous rapids which should be attempted only by the very best canoeists under carefully controlled conditions. Paddling Class VI rapids is a life-threatening experience!

## Temperature chart

Average daily maximum temperatures at selected points across Canada, in degrees Fahrenheit.

| | May | | June | | July | | Aug. | | Sept. | | Oct. | |
|---|---|---|---|---|---|---|---|---|---|---|---|---|
| | low | high | low | high | low | high | low | high | low | high | low | high |
| **British Columbia** | | | | | | | | | | | | |
| Kamloops | 45 | 72 | 52 | 79 | 55 | 84 | 54 | 83 | 46 | 73 | 39 | 57 |
| Penticton | 43 | 70 | 50 | 77 | 54 | 84 | 52 | 81 | 45 | 72 | 37 | 57 |
| Prince Rupert | 43 | 57 | 46 | 59 | 50 | 63 | 52 | 63 | 48 | 59 | 43 | 52 |
| Vancouver | 48 | 64 | 54 | 70 | 57 | 75 | 55 | 73 | 52 | 68 | 45 | 59 |
| Victoria | 46 | 64 | 50 | 70 | 52 | 75 | 52 | 73 | 50 | 68 | 46 | 59 |
| **Alberta** | | | | | | | | | | | | |
| Banff | 34 | 57 | 39 | 64 | 45 | 72 | 43 | 70 | 36 | 61 | 30 | 50 |
| Calgary | 37 | 61 | 45 | 66 | 50 | 75 | 46 | 72 | 39 | 63 | 30 | 54 |
| Edmonton | 41 | 63 | 48 | 68 | 54 | 73 | 50 | 72 | 41 | 63 | 32 | 52 |
| Jasper | 34 | 61 | 41 | 68 | 46 | 73 | 45 | 72 | 37 | 63 | 30 | 52 |
| Lethbridge | 39 | 64 | 48 | 70 | 52 | 79 | 50 | 77 | 43 | 68 | 34 | 57 |
| **Yukon** | | | | | | | | | | | | |
| Whitehorse | 34 | 59 | 43 | 68 | 46 | 70 | 45 | 66 | 37 | 57 | 27 | 41 |
| **Northwest Territories** | | | | | | | | | | | | |
| Frobisher | 19 | 32 | 32 | 45 | 39 | 54 | 39 | 50 | 32 | 41 | 18 | 28 |
| Inuvik | 21 | 39 | 39 | 61 | 45 | 66 | 41 | 61 | 30 | 45 | 12 | 25 |
| Yellowknife | 30 | 48 | 45 | 63 | 52 | 70 | 50 | 66 | 39 | 52 | 25 | 36 |
| **Saskatchewan** | | | | | | | | | | | | |
| Price Albert | 36 | 63 | 45 | 70 | 52 | 77 | 48 | 73 | 39 | 63 | 28 | 50 |
| Regina | 37 | 64 | 48 | 72 | 54 | 79 | 50 | 77 | 39 | 66 | 28 | 54 |
| Saskatoon | 39 | 64 | 48 | 72 | 54 | 79 | 52 | 77 | 41 | 64 | 32 | 54 |
| **Manitoba** | | | | | | | | | | | | |
| Churchill | 21 | 34 | 36 | 52 | 45 | 63 | 46 | 61 | 37 | 48 | 27 | 36 |
| Winnipeg | 39 | 63 | 50 | 73 | 57 | 79 | 54 | 77 | 45 | 64 | 34 | 54 |
| **Ontario** | | | | | | | | | | | | |
| Hamilton | 46 | 66 | 57 | 77 | 63 | 82 | 61 | 81 | 52 | 72 | 43 | 61 |
| Kitchener | 45 | 64 | 54 | 77 | 57 | 81 | 57 | 79 | 50 | 70 | 41 | 59 |
| London | 45 | 64 | 54 | 75 | 59 | 79 | 57 | 79 | 50 | 70 | 41 | 59 |
| Ottawa | 45 | 66 | 55 | 75 | 59 | 81 | 57 | 79 | 50 | 68 | 39 | 57 |
| Sault Ste. Marie | 39 | 57 | 48 | 70 | 54 | 75 | 54 | 73 | 48 | 64 | 39 | 55 |
| Sudbury | 43 | 63 | 52 | 73 | 57 | 77 | 55 | 75 | 48 | 66 | 39 | 54 |
| Thunder Bay | 36 | 59 | 45 | 68 | 54 | 75 | 52 | 73 | 45 | 63 | 36 | 54 |
| Toronto | 45 | 64 | 55 | 77 | 63 | 81 | 61 | 79 | 54 | 72 | 45 | 59 |
| Windsor | 46 | 68 | 57 | 79 | 63 | 82 | 61 | 81 | 54 | 73 | 43 | 63 |

**Quebec**

| Gaspe | 37 | 54 | 46 | 64 | 55 | 73 | 52 | 72 | 43 | 64 | 36 | 54 |
| Montreal | 48 | 64 | 59 | 75 | 63 | 79 | 61 | 77 | 54 | 68 | 43 | 47 |
| Quebec City | 43 | 63 | 54 | 72 | 59 | 77 | 57 | 75 | 48 | 66 | 39 | 54 |

**New Brunswick**

| Fredericton | 39 | 63 | 48 | 73 | 55 | 79 | 54 | 75 | 46 | 68 | 36 | 55 |
| Moncton | 39 | 61 | 48 | 72 | 55 | 77 | 54 | 75 | 46 | 68 | 37 | 57 |
| Saint John | 41 | 59 | 48 | 66 | 54 | 73 | 55 | 73 | 50 | 66 | 41 | 57 |

**Nova Scotia**

| Halifax/Dartmouth | 41 | 57 | 50 | 68 | 57 | 73 | 57 | 73 | 52 | 66 | 45 | 55 |
| Yarmouth | 41 | 55 | 48 | 63 | 54 | 70 | 54 | 70 | 50 | 64 | 43 | 57 |

**Price Edward Island**

| Charlottetown | 39 | 57 | 50 | 68 | 57 | 75 | 57 | 73 | 50 | 66 | 41 | 55 |

**Newfoundland/Labrador**

| Corner Brook | 37 | 52 | 45 | 63 | 54 | 72 | 54 | 70 | 46 | 63 | 39 | 52 |
| Goose Bay | 32 | 50 | 43 | 63 | 52 | 70 | 50 | 66 | 41 | 57 | 32 | 48 |
| St. John's | 36 | 52 | 43 | 61 | 52 | 70 | 54 | 68 | 46 | 63 | 39 | 54 |

*From *Canada Travel Information 1982/83. Courtesy of the Canadian Government Office of Tourism.*

# Index